ULTIMATE
BOOK
OF
PUZZLES

Publications International, Ltd.

Puzzle Consultants: Adam Cohen, Julie K. Cohen, Shawn Kennedy, Amy Reynaldo

Introduction: Holli Fort

Cover Puzzles: Myles Callum, Conceptis Puzzles, Harvey Estes, Erich Friedman, Stephen Schaefer

Puzzle Constructors: Cihan Altay, Myles Callum, Philip Carter, Clarity Media, Kelly Clark, Andrew Clarke, Barry Clarke, Jeff Cockrell, Conceptis Puzzles, Don Cook, Jeanette Dall, Mark Danna, Jacque Day, Harvey Estes, Josie Faulkner, Adrian Fisher, Connie Formby, Holli Fort, Erich Friedman, The Grabarchuk Family, Ray Hamel, Bob Harris, Luke Haward, Dick Hess, Tyler Hinman, Marilynn Huret, Lloyd King, Catherine Leary, Dan Meinking, Kate Mepham, Patrick Merrell, David Millar, Michael Moreci, Elsa Neal, Alan Olschwang, Ellen F. Pill, Planet X Graphics, Stephen Ryder, Gianni Sarcone, Pete Sarjeant, Stephen Schaefer, Paul Seaburn, Fraser Simpson, Shavan R. Spears, Terry Stickels, Howard Tomlinson, Kristen Tomlinson, Linda Washington, Wayne Robert Williams

Illustrators: Helem An, Connie Formby, Elizabeth Gerber, Robin Humer, Nicole H. Lee, Anna Lender, Pat Murray, Jay Sato, Shavan R. Spears, Jen Torche

GET READY, GET SET . . .

For a true value-added proposition, all you really need to bring to the table is the *Ultimate Book of Puzzles*. We've packed these pages with puzzle after puzzle, each gleefully designed to challenge your mind without hurting your pocketbook. To further push the envelope, the puzzles get tougher as you work your way through the book, giving you a chance to take your mental skills to the next level.

With more than 500 puzzles to choose from, there is sure to be plenty to pique your curiosity. You can mix and match from all sorts of different brain stumpers:

- Word puzzles: crosswords, anagrams, word searches, and more
- Math puzzles: story problems, number crosswords, and others
- Visual puzzles: hidden objects, mazes, and observation and perspective exercises
- Logic puzzles: sudoku, hashi, sequencing, and more

Think you've got a handle on the situation? You may hit the ground running with the easier puzzles in the beginning, but by the time you've crossed the last word and solved the final maze, you'll really understand why this is the *Ultimate Book of Puzzles*!

Don's Diner and Part-Time Arcade found on page 287.

SHROUDED SUMMARY

Hidden in the word search is a synopsis of a well-known story. The words you need to find are listed below, but in the word search they are presented in an order that will make a little more sense. The words can be found vertically, horizontally, or diagonally. Can you name the book title?

BEFORE

BUT

FAMILY

FINDING

FOR

GANG

HAS

HIDES

HIM

LEADER

ORPHAN

OTHER

OUT

PLANS

REAL

THIEVES

WITH

```
B O R P H A N I N P L T K W
H A H D I O T H W I H O P N
E F K J D L S N R E G G R N
N S Y S E R H Y M T B F I P
L T L H S O U T O T B H O W
O E O N W E A E V A U A R H
T I A I K I R I I A I N A K
P I B D H T T L T C E G I K
P H F I L H H H P S U A N V
R N A R N M I A R H M N C W
I Y L A R N E Q C R P O N S
O T L C A L V S N I B I O J
R E G O J B E F O R E N G M
A I A D L F S I I E K S T A
I M L I T L T N N A N I N C
Z C I Y D N E D G L J L P A
W Y W J T K I I F A M I L Y
F A P O S N C N B W N L E M
I D L F N T R G U P R H A S
H T R O T H E R T L S T D U
T U A R D A I E G A N G E F
D S I F G L F M A N I A R B
N W R A T V W L D S D G D L
```

Synopsis and book title: _____

_____

Answers on page 353.

TRUE OR FALSE?

Each group of scrambled letters can be rearranged to reveal a number. Following the mathematical functions indicated, mark each problem true or false. For example, ORFU + VIFE = HIGET, or 4 + 5 = 8, would be false.

1. REHET + VEENEL = ERONETUF

2. TETOWWYNT – TINNENEE = OWT

3. EFFENIT + NEXTIES = HORINTTEY

4. TINNEY – VETELW = GHYTIGETHIE

5. FYTVORIFE – TROFY = XYROFIST

6. VESNE + NELVEE = INEGETHE

7. HYGITE – TYNEWT = NETYVES

8. TENSYEV + HERITTEN = THETHIGREEY

9. HOWIRTTYT – OTEWENYNT = WELTEV

NAME CALLING

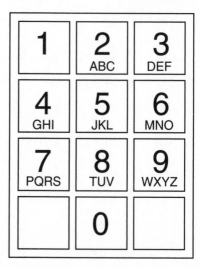

Decipher the encoded word in the quip below from physicist-philosopher Niels Bohr by using the numbers and letters on the phone pad. Remember that each number can stand for 3 or 4 possible letters.

It is difficult to make predictions, especially about the 3–8–8–8–7–3.

WORD SQUARE

Complete the word square below using 4 words that mean, in this order: get ready for, big, a jungle cat, and the back of a ship. Words will be spelled the same across and down.

S	A	L	T	S
A				
L				
T				
S				

RHYME TIME

Each clue leads to a 2-word answer that rhymes, such as BIG PIG or STABLE TABLE. The numbers in parentheses after the clue give the number of letters in each word. For example, "cookware taken from the oven (3, 3)" would be "hot pot." As a bonus, can you figure out the theme of this puzzle?

1. Bisected a cherry stone (5, 3): _____ _____

2. Tidy avenue (4, 6): _____ _____

3. Constructed a leg pole for a clown (5, 5): _____ _____

4. Close-in-score boxing match (5, 5): _____ _____

5. One more than 7 in a row (5, 8): _____ _____

Theme: _____

Answers on page 353.

CRIMINALS

How many different kinds of criminals can you find here? We count 8. To spell out a criminal, keep moving from one letter to the next in any direction—up, down, across, or diagonally. You may move in several different directions for each word. You can also use letters more than once—but not in the same word.

M	O	B	B	O	O
T	U	R	E	R	K
B	L	G	G	T	C
R	A	G	S	I	H
W	I	N	D	E	F

APTAGRAMS

What's an aptagram? That's our word for anagrams that are especially apt because the rearranged word or phrase relates closely to the original word or phrase. Examples: An astronomer is a MOON STARER; many a dormitory is a DIRTY ROOM; and with Marie Curie, RADIUM CAME. Get it? Try your hand at these:

1. GUT HOUND ____________________
2. SO LET'S PINCH ____________________
3. HINT: HOTEL ____________________
4. LIBERAL BOD ____________________

Answers on page 353.

LIP SERVICE

ACROSS

1. "Yikes"
5. Lumberyard tools
9. "Hungarian Rhapsodies" composer Franz
14. Employee's move, for short
15. "_____ Silver! Away!"
16. "…an old woman who lived in _____"
17. Comfy footwear: 2 wds.
20. Popular swimwear brand
21. Leaves the dock
22. One of Alcott's "Little Women"
24. Agnus _____ (Lamb of God)
25. Nine-digit ID org.
26. Scrooge's expletive
29. Practice boxing
31. Session: abbr.
33. Jai _____
35. Swift, compact horse
37. Exhorts
41. Shears for a hair pro: 2 wds.
44. Foe
45. Beer foam
46. Basic seasoning
47. Harden
49. Miffed state
51. Domicile: abbr.
52. Spot of land in the Seine
55. Opening
57. Mrs. David Copperfield
59. Tinny-sounding
62. "Give a ring sometime!"
66. Griddle utensils: 2 wds.
68. Soft Dutch cheeses
69. Repetitive learning process
70. Does a gardening chore
71. Zaps with a stun gun
72. Lith. and Ukr., formerly
73. Assistant

DOWN

1. Eyes, poetically
2. Dickens's Uriah
3. Like many a New England "shoppe"
4. Mount in Exodus
5. Have a good day on the links: 2 wds.
6. Prepare to fire
7. "Swiss Family Robinson" author Johann
8. Did a cobbler's job
9. Enjoys thoroughly, as praise, slangily: 3 wds.
10. AOL and others
11. Old Mets' stadium's dedicatee, et al.
12. Geisha's footwear
13. Inventor and electrical engineer Nikolai
18. Praise-filled poems
19. News bit
23. Severe
26. Like a _____ in the woods
27. Actor Alda
28. Loser to the tortoise
30. Track meet events
32. Orgs.
34. Some PCs
36. Not at all spicy
38. Equipment
39. _____ Stanley Gardner
40. Retired sound-breakers
42. Monocle
43. Extreme follies
48. Use a phone
50. Ensnare
52. Egg on
53. "You can _____ horse to water…"
54. Old lab burners
56. Marina sights
58. First Greek letter
60. Topmost
61. Corp. money chiefs
63. First of 13 popes
64. Classic TV's talking horse
65. Caesar's existence
67. Env. content, maybe

RHYME TIME

Each clue leads to a 2-word answer that rhymes, such as BIG PIG or STABLE TABLE. The numbers in parentheses after the clue give the number of letters in each word. For example, "cookware taken from the oven (3, 3)" would be "hot pot."

1. Less-optimistic orator (7, 7): _____ _____

2. Unhappy diploma recipient (3, 4): _____ _____

3. Pale-red cocktail (4, 5): _____ _____

4. Enormous marine mammal of fragile health (5, 5): _____ _____

5. What formaldehyde and fluoride do (5, 5): _____ _____

6. Tiny pears, apples, or bananas (6, 5): _____ _____

7. Hypothesis with a bright outlook (6, 6): _____ _____

8. Song for a barroom piano (6, 4): _____ _____

Answers on page 353.

CONTINUOUS LINE BET

Draw 4 straight lines to bisect these circles. Do not lift your pencil from the page. Do not double back.

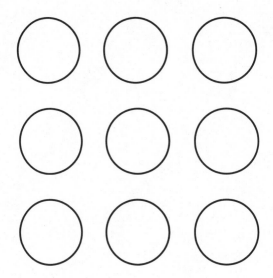

NAME CALLING

In some areas of the United States, you can find out the time by picking up the phone and dialing N–E–R–V–O–U–S (637–8687). In the same way, the 8 phone numbers below can be translated into the names of 8 states. What are they?

A. 252–2262

B. 356–7432

C. 436–7442

D. 463–4262

E. 666–8262

F. 639–9675

G. 837–6668

H. 996–6464

Answers on page 353.

WHERE ARE THE ANIMALS?

Find the names of 2 animals in each group of letters below. The letters for each animal are in their proper order.

1. DOCAGT _____ _____

2. SEKLUNKK _____ _____

3. DEOWERL _____ _____

4. FOSNAXKE _____ _____

5. WHOORLSEF _____ _____

6. RELAEBPHABINTT _____ _____

7. TILIGONER _____ _____

8. MEONAGKLEYE _____ _____

9. SWEHALALE _____ _____

10. PEAREROLT _____ _____

FITTING WORDS

In this miniature crossword, the clues are listed randomly and are numbered for convenience only. It is up to you to figure out the placement of the 9 answers. To help you, we've inserted one letter in the grid, and this is the only occurrence of that letter in the puzzle.

CLUES

1. Simple

2. Does pressing work

3. Packed with the latest information

4. Forehead

5. Related (to)

6. Stroll

7. Oliver Twist's request

8. "M*A*S*H" setting

9. Microscope part

Answers on page 353.

SUDOKU

Use deductive logic to complete the grid so that each row, each column, and each 3 by 3 box contains the numbers 1 through 9 in some order. The solution is unique.

	9		1		6		8	
	2	1						4	9
		3		4		2		
9			7		3			8
		6		1		4		
3			2		4			5
		8		7		5		
6	7						2	3
	2		4		8		1	

THEME PARK

This "ride" has a theme, but we can't tell you what it is. Place all the words in the boxes on the left—when you do, read the word created in the outlined boxes, from top to bottom, to reveal what the theme is.

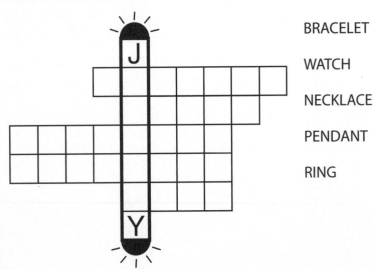

J

Y

BRACELET

WATCH

NECKLACE

PENDANT

RING

Answers on page 353.

BASEBALL TEAMS LETTERBOX

The letters in BRAVES can be found in boxes 1, 4, 6, 10, 12, and 21, but not necessarily in that order. Similarly, the letters in all the other baseball teams can be found in the boxes indicated. Your task is to insert all the letters of the alphabet into the boxes. If you do this correctly, the shaded cells will reveal the name of another baseball team.

Hint: Compare BRAVES and BREWERS to get the value of **W**, then BRAVES and PADRES for the value of **A**.

1	2	3	4	5	6	7	8	9	10	11	12	13

14	15	16	17	18	19	20	21	22	23	24	25	26
										F	Q	Z

ASTROS: 1, 6, 10, 22, 23

BLUE JAYS: 1, 4, 5, 6, 7, 9, 12, 18

BRAVES: 1, 4, 6, 10, 12, 21

BREWERS: 4, 6, 10, 12, 17

CARDINALS: 1, 2, 5, 6, 10, 13, 16, 20

CUBS: 6, 9, 12, 20

MARLINS: 1, 2, 5, 6, 10, 14, 16

PADRES: 1, 4, 6, 10, 11, 13

RED SOX: 4, 6,10, 13, 15, 23

TIGERS: 3, 4, 6, 10, 16, 22

WHITE SOX: 4, 6, 15, 16, 17, 19, 22, 23

YANKEES: 1, 2, 4, 6, 7, 8

Answer on page 353.

JIGSHAPE

Can you visually rotate and fit these 4 pieces together to form a square with rounded corners? There's no need to flip any pieces.

CONTAIN YOURSELF

For the clues below, you are looking for a small word that fits in a larger "container" word. For example, "vegetable in a weapon (3 letters in 5 letters)" would be "s(pea)r."

Writing implement in a description of price (3 letters in 9 letters) _____

Satanic character in old-style theatrical entertainment (5 letters in 10 letters) _____

"Messiah" composer in overhead light fixture (6 letters in 10 letters) _____

Answers on page 353.

GEMS

Every gem and term listed is contained within the group of letters below. Words can be found in a straight line horizontally, vertically, or diagonally. They may read either backward or forward. The leftover letters will spell out a song title related to the theme.

AGATE

AMETHYST

CARNELIAN

CAT'S-EYE

CHALCEDONY

EMERALD

GARNET

JADE

JARGON

KUNZITE

ONYX

OPAL

PERIDOT

RUBY

SARD

TOPAZ

ZIRCON

```
                    D
                  A   N   P
                G   O   I   D   E
              A   C   L   L   O   Y   R
            T   R   A   A   A   M   N   O   I
          E   I   E   R   P   T   N   O   Y   D   D
        N   Z   S   E   N   O   A   S   D   R   X   E   O
      A   G   O   M   I   E   R   A   M   E   T   H   Y   S   T
        K   E   G   R   L   U   A   L   C   Y   S   B   J
          U   E   R   I   B   S   G   L   Z   E   A
            N   T   A   Y   F   S   A   R   D
              Z   N   J   R   P   H   E
                I   I   O   E   C
                  T   N   D
                    E
```

Hidden song title: _____

ACROSTIC ANAGRAM

Unscramble the letters below to form words, then place the letters in their corresponding spots in the grid to reveal a quote from Agnes Repplier. The letter in the upper-right corner of each grid square refers to the clue the letter comes from. A black square indicates the end of a word.

A.   A   C   I   N   B

  ___ ___ ___ ___ ___
  10 30 35 40 12

B.   M   O   P   S   Y   C   H   I   N

  ___ ___ ___ ___ ___ ___ ___ ___ ___
  36 42 50   4   8 74 75 69 18

C.   E   E   L   V   L

  ___ ___ ___ ___ ___
   5 33 66 58 28

D.   N   P   I   Y   T   G

  ___ ___ ___ ___ ___ ___
  56 49   1 67 55 20

E.   A   A   W   R   D   H   E

  ___ ___ ___ ___ ___ ___ ___
  59 43 44 53 45 60 39

F.   C   A   P   N   E

  ___ ___ ___ ___ ___
  29   6 64 71 21

G.   I   A   L   Z   N   F   E   I

  ___ ___ ___ ___ ___ ___ ___ ___
  63 22 13 25 68 54 23 24

H.   E   H   C   O   R

  ___ ___ ___ ___ ___
  52 57 62 48   2

I.   O   I   A   T   A   V   R

  ___ ___ ___ ___ ___ ___ ___
  27 46 65 34 15 14 16

J.   L   I   R   Y   W   E   A

  ___ ___ ___ ___ ___ ___ ___
   7 17 11 38 73 32 61

K.   O   B   O   E   Z

  ___ ___ ___ ___ ___
  31 19   3 70 47

L.   T   P   U   U   T   O

  ___ ___ ___ ___ ___ ___
   9 51 41 26 37 72

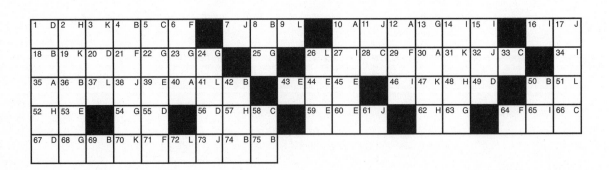

Answers on page 354.

DREAM MAN

A rebus follows its own type of alphabet: a mixture of letters, symbols, and pictures. Look carefully at the rebus below. You should be able to "read" the solution to the clue in the puzzle's title.

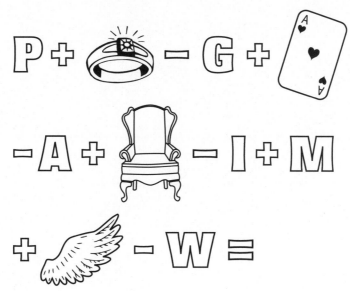

WACKY WORDY

Can you "read" the title below?

HOLLOW

Ö

CITIES AND STATES

Without scrambling any of the given letters below, can you spell the names of 6 United States cities or states by adding one letter to each word? Letters may be inserted anywhere in the words.

FARO

INDIAN

MINE

SALE

SETTLE

TEAS

WORD LADDERS

Use the clues to change just one letter on each line to go from the top word to the bottom word. Do not change the order of the letters. You must have a common English word at each step.

1. PEACH

_____ shore

_____

LEECH

2. SHOW

_____ not quick

_____ do farm work

_____

_____ theatrical production oblect

DROP

Answers on page 354.

IT'S ELEMENTARY

Remember the periodic table? Hopefully, you won't need any extra oxygen as you go through these lists and pick out the real element in each group.

1. a) nemonium
   b) goofonium
   c) plutonium
   d) pocohontium

2. a) billium
   b) lawrencium
   c) rogerium
   d) peterium

3. a) californium
   b) nevadium
   c) washingtonium
   d) floridium

4. a) coliseum
   b) stadium
   c) palladium
   d) rostrum

5. a) bolivium
   b) spainium
   c) brazilium
   d) francium

6. a) geranium
   b) germanium
   c) gorrilium
   d) gerrymanderium

7. a) frankincense
   b) gold
   c) bronze
   d) myrrh

8. a) fluoride
   b) fluorine
   c) formaldehyde
   d) fluorescence

PARDON MY FRENCH

Cryptograms are messages in substitution code. Break the code to read the quote and its author. For example, THE SMART CAT might become FVO QWGDF JGF if **F** is substituted for **T,** **V** for **H, O** for **E,** and so on.

"EJPF'O FJK YXKHUJ YTX 'YRQQSK-QK-QKK'?"

—SKERO UPXXTSS

FIND THE WORD

Ignoring spaces, capitalization, and punctuation, can you find a girl's name in each of the sentences below?

1. She couldn't believe that she won the lottery.

2. "In summary, we've had a very profitable year," Larry said.

3. "Macbeth is a classic treat for any connoisseur," Tom loftily replied.

4. "What time is it?" Paul asked.

5. "To tell ends a friendship, to not tell would make me very uncomfortable," she said.

6. "Wal-Mart has stuff like that," Hank observed.

7. "A man dared to refuse you? What is the world coming to these days?" she asked, astonished.

8. "Yes! That helm! And keep her steady!" he growled, ducking another wave and dancing across the wildly pitching deck.

9. "She isn't too bright, is she? I laid my clothes out the night before," she said, sniffing in obvious disdain.

10. "He's a man that thinks before he speaks," she said, gazing at him with loving eyes.

TASTY SCRAMBLEGRAM

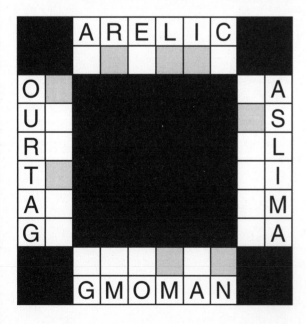

Four 6-letter words, all of which revolve around the same theme, have been jumbled. Unscramble each word, and write the answer in the accompanying space. Next, transfer the letters in the shaded boxes into the shaded keyword space, and unscramble the 8-letter word that goes with the theme. The theme for this puzzle is food.

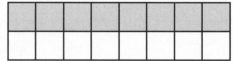

Answers on page 354.

RED, RED, RED

Every word listed below is contained within this group of letters. Words can be found horizontally, vertically, or diagonally. They may read either backward or forward. Leftover letters spell the name of the pictured object.

APPLE

BEET

BLOOD

BRICK

CHERRY

MEAT

STOPLIGHT

SUNBURN

TOMATO

WINE

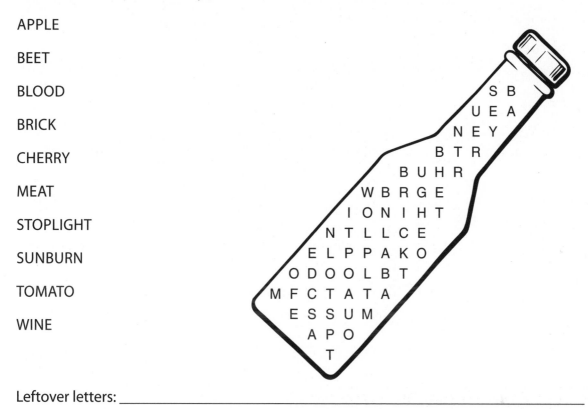

Leftover letters: _____

WACKY WORDY

Can you "read" the phrase below?

THE WHETHER

THE WEATHER

Answers on page 354.

SUDOKU

Use deductive logic to complete the grid so that each row, each column, and each 3 by 3 box contains the numbers 1 through 9 in some order. The solution is unique.

	6	7	2			9		3
	8	2				6		
			5			7	2	
2		5						
		1	9	5	3	4		
						8		7
	9	4			6			
		6				3	9	
1		8			9	2	7	

WHO'S THERE?

Cryptograms are messages in substitution code. Break the code to read the humourous quote and its author. For example: THE SMART CAT might become FVO QWGDF JGF if **F** is substituted for **T, V** for **H, O** for **E,** and so on.

"YVHH, MR M STHHVO BQV YCGKN KDLWVC, YQX OMO XGD

TKEYVC BQV JQGKV?"

—PTLVE BQDCWVC

Answers on page 354.

IT HAS A RING

Every word listed below is contained within this group of letters. Words can be found horizontally, vertically, or diagonally. They may be read either backward or forward.

BATHTUB

BOXER

BRIDE

CHIMES

CIRCUS

DOORBELL

GONG

GROOM

JEWEL BOX

JEWELER

JINGLE BELLS

SATURN

SLEIGH BELLS

TELEPHONE

WEDDING

XYLOPHONE

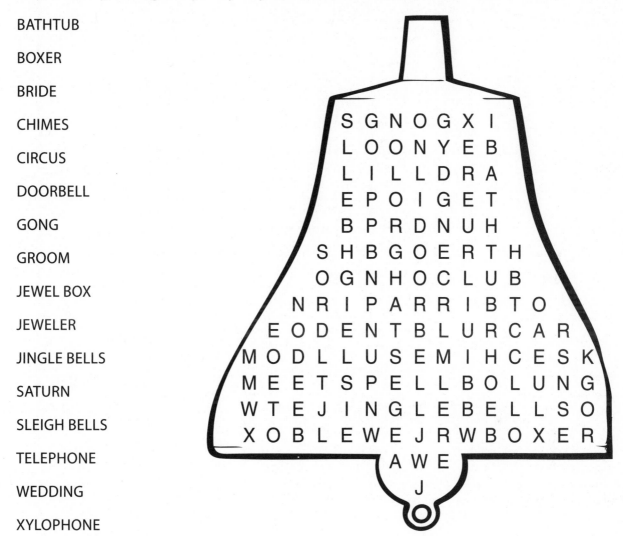

```
S G N O G X I
L O O N Y E B
L I L L D R A
E P O I G E T
B P R D N U H
S H B G O E R T H
O G N H O C L U B
N R I P A R R I B T O
E O D E N T B L U R C A R
M O D L L U S E M I H C E S K
M E E T S P E L L B O L U N G
W T E J I N G L E B E L L S O
X O B L E W E J R W B O X E R
A W E
J
```

VERSATILE VERBIAGE

One 4-letter word can be placed after each word below to form a new word or phrase. What's the all-purpose word?

BIG   ELASTIC   HEAD   SWEAT

TAKE A VACATION

ACROSS

1. Feminist leader Lucretia
5. Tex-Mex fare
10. City in Iowa
14. Khayyam
15. Rage
16. Electrical unit
17. Place for a vacation: 2 wds.
19. _____ cap mushroom
20. Islands in the Indian Ocean
21. Quarrels
23. Military investigative group: abbr.
24. Write down
26. Things to keep
30. What many a surgeon does
33. Chum
34. " . . . held his pen in trust _____" (Dobson)
36. 100 square meters
37. Sounds at a séance
38. Rhythms
39. Campbell's "Exile of _____"
40. Adventurer Johnson
41. Sharp mountain ridge
42. Islands: Sp.
43. Dewey's system
45. Sextuplet in music
47. Gets up
49. Military go-between
50. Abba and family
51. On the loose
55. Garden bloom, for short
56. Place for a vacation: 2 wds.
59. Domestic slave of yore
60. Awaken
61. Hunter, the writer
62. Congou and hyson
63. Author of "The Three Musketeers"
64. IOU

DOWN

1. Matriarch, for short
2. Portent
3. Move to takeoff position
4. Cocked hats
5. Petty: hyph.
6. Strong box: Sp.
7. Small terrier
8. Mel of Cooperstown fame
9. Pettifoggers
10. Emulate Wiley Post
11. Place for a vacation: 2 wds.
12. Fraternal organization members
13. Farm residence
18. New York's _____ Island
22. Ago
25. Harangues
26. Young fish
27. Expunge
28. Place for a vacation
29. Founder of "The Tatler"
31. Error's partner
32. Comprehend
35. Kind of grass
38. Part of a suit of armor
39. Impeded
41. Dictator Idi
42. Island of the Hebrides
44. Turkish decrees
46. Inks: Fr.
48. Glandular secretion
50. Otherwise
52. Site of ancient ruins in Iran
53. Overhang
54. Dreary
55. Catch on
57. Five-centime piece
58. Man of the Round Table: abbr.

WORD JIGSAW

Fit the pieces into the frame to form common words reading across and down. There's no need to rotate the pieces; they'll fit as shown, with each piece used once.

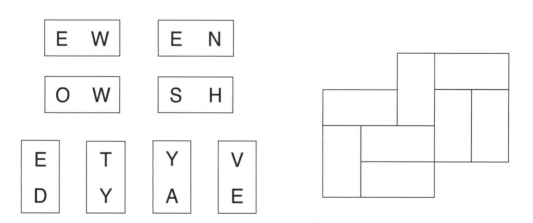

Answers on page 354.

SPACE HOP

Get the spaceship to the star at the bottom right corner of the maze by moving through alternating shapes. You can only move vertically or horizontally.

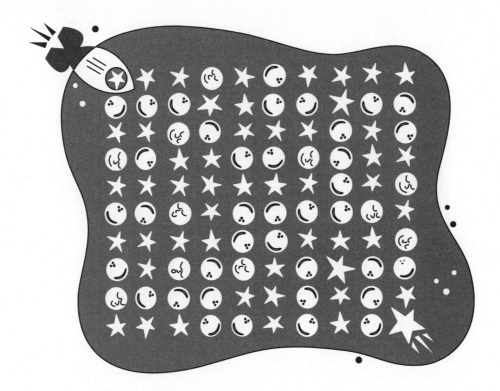

CROSSWORD SNACK

Solve the clues to fill in this 5 by 5 crossword square.

1	2	3	4	5
6				
7				
8				
9				

ACROSS

1. Drabs partner
6. Internet search engine
7. The Donald's first
8. At no time
9. Sharon of "Cagney & Lacey"

DOWN

1. "_____ is easy. Comedy is hard."
2. Bolero composer
3. "_____ a dream . . ."
4. Skeleton parts
5. Flies high

Answers on page 354.

ALPHABETICS

Determine the single letter each clue suggests. Use each letter only once.

1. Failing grade in school

2. _____ whiz

3. Washington, _____.C.

4. Hive dweller

5. Garden vegetable that grows in a pod

6. Look at

7. J. _____. Ewing of "Dallas"

8. Cartoon snoring letter

9. "Mad" magazine's Alfred _____. Neuman

10. Mark on the spot where treasure is buried

11. "Dial _____ for Murder"

12. Letter followed by "U" in every word it starts with

13. Hot drink

14. Single word meaning "for what reason"

15. Highest grade in school

16. "M*A*S*_____"

17. A name to call myself

18. O. _____. Simpson

19. "W_____RP in Cincinnati"

20. California city abbr.: _____.A.

21. Letter on Superman's chest

22. Double letter

23. I Luv _____

24. Victory symbol

25. Letter used in place of "and"

26. Letter that looks like a zero

A B C D E F G H I J K L M N O P Q R S T U V W X Y Z

Answers on page 355.

SOUPY SAILFISH

Can you reel in the path it takes to get through this swordfish?

Answer on page 355.

FLOWER GIRLS LETTERBOX

The letters in CAMELLIA can be found in boxes 2, 6, 7, 8, 9, and 14, but not necessarily in that order. Similarly, the letters in all the other girls' names can be found in the boxes indicated. Your task is to insert all the letters of the alphabet into the boxes. If you do this correctly, the shaded cells will reveal another flower-inspired girl's name.

Hint: Compare VIOLA and VIOLET to get the value of **A,** then VIOLET and ROSE for the value of **T.**

1	2	3	4	5	6	7	8	9	10	11	12	13

14	15	16	17	18	19	20	21	22	23	24	25	26
						B	F	K	Q	W	X	Z

CAMELLIA: 2, 6, 7, 8, 9, 14

DAISY: 6, 7, 10, 12, 18

HEATHER: 2, 3, 7, 13, 16

HOLLY: 12, 14, 16, 19

IRIS: 6, 10, 13

JASMINE: 2, 5, 6, 7, 9, 10, 17

LILY: 6, 12, 14

MAGNOLIA: 5, 6, 7, 9, 14, 15, 19

MARGUERITE: 2, 3, 4, 6, 7, 9, 13, 15

MARIGOLD: 6, 7, 9, 13, 14, 15, 18, 19

MYRTLE: 2, 3, 9, 12, 13, 14

POPPY: 1, 12, 19

ROSE: 2, 10, 13, 19

VIOLA: 6, 7, 11, 14, 19

VIOLET: 2, 3, 6, 11, 14, 19

Answer on page 355.

E PYRAMID

To build this pyramid, we begin by placing an **E** at the very top. Each clue can be answered by adding one letter to the previous line in order to fill the remaining rows in the pyramid. Do not change the order of the letters from one line to the next.

E

1. Masculine pronoun
2. Feminine pronoun
3. Storage building
4. Avoided
5. Protect

FIND THE WORD

Ignoring spaces, capitalization, and punctuation, how many occurrences of the consecutive letters **DOG** can you find in the paragraph below?

Fred, ogre of the land of Prado Gamma, declared that the dogma of endogamy, requiring him to wed ogres only, was unfair. Fred doggedly courted Endogia, a lover of avocado gum, but not a weirdo girl. He wrote her doggerel, sent her hot dogs, and took her to a black-tie dinner, but his tuxedo got caught on a nail, and everyone saw his Speedo garment underneath. Fred moped in his condo garage until Endogia's parents, after much ado, gave their permission to wed. Ogres from Prado Gamma thought the wedding was a boondoggle, and they were proven right when Fred ogled the maid of honor and Endogia said, "No can do—goodbye!"

Answers on page 355.

INITIALLY YOURS

We hope you don't come up short trying to figure out what these famous abbreviations stand for!

1. BMOC, at a college _____

2. BOMC, a famous mail-order company _____

3. C.O.D., in parcel post _____

4. ESP, in parapsychology _____

5. HDTV _____

6. MGS, in weather reports about skiing conditions _____

7. PT, as in PT boat _____

8. SRO, in the theatre _____

9. UFO _____

10. WD, in the product name WD-40 _____

CODE-DOKU

Solve this puzzle just as you would a sudoku. Use deductive logic to complete the grid so that each row, each column, and each 3 by 3 box contains each of the letters in the words WASN'T HELD. When you have completed the puzzle, read the shaded squares to reveal a traditional saying.

T	D		H	W				E
		H			A			
S				D			N	
N				D				
					H			N
		E		A	L		T	
			A			H		
		T					A	
E	H					W	S	D

Answer: _____

Answers on page 355.

DONUT MAZE

Nothing eases the Monday-morning blues like a donut. If you can find your way through this maze, you'll be on your way to a great week!

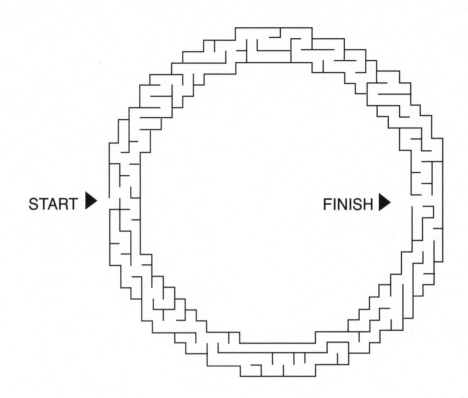

START ▶   FINISH ▶

WACKY WORDY

Can you "read" the phrase below?

SUDDEN DEATH

TIME

Answers on page 355.

PLAY BALL

Ignoring spaces, capitalization, and punctuation, can you find a baseball-related word in each of the sentences below?

1. The cat chewed the toy mouse.

2. Barry buttered the bun then ate it.

3. Grab a seat quickly when you play musical chairs.

4. Would you sing less loudly, please?

5. "Does your scalp itch?" Ernie asked.

6. The bump I received was a hard one.

7. Mark went on a hiking trip led by Al.

8. We put on shorts to play soccer.

9. Lily gave the woman a geranium.

10. The captain said I am on duty tonight.

NUMBER CROSSWORD

Fill in this crossword with numbers instead of letters. Use the clues to determine which of the numbers 1 through 8 belongs in each square. No zeros are used.

¹	²	³	■
⁴			⁵
⁶			
■	⁷		

ACROSS
1. An even number
4. Consecutive digits, ascending
6. Each of its digits (after the first one) is double the previous digit
7. An even number

DOWN
1. Consecutive digits, out of order
2. A number in the form of aabb
3. Consecutive digits, descending
5. A palindrome

Answers on page 355.

DOGGONE LOGIC

Lisa, Jeremy, Mike, and Alyssa take their dogs to the park every day. The dogs' names are Sam, Mr. Big, Shasta, and Maggie. The dogs are a Dalmatian, a beagle, a German shepherd, and a Chihuahua. One day all of the dogs escape the park! Can you help find them? Use the clues below to discover each dog's name, its breed, and its owner.

Lisa's dog's name is Maggie.

The Dalmatian belongs to Jeremy.

Alyssa's dog, named Shasta, is not the beagle.

A boy owns the Chihuahua.

Sam is not the Chihuahua.

WORD LADDER

Use the clues to change just one letter on each line to go from the top word to the bottom word. Do not change the order of the letters. You must have a common English word at each step.

ALDA

_____ mater

_____ may be found in a poor box

_____ aspirations

_____ is under the weather

_____ wire diameter units

_____ fail to catch

_____ a Sunday ritual

"M*A*S*H"

Answers on pages 355.

CROSSED WORDS

Use each of the words below to complete this clue-less crossword grid. The puzzle has only one solution.

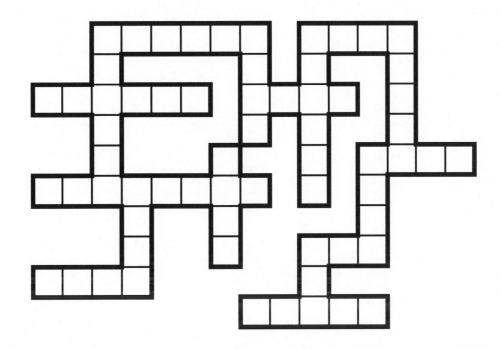

3 letters

CAR

CAT

4 letters

BABY

BELL

BOAT

FISH

PLAY

ROSE

SHOE

SNOW

5 letters

HORSE

HOUSE

6 letters

FARMER

FATHER

FLOWER

MOTHER

8 letters

AIRPLANE

Answer on page 355.

YOU AUTO LIKE THIS

Every word or phrase listed below is contained within this group of letters. Words can be found in a straight line horizontally, vertically, or diagonally. They can be read backward or forward.

AIR BAGS

ALARM

ANTENNA

AXLE

BODY

BRAKES

BULB

CARBURETOR

CLUTCH

DASHBOARD

DOORS

ENGINE

FENDER

FILTER

FRAME

```
T Z A B O D Y M A N N E T N A
A E L L I R G E S O H D R S I
C Y A U D A S H B O A R D F R
H E R B A S K K O V J O O O B
O G M L R R L D C R R Q O O A
M U F F L E R M X O N V R R G
E A P M U P T J T W L H S N S
T G Z C Z I R E D N E F H U T
E A Q E L W R R M A M I B S L
R S P M E U T A D O J L C L E
O K E A B N T L Z G D T G E B
R E D R Y S I C A X L E P N T
R T A F Z G G G H M A R E A A
I C L W H E E L N R P L Y P E
M R S T I R E S S E K A R B S
```

GASKET	LAMP	RODS
GAUGE	LOCKS	SEAT BELTS
GEARS	MATS	SPEEDOMETER
GRILLE	MIRROR	SUNROOF
HEADLIGHT	MUFFLER	TACHOMETER
HOOD	PANELS	TIRES
HORN	PEDALS	WHEEL
HOSE	PUMP	WIPERS
	RADIO	

Answers on page 355.

WORD LADDER

Change just one letter on each line to go from the top word to the bottom word. Do not change the order of the letters. You must have a common English word at each step.

HATE

———

———

———

LOVE

WORD JIGSAW

Fit the pieces into the frame to form common words reading across and down. There's no need to rotate the pieces; they'll fit as shown, with each piece used once.

N	E

A	W

O	Y

G	L

G
O

H
O

L
I

I
B

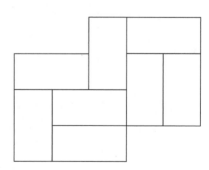

Answers on page 355.

ACROSTIC ANAGRAM

Unscramble the letters below to form words, then place the letters in their corresponding spots in the grid to reveal a quote from Jules Renard. The letter in the upper-right corner of each grid square refers to the clue the letter comes from. A black square indicates the end of a word.

A. N I E I D O

— — — — — —
24 62 51 50 14 12

B. L F E R Y O W

— — — — — — —
60 15 56 27 43 30 74

C. U U F R S O I

— — — — — — —
20 54 2 5 38 63 58

D. S Y P W I

— — — — —
1 3 45 17 46

E. N C U Y O T R

— — — — — — —
53 19 57 32 4 49 16

F. C S O L O H

— — — — — —
9 37 11 13 47 55

G. E N O I M N E

— — — — — — —
26 33 70 8 68 31 29

H. N S O E R

— — — — —
22 35 71 66 73

I. R O O N D T A

— — — — — — —
10 34 18 67 65 42 69

J. G I E E S

— — — — —
23 52 36 7 64

K. I U N R E N O

— — — — — — —
44 21 48 39 41 25 6

L. N I Y S H

— — — — —
40 28 59 72 61

1 D	2 C	3 D	4 E	5 C	6 K	7 J		8 G	9 F		10 I	11 F	12 A		13 F	14 A	15 B	16 E
17 D	18 I	19 E	20 C	21 K	22 H	23 J	24 A	25 K	26 G		27 B	28 L	29 G	30 B	31 G		32 E	33 G
34 I	35 H	36 J		37 F	38 C	39 K	40 L	41 K	42 I	43 B	44 K	45 D		46 D	47 F	48 K		49 E	50 A
51 A	52 J	53 E	54 C	55 F	56 B	57 E	58 C		59 L	60 B		61 L	62 A	63 C		64 J	65 I	66 H	67 I
	68 G	69 I		70 G	71 H	72 L	73 H	74 B									

Answers on page 355.

THE BUT-NOT GAME

The object of the But-Not Game is to uncover the common element in each statement.

Carol likes archery but not arrows.

Carol likes brothers but not sisters.

Carol likes fishers but not fish.

So…what does Carol like?

CLASS LOGIC

Four friends attend school together. Each one has a favorite subject, and every subject is taught by a different teacher. Although each item is in the correct column, only one item in each column is correctly positioned. Use the clues to figure out the students' favorite subject and teacher.

1. Bethany's favorite subject is taught by Mrs. Simpson.

2. The subject Jordan likes best is history.

3. Mrs. Jennings teaches art.

4. Mary's favorite teacher is Mr. Smith, but he doesn't teach computers.

5. Mr. Jackson is one place below Bethany and two places above science.

Student	Subject	Teacher
Bethany	History	Mr. Smith
Mary	Computers	Mrs. Simpson
Jordan	Art	Mrs. Jennings
Kateline	Science	Mr. Jackson

ROCK AROUND THE RECORD MAZE

Don't get dizzy as you spin through this record from start to finish.

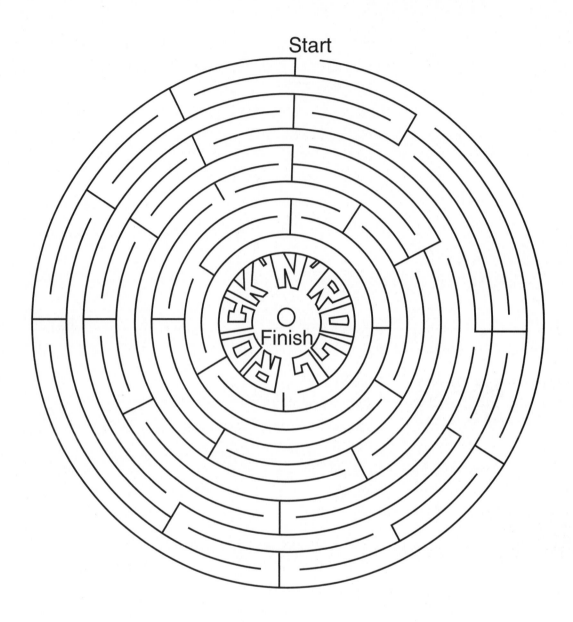

Answer on page 356.

WHERE ARE THEY?

Ignoring spaces, capitalization, and punctuation, how many occurrences of the consecutive letters **ARE** can you find in the paragraph below?

On a dare, Carey called Marie, a regular at his favorite bar, expecting to get her cell phone. Marie scares easily so she compared his number to her speed-dial list and didn't answer. Carey ate a pear and decided to visit Bar, ex-wife number two, but car engine trouble forced him to take a cab and share fare with a fair-haired lass named Claire, who told him he didn't have a prayer with her. Bar doesn't care for Carey, so she had current boyfriend Gary blare a red horn to scare Carey away.

NUMBER CROSSWORD

Fill in this crossword with numbers instead of letters. Use the clues to determine which of the numbers 1 through 8 belongs in each square. No zeros are used.

ACROSS
1. A multiple of 9
3. Consecutive digits, ascending
6. Consecutive digits, ascending
7. A multiple of 11

DOWN
1. A palindrome
2. Three different digits
4. Three different digits
5. Consecutive even digits, ascending

Answers on page 356.

BACKYARD BARBECUE

Throw some shrimp (and some anagrams!) on the barbie! Below are 10 jumbled words or phrases indicated by capital letters. Each is an anagram (rearrangement) of a word or phrase that fits the story. Can you decipher all 10?

The kids were playing on the WET SIGNS, Uncle Frank and Jack from next door were playing a game of HOSS HEROES, and it was time to grill. The THICK TRIO was lighted, and the TOAST PIE had been dusted off. Kristen, their teenager, was stretched out on the EAGLE CUSHION and talking on her CLONE HELP as usual. The RUM LABEL offered some shade, and it was time for the announcement: "NO HBO CONCERT!" This was followed by PRESCRIBE MAD HUB and a genial reminder: TO CHOKE SKIS!

EVENS/ODDS

Arrange the numbers 2, 4, and 6 horizontally and vertically in groups of 3. Similarly, arrange the numbers 1, 3, and 5 into groups of 3. Combinations connect with one another on shared numbers (a vertical 135 can connect with a horizontal 513) and the even and odd numbers will intertwine.

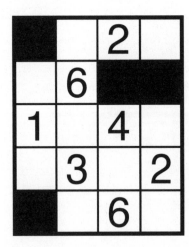

Answers on page 356.

PERFECT HARMONY BY ALPHA SLEUTH™

Move each of the letters below into the grid to form common words. You will use each letter once. The letters in the numbered cells of the grid correspond to the letters in the phrase at the bottom. Completing the grid will help you complete the phrase and vice versa. When finished, the grid and phrase will be filled with valid words, and you will have used all the letters in the letter set.

Hint: The numbered cells in the grid are arranged alphabetically, so the letter in the cell marked 1 will appear in the alphabet before the letter in the cell marked 2, and so on.

A B C D E F G H I J K L M N O P Q R S T U V W X Y Z

Answer on page 356.

Use deductive logic to complete the grid so that each row, each column, and each 3 by 3 box contains the numbers 1 through 9 in some order. The solution is unique.

		4		9		1		
	3			7			6	
6			2		4			8
		3	5		2	6		
7	8						5	2
		5	3		7	9		
9			8		6			5
	6			1			7	
		2		5		8		

DON'T FORGET TO COUNT THE DONUTS

On Police Officer Appreciation Day at the Bear Clause Donut Shop and Law Firm, all local officers who came in uniform got to eat as many donuts as they wanted. Thirty men and women in blue showed up and chowed down. When the cloud of powdered sugar finally settled and the satisfied officers left, the clerk realized she forgot to write down how many donuts each officer ate. The legal branch of the Bear Clause Donut Shop and Law Firm informed her that by some obscure law, she must report the total number of officers who ate 6, 7, 8, or 9 donuts so they can be written off as a charitable donation (or in this case, a "donution"). All the poor clerk can remember is that 10 of the officers ate fewer than 6 donuts, 8 ate more than 7 donuts, 5 ate more than 8 donuts, and one ate more than 9 donuts. Can you help the clerk stay out of trouble with her bosses and figure out how many officers ate 6, 7, 8, or 9 donuts?

Answers on page 356.

RHYME TIME

Each clue leads to a 2-word answer that rhymes, such as BIG PIG or STABLE TABLE. The numbers in parentheses after the clue give the number of letters in each word. For example, "cookware taken from the oven (3, 3)" would be "hot pot."

1. Someone who lives in the basement (6, 7): _____ _____

2. A bloody tale (4, 5): _____ _____

3. Flower that doesn't want to work (4, 5): _____ _____

4. Friend who falls into a puddle (5, 5): _____ _____

5. Hilarious rabbit (5, 5): _____ _____

6. Small violin (6, 6): _____ _____

7. A lawful bird (5, 5): _____ _____

8. Stomach full of jam (5, 5): _____ _____

9. Poodle caught in a thunderstorm (5, 5): _____ _____

10. An improved correspondence (6, 6): _____ _____

TIMES SQUARE

Fill each square in the grid with a number from 1 through 6. When the numbers in each row are multiplied, you should arrive at the total in the right-hand column. When the numbers in each column are multiplied, you should arrive at the total on the bottom line. The numbers in each diagonal must multiply to the totals in the upper- and lower-right corners.

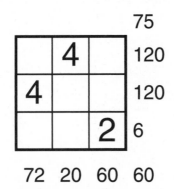

Answers on page 356.

SPIN THE DIALS

Imagine that each of the dials below can spin. Turn each dial to form a 6-letter word reading straight across the middle of the 3 dials.

QUILT QUEST

The small, tricolored pattern at right appears exactly twice in the quilt. Note that the pattern may be rotated but not overlapped and/or mirrored. Can you find both instances?

Answers on page 356.

FLYING HIGH

Unscramble the names of these common birds, then use the letters in the numbered squares to solve the second puzzle below, a related idiom.

COANFL ☐☐☐☐☐☐
1

RIOBN ☐☐☐☐☐
8

CAALINRD ☐☐☐☐☐☐☐☐
7 11

NAARYC ☐☐☐☐☐☐
10

BIRDULEB ☐☐☐☐☐☐☐☐
4

WOCR ☐☐☐☐
2

EGLAE ☐☐☐☐☐
3

WSROPRA ☐☐☐☐☐☐☐
5

GASLIRNT ☐☐☐☐☐☐☐☐
6 9

☐☐☐☐ ☐☐ ☐ ☐☐☐☐
1 2 3 4   5 6   7   8 9 10 11

WORD LADDER

Use the clues to change just one letter on each line to go from the top word to the bottom word. Do not change the order of the letters. You must have a common English word at each step.

LEAP

_____ a big pile

_____

_____ a camel has one

JUMP

Answers on page 356.

SHENANIGANS

A rebus follows its own type of alphabet: a mixture of letters, symbols, and pictures. Look carefully at the rebus below. You should be able to "read" the solution to the clue in the puzzle's title.

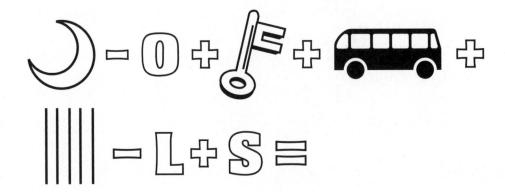

CROSS-MATH

Place the numbers 1 through 9 in the empty white squares so that the 3 horizontal and 3 vertical equations are true. Each digit will be used once. Calculations are done from left to right and from top to bottom.

	-		÷		=	1
+		+		×		
	×		-		=	66
÷		×		-		
	-		-		=	2
=		=		=		
2		10		14		

Answers on pages 356–357.

LET'S PLAY SOME MUSIC

Every word listed below is contained within this group of letters. Words can be found vertically or diagonally. They may read either backward or forward. Leftover letters spell the name of the pictured object.

BASSOON

CELLO

CORNET

FLUTE

HARP

HORN

LUTE

OBOE

PIANO

SAXOPHONE

VIOLIN

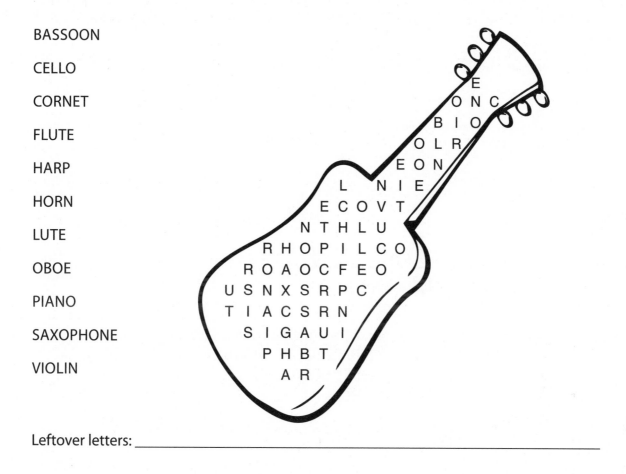

Leftover letters: _____

WORD LADDER

Use the clues to change just one letter on each line to go from the top word to the bottom word. Do not change the order of the letters. You must have a common English word at each step.

COLD

_____ phone wire

_____ a single element of speech or writing

_____ low animal

WARM

Answers on page 357.

MANY MICE

Ignoring spaces, capitalization, and punctuation, how many occurrences of the consecutive letters **MICE** can you find in the paragraph below?

Tami centered the ceramic egg that Mick eventually gave her so she wouldn't miss him while he worked for the Atomic Energy commission. Tami smoothed the egg with a pumice stone, the only one in her domicile. Tami enjoyed the egg, but Mike's gift of an imported salami cemented their relationship and helped her to miss him less.

NAME CALLING

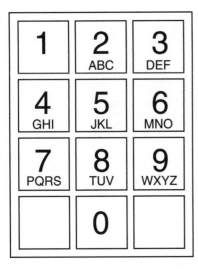

Decipher the encoded word in the humorous observation below by using the numbers and letters on the phone pad. Remember that each number can stand for 3 or 4 possible letters.

The hardest thing when learning how to 7–5–2–8–3 is probably the ice.

Answers on page 357.

TREES IN WORDS

Each of the 7 words below contains the name of a tree. Can you find them all?

1. Beefsteaks _____

2. Eyewitness _____

3. Harmlessly _____

4. Red-letter _____

5. Sleepiness _____

6. Soothsayer _____

7. Spendthrift _____

ODDBALL OF THE GROUP

Which figure is the odd one out, based on a simple design difference?

A

B

C

D

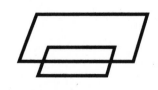
E

F

Answers on page 357.

BIRTHDAY PARTY

A rebus follows its own type of alphabet: a mixture of letters, symbols, and pictures. Look carefully at the rebus below. You should be able to "read" the solution to the clue in the puzzle's title.

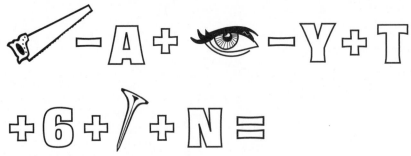

COLORS LETTERBOX

The letters in the word PINK can be found in boxes 1, 8, 16, and 19, but not necessarily in that order. Similarly, the letters in the colors listed below can be found in the boxes indicated. Your task is to insert all the letters of the alphabet into the boxes. If you do this correctly, the names of two more colors will be revealed in the shaded cells.

Hint: Compare TAWNY and GRAY to get the value of **Y,** then TAWNY and TURQUOISE for the value of **T.**

AZURE: 2, 6, 14, 21, 22

BEIGE: 4, 15, 19, 21

CREAM: 6, 7, 21, 22, 23

FAWN: 1, 6, 10, 17

GRAY: 6, 15, 22, 26

GREEN: 1, 15, 21, 22

JADE: 6, 12, 21, 25

KHAKI: 6, 8, 18, 19

MAUVE: 2, 6, 21, 23, 24

PINK: 1, 8, 16, 19

PURPLE: 2, 5, 16, 21, 22

RED: 21, 22, 25

SAXE: 6, 11, 13, 21

SILVER: 5, 13, 19, 21, 22, 24

TAWNY: 1, 6, 17, 20, 26

TURQUOISE: 2, 3, 9, 13, 19, 20, 21, 22

YELLOW: 3, 5, 17, 21, 26

1	2	3	4	5	6	7	8	9	10	11	12	13

14	15	16	17	18	19	20	21	22	23	24	25	26

Answers on page 357.

ANSWER IN THE ROUND

What has four legs, a head, and leaves? To find the answer to this riddle, look at the words in the circles below. Cross off all the words that appear in all 3 circles. The words that remain will reveal the answer.

Circle 1: double rude daydream decorate tree rush term tangle range remove trash railroad recess deal dining thief diary thoughtful root

Circle 2: root room thoughtful decorate rush tree diary trash tangle railroad remove recess range rude thief deal term daydream double

Circle 3: diary rude trash rush railroad tree range deal daydream tangle decorate remove term table recess thief double root thoughtful

Answer on page 357.

SOLVE THIS ASAP!

We hope you don't come up short trying to figure out what these famous abbreviations stand for!

1. B&O, the railroad _____

2. CARE, the foreign-aid organization _____

3. ECG, at a hospital _____

4. GMT _____

5. ISBN, to a librarian _____

6. LED, in electronics _____

7. NASA _____

8. RSVP, on an invitation _____

9. SAM, the military weapon _____

10. SWAK, on a love letter _____

HASHI

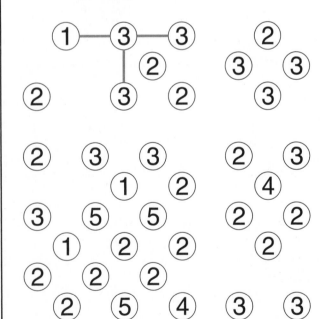

Each circle represents an island, with the number inside indicating the number of bridges connected to it. Draw bridges between islands using the number given, but there can be no more than 2 bridges going in the same direction and there must be a continuous path connecting all islands. Bridges can only be vertical or horizontal and may not cross islands or other bridges. We've drawn some bridges to get you started.

Answers on page 357.

EDIBLE ANAGRAMS

Fill in the blanks in each sentence below with words that are anagrams (rearrangements of the same letters) of each other.

1. Elizabeth kept a daily _____ and wrote about her trip to see the cows at the _____ farm.

2. "I tried to wash off the _____," said the cook, "but it was a lost _____."

3. "Go _____, young man," said the trail boss, as he was dipping into the cook's mulligan _____.

4. "At my _____ checkup," said Sam, "the doc said I needed to cut down on _____."

5. At the pep talk to his losing _____, the coach said, "You boys are looking a bit anemic. Eat some red _____!"

GO FIGURE

Fill in the empty squares with numbers between 1 and 9. The numbers in each row must add up to the numbers in the right-hand column. The numbers in each column must add up to the numbers on the bottom line. The numbers in each diagonal must add up to the numbers in the upper- and lower-right corners.

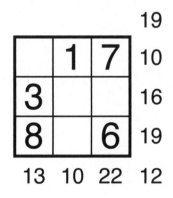

Answers on page 357.

CROSSWORD FOR DUMMIES

ACROSS

1. Prima donna
5. Chemical banned in the U.S. in 1972
8. Male clotheshorses
12. Surpassed
14. Dog in "Garfield"
15. One who works with a dummy
17. Superlative ending
18. Bankbook increase: abbr.
19. Wrist bones
20. Slow run
21. _____ Moines, Iowa
22. Cry from a roller coaster
25. Stage signal
26. Shriner's topper
29. Game played with a dummy: 2 wds
33. Sporty Pontiac model
34. Start for Quentin or Diego
35. Skillet metal
36. Long-jawed fish
37. Mai _____
39. Western African nation
42. Big donating org.
43. Belittle, slangily
46. It involves putting a dummy in a car: 2 wds.
49. Not fat
50. Common school fund-raiser, once: 2 wds.
51. Be misanthropic
52. Org. with many examiners
53. Kind of school

DOWN

1. White bird
2. Currier's partner
3. Air duct
4. Gallery showing
5. "Nothing _____!" ("No way!")
6. Oaf
7. Potential fight ender
8. Sports gaffes
9. One-eyed Norse god
10. Leaning Tower city
11. Hardens, as concrete
13. Tony Orlando and Dawn, e.g.
16. Unusually different
20. Fighter plane
21. Name
22. Move back and forth, as a finger
23. Simple abode
24. Prefix with system
25. "The Situation Room" network
26. HST's predecessor
27. Self-importance
28. School of Buddhism
30. Bartender on "The Love Boat"
31. Boat mover
32. Number on a grandfather clock
36. Garden statue
37. Pieces of work
38. Stomach trouble
39. Knife cut
40. _____ hoop
41. Fighting
42. Former host of "The Tonight Show"
43. Letter opener?
44. Remote getaway
45. Put one's foot down?
47. Baseball stat
48. One-third of a tbsp.

NAME CALLING

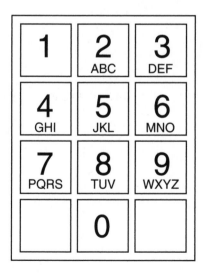

Decipher the encoded word in the quips below using the numbers and letters on the phone pad. Remember that each number can stand for 3 or 4 possible letters.

1. A virtuoso is a musician with very high 6–6–7–2–5 standards.

2. 8–4–7–8–8–3 is its own punishment.

3. The 4–4–7–2–3–3–3 is the highest form of animal life.

4. Help Wanted: Dynamite Factory. Must be willing to 8–7–2–8–3–5.

5. Remember, paper is always 7–8–7–6–6–4–3–7 at the perforations.

Answers on page 357.

A-MAZE-ING RACE

Can you get from Alaska to Zanzibar? Actually, we'll settle for from A to Z.

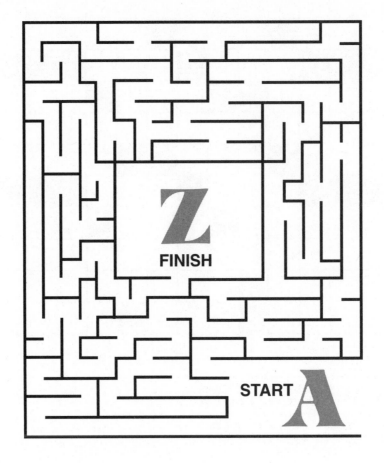

HO-HUM ADVICE

Cryptograms are messages in substitution code. Break the code to read the quote and its author. For example, THE SMART CAT might become FVO QWGDF JGF if **F** is substituted for **T, V** for **H, O** for **E,** and so on.

"UJPC HC RFQVO, MHCL BFQR."

—KFVPKO APKKHBB

Answers on page 357.

HONEYCOMB

There are 16 letters in the honeycomb below that are surrounded by 6 different letters (no letters are repeated). Can you find them all?

WORD COLUMNS

Find the hidden quote from Ludwig Wittgenstein by using the letters directly below each of the blank squares. Each letter is used once. A black square indicates the end of a word.

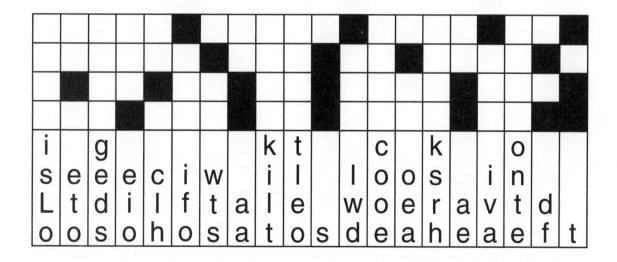

Answers on page 357.

INHERIT THE WIN

Cryptograms are messages in substitution code. Break the code to read the humorous message. For example, THE SMART CAT might become FVO QWGDF JGF if **F** is substituted for **T, V** for **H, O** for **E,** and so on.

HZWLBW IBLK'D HOJQ TOK DS FZXL RZDQ, GOD DQLV

HIUL PBLID IKJLWDSBW!

A WHALE OF A CHALLENGE

While in pursuit of plankton, this whale went to pieces. Can you visually put him back together? The pieces haven't been flipped or rotated.

Answers on page 357.

TEN-FIVE, GOOD BUDDY

This trucker's been driving all night, and some strange things are happening. Is it all in his mind? Nope! We count 9 things wrong with this picture. How many can you find?

WORD COLUMNS

Find the hidden humorous observation by using the letters directly below each of the blank squares. Each letter is used once. A black square or end of a line indicates the end of a word.

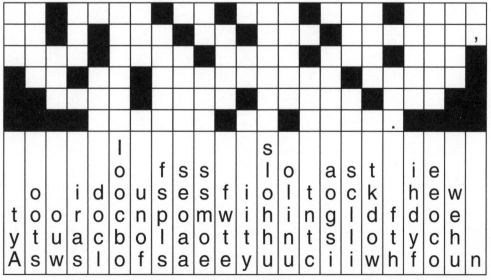

STRIKE A POSE

Every word listed below is contained within this group of letters. Words can be found horizontally vertically, or diagonally. They may read either backward or forward. The leftover letters reveal a quote from Madonna.

BLOND AMBITION

BUSTIER

CATHOLIC

CICCIONE

DANCER

"DICK TRACY"

DIVORCES

"EVITA"

FISHNETS

GUY RITCHIE

"HUNG UP"

KABBALAH

"LIKE A VIRGIN"

LOURDES

"MATERIAL GIRL"

MAVERICK (Records)

MUSIC VIDEOS

PEPSI

SEAN PENN

TOURS

"TRUTH OR DARE"

"VOGUE"

```
B G C I L O H T A C E T M
T Y U E O R O P U G N U H
T C O Y U U L I V L S E O
M A T E R I A L G I R L N
K R E S D I Y E C K P N K
A T I V E A T V R E A N C
B K S A S T I C P A I E I
B C G R T D E S H V R P R
A I B T E C I C C I O N E
L D U O N C H A N R E A V
A A S H H U N N D G U E A
H R T E S D A A S I G S M
N O I T I B M A D N O L B
S H E E F S E C R O V I D
E T R U T H O R D A R E P
```

Leftover letters: _____

Answers on page 358.

A TUNEFUL LOVE STORY

Solve the clues below, then transfer the corresponding letters to the grid. The letter in the upper-right corner of each grid square refers to the clue the letter comes from. A black square indicates the end of a word. When you're finished, you'll be rewarded with a quote from the film "Meet Me in St. Louis."

A. "Clang, clang, clang went _____": 2 wds.

___ ___ ___ ___ ___ ___ ___ ___ ___ ___
38 72 9 71 48 76 29 67 15 11

B. Panda food

___ ___ ___ ___ ___ ___
75 5 51 19 47 18

C. "Have _____ a Merry Little Christmas"

___ ___ ___ ___ ___ ___ ___ ___
22 53 13 6 64 45 30 69

D. Enlarging in appearance

___ ___ ___ ___ ___ ___ ___ ___ ___ ___
1 43 14 57 50 31 26 61 33 24

E. Judy's role

___ ___ ___ ___ ___ ___
70 78 59 8 42 54

F. Cried "Yee-haw!"

___ ___ ___ ___ ___ ___ ___
7 60 12 27 52 49 34

G. Judy's onscreen beau: John _____

___ ___ ___ ___ ___ ___
55 44 36 40 58 17

H. Showing hospitality to

___ ___ ___ ___ ___ ___ ___ ___ ___ ___ ___ ___
4 62 37 25 41 16 23 65 74 32 10 63

I. Duet sung by Mr. and Mrs. Smith: 3 wds.

___ ___ ___ ___ ___ ___ ___
77 35 28 73 66 3 68

J. Utter chaos

___ ___ ___ ___ ___ ___
21 56 2 39 20 46

1 D	2 J		3 I	4 H	5 B	6 C			7 F	8 E	9 A	10 H		11 A	12 F	13 C		14 D	15 A	16 H		17 G	18 B
	19 B	20 J		21 J	22 C		23 H	24 D	25 H		26 D	27 F	28 I	29 A	30 C		31 D	32 H	33 D	34 F		35 I
36 G	37 H		38 A	39 J	40 G	41 H	42 E		43 D	44 G	45 C		46 J	47 B	48 A	49 F		50 D	51 B	52 F	53 C	54 E
55 G	56 J	57 D	58 G		59 E	60 F	61 D	62 H	63 H	64 C		65 H	66 I		67 A	68 I	69 C	70 E		71 A	72 A	73 I
74 H		75 B	76 A	77 I	78 E																

ANIMAL HOUSE

Four animals have to pay their rent, but the landlord cannot remember in what order they usually pay. He also has their details mixed up in his notebook. Although each item appears in the correct column, only one item in each column is correctly positioned. The following facts are true about the correct order:

1. The animal named Dolly is either the flamingo or the elephant, and her location is either the field or shed.

2. Neither the cave nor the field is second.

3. Either Andy or Dolly lives in either the wood or the field, and the animal directly above is neither Brenda nor Dolly and is either the goat or elephant.

4. Either Brenda or Dolly is first.

5. Neither the goat nor the elephant is third.

6. The horse is not last.

Can you determine the correct name, animal, and location for each position?

	Name	Animal	Location
1	Andy	elephant	cave
2	Brenda	flamingo	field
3	Clive	goat	shed
4	Dolly	horse	wood

WORD LADDER

Use the clues to change just one letter on each line to go from the top word to the bottom word. Do not change the order of the letters. You must have a common English word at each step.

SOFT

_____ type of

_____ painful

_____ apple center

_____ phone wire

_____ postal message

HARD

Answers on page 358.

RHYME TIME

Each clue leads to a 2-word answer that rhymes, such as BIG PIG or STABLE TABLE. The numbers in parentheses after the clue give the number of letters in each word. For example, "cookware taken from the oven (3, 3)" would be "hot pot."

1. Became overheated (3, 3): _____ _____

2. Rudely ignore Chicago baseballer (4, 3): _____ _____

3. Sluggish river current (4, 4): _____ _____

4. College housing application (4, 4): _____ _____

5. More elegant cruise ship (5, 5): _____ _____

6. Earthquake cause (4, 5): _____ _____

7. Reading room with tracked-in muck (5, 5): _____ _____

8. Arrive at sandy expanse (5, 5): _____ _____

9. Unpleasant surprise from a market decline (5, 5): _____ _____

10. Majestic raptor (5, 5): _____ _____

SUDOKU

Use deductive logic to complete the grid so that each row, each column, and each 3 by 3 box contains the numbers 1 through 9 in some order. The solution is unique.

2				1				8
	3	8						6
		6		9		5		
	9	7		8				2
		1	7	2	3	5		
5			9			8	7	
	8		1			7		
9						1	8	
3			4					9

LIFE'S LITTLE MYSTERIES

Cryptograms are messages in substitution code. Break the code to read the ironic questions below. For example, THE SMART CAT might become FVO QWGDF JGF if **F** is substituted for **T, V** for **H, O** for **E,** and so on. The code is the same for each question.

1. BFZ ED WFJZ HCRR UW C WN LJW

   BFJM ZDO DMRZ KJW DMJ?

2. BFZ UL UW WFCW BFJM ZDO

   WICMLGDIW LDQJWFUMK YZ HCI,

   UW'L C LFUGQJMW, YOW BFJM ZDO LJME UW YZ

   LFUG, UW'L HCRRJE HCIKD?

3. FDB EDJL WFJ KOZ BFD EIUNJL WFJ LMDBGRDB

   KJW WD BDIA UM WFJ QDIMUMK?

4. HCM CM CQYUEJPWIDOL GJILDM

   QCAJ CM DVVFCME IJQCIA?

5. BFZ EDM'W WFJZ XOLW QCAJ VDDE

   LWCQGL JEUYRJ?

Answers on page 358.

PLAYING THE MARKET

Steve the simple stockbroker owned thousands and thousands of premium shares of stock in the Sterling Silver Silverware Company. One day, simple Steve was reading the stock listings in the paper and noticed that his thousands of shares of premium stock were worth much less than they had been the day he bought them. In fact, his shares of the Sterling Silver Silverware Company were almost worthless. Steve wasn't worried though. He could sell all of his holdings and still be a millionaire.

How was this possible?

WORD JIGSAW

Fit the pieces into the frame to form common words reading across and down. There's no need to rotate the pieces; they'll fit as shown, with each piece used once.

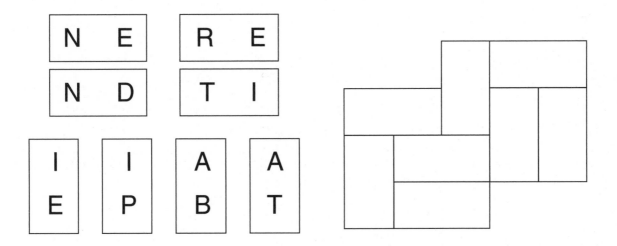

GONE FISHIN'

Just about every week, John likes to cast a line or 2 in the river. But this week, everything seemed to go wrong. We count 6 things wrong in this picture. How many can you find?

GRID FILL

To complete this puzzle, place the given letters and words into the shapes in this grid. Words and letters will run across, down, and wrap around each shape. When the grid is filled, each row will contain one of the following words: dinner, drinks, friends, hangout, ice cream.

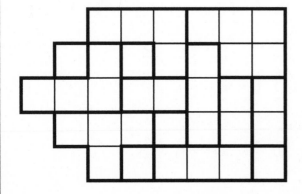

1. F, G, I, R, S

2. AU, CR, MT

3. INK, NEO

4. DINE, HAND, RICE

5. NERDS

Answers on page 358.

ANAGRAMMED TO HOMONYMS

An anagram is a word made up of the rearranged letters of another word (as in MADE and DAME). Homonyms are 2 words that have the same sound but different spellings (as in HERE and HEAR). Rearrange the letters in each pair of words below to form a pair of homonyms.

EARL / LEER _____ _____

KEEL / LAKE _____ _____

LEAN / NAIL _____ _____

MATE / TEEM _____ _____

OARS / ROSE _____ _____

ALL 26

Use all 26 letters of the alphabet once to complete this mini-crossword puzzle.

ACROSS
2. Perpendicular measurement
5. Military organization: abbr.
8. Alcoholic beverages
9. Sports center, for short

DOWN
1. Second month: abbr.
3. Entertaining machine: abbr.
4. Doves' opponents
6. Bring bad luck
7. Comfy

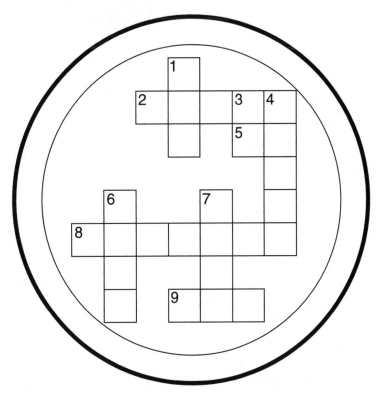

Answers on page 358.

1-2-3

Place the numbers 1, 2, or 3 in the circles below. The challenge is to have only these 3 numbers in each connected row and column—no number should repeat. Any combination is allowed.

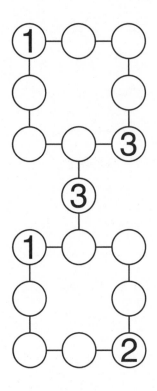

SIX-LETTER ANAGRAMS

What 2 words, formed by different arrangements of the same 6 letters, can be used to complete the sentence below?

The fiery _____ hurtled through the sky before crashing to Earth in a _____, uninhabited part of Tajikistan.

Answers on page 358.

STAR POWER

Fill in each empty square of the grid so that each star is surrounded by the numbers 1 through 8 with no repeats.

3	7		★		8	6
1	★	4		7	★	4
5	2		★		3	5
8	★				★	7
7	1		★		1	4
★		1	2	7	★	★

VEX-A-GON

Place the numbers 1 through 6 into the triangles of each hexagon. The numbers may be in any order, but they do not repeat within each hexagon shape.

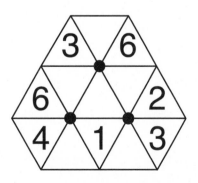

Answers on pages 358–359.

SAILING SMARTS

ACROSS

1. Gang's domain
5. Gripe
9. [as printed]
12. German auto
13. _____ avis
14. Ambient musician Brian
15. Hidden-radar road section: 2 wds.
17. E'en if
18. Labor leader Chavez
19. Groceries unit
21. "What _____ you getting at?"
22. Big name in lotion
25. "_____ La Douce"
26. Last name of the Bee Gees
27. "Know what _____?"
28. Prudence on a Long Island waterway?: 2 wds.
32. Montreal team of old
33. Beech or birch
34. Setting for "The King and I"
35. "Hey, over here!"
36. Site for three men in a tub?
39. Stick fast
41. Des Moines resident, e.g.
43. Fannie _____
44. Like a hobo's clothes: 2 wds.
47. Bambi's aunt
48. Break under strain
49. Leave the ground, with "off"
50. Norm: abbr.
51. Brontë's Jane
52. Spoken

DOWN

1. Puccini opera
2. Word before crust or hand
3. Pee Wee or Della
4. Dog botherer
5. "The A-Team" star
6. Galley slave's tool
7. Sheik's land, in song
8. Big wine valley
9. Emancipate: 2 wds.
10. More than cruel
11. Radiator content
16. Sci-fi robots
20. Greedy demand
23. JFK's successor
24. Borders on
26. A garden figurine, often
27. "No need to explain"
28. Plants with edible seeds
29. Rust producer
30. Further on
31. Highest deg. holders
35. Loafer insert
36. Say "*#!$#*"
37. Hooded jacket
38. Photographer Adams
40. Stand
42. "Beatle Bailey" dog
45. Paving material
46. Do an impression of

WACKY WORDY

Can you "read" the phrase below?

SHGETAPE

Answers on page 359.

WORD MATH

This puzzle works exactly like a regular math problem, but instead of using numbers in the equation you use letters. First, fill in the blanks with the proper name for each picture. Then solve the equation.

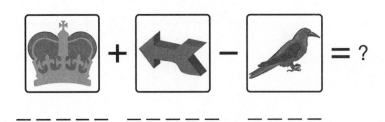

_ _ _ _ _ _ _ _ _ _ _ _ _ _

THREE-LETTER ANAGRAMS

What 2 words, formed from different arrangements of the same 3 letters, can be used to complete the sentences below?

1. _____ that I have my _____ car, I can drive anywhere I like.

2. She caught _____ butterflies in her _____.

3. _____ taught you _____ to dance?

4. She kept sticks of _____ in a _____ on her desk.

Answers on page 359.

THE DARK SIDE

Solve the clues below, and then place the letters in their corresponding spots in the grid to reveal a quote from director Tim Burton. The letter in the upper-right corner of each grid square refers to the clue the letter comes from. A black square indicates the end of a word.

A. More than usual, like many Burton films

‾‾ ‾‾ ‾‾ ‾‾ ‾‾ ‾‾
31 18 68 72 8 14

B. 2005 film "_____ Bride"

‾‾ ‾‾ ‾‾ ‾‾ ‾‾ ‾‾
23 30 47 42 9 44

C. Exotic fruit

‾‾ ‾‾ ‾‾ ‾‾ ‾‾
19 82 66 20 64

D. 2001 Tim Burton remake of a classic: 4 wds.

‾‾ ‾‾ ‾‾ ‾‾ ‾‾ ‾‾ ‾‾ ‾‾ ‾‾ ‾‾ ‾‾ ‾‾ ‾‾ ‾‾ ‾‾
40 71 74 37 24 58 12 53 83 2 57 79 43 60 22

E. Spoiled, perhaps

‾‾ ‾‾ ‾‾ ‾‾ ‾‾ ‾‾
29 4 28 85 45 78

F. 1988 Tim Burton hit "Beetle _____"

‾‾ ‾‾ ‾‾ ‾‾ ‾‾
7 73 84 69 50

G. Unparalleled technical skill

‾‾ ‾‾ ‾‾ ‾‾ ‾‾ ‾‾ ‾‾ ‾‾ ‾‾ ‾‾
35 17 54 15 41 34 6 21 32 52

H. 2003 tall-tale Burton flick: 2 wds.

‾‾ ‾‾ ‾‾ ‾‾ ‾‾ ‾‾ ‾‾
80 36 38 46 76 63 16

I. Recommended screening procedure

‾‾ ‾‾ ‾‾ ‾‾ ‾‾ ‾‾ ‾‾ ‾‾ ‾‾
65 26 49 13 81 67 61 39 56

J. Show place

‾‾ ‾‾ ‾‾ ‾‾ ‾‾ ‾‾ ‾‾
77 59 62 70 10 5 25

K. Spaghetti partner, sometimes

‾‾ ‾‾ ‾‾ ‾‾ ‾‾ ‾‾ ‾‾ ‾‾ ‾‾
33 3 48 1 51 55 75 27 11

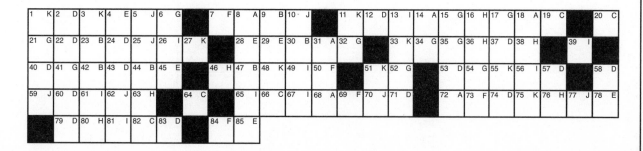

Answers on page 359.

SUDOKU

Use deductive logic to complete the grid so that each row, each column, and each 3 by 3 box contains the numbers 1 through 9 in some order. The solution is unique.

2			1	4	5			
5	4							
		9		8	2			4
		1		9		6		8
	7			2			3	
8		5		3		4		
1			8	7		3		
							9	7
			4	5	9			2

FRAME GAMES™

Can you "read" the phrase below?

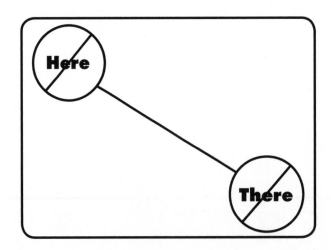

Answers on page 359.

GIRLS' NAMES LETTERBOX

The letters in the name ZOE can be found in boxes 4, 17, and 19, but not necessarily in that order. Similarly, the letters in all the other girls' names can be found in the boxes indicated. Your task is to insert all the letters of the alphabet into the boxes. If you do this correctly, the shaded cells will reveal another girl's name.

Hint: Compare KATE and LAURA to get the value of **A,** then KATE and QUEENIE for the value of **E.**

1	2	3	4	5	6	7	8	9	10	11	12	13

14	15	16	17	18	19	20	21	22	23	24	25	26

BETH: 5, 7, 17, 25

BRENDA: 5, 15, 17, 18, 20, 23

CILLA: 21, 22, 23, 24

DAVINA: 15, 16, 20, 21, 23

FRANCES: 6, 10, 17, 18, 20, 22, 23

GLADYS: 6, 12, 14, 15, 23, 24

JOSIE: 1, 6, 17, 19, 21

KATE: 3, 17, 23, 25

LAURA: 13, 18, 23, 24

MARY: 14, 18, 23, 26

MAXINE: 2, 17, 20, 21, 23, 26

PATSY: 6, 11, 14, 23, 25

QUEENIE: 8, 13, 17, 20, 21

WANDA: 9, 15, 20, 23

ZOE: 4, 17, 19

Answer on page 359.

CROSSED WORDS

Use each of the words and phrases below to complete this clue-less crossword grid. The puzzle has only one solution.

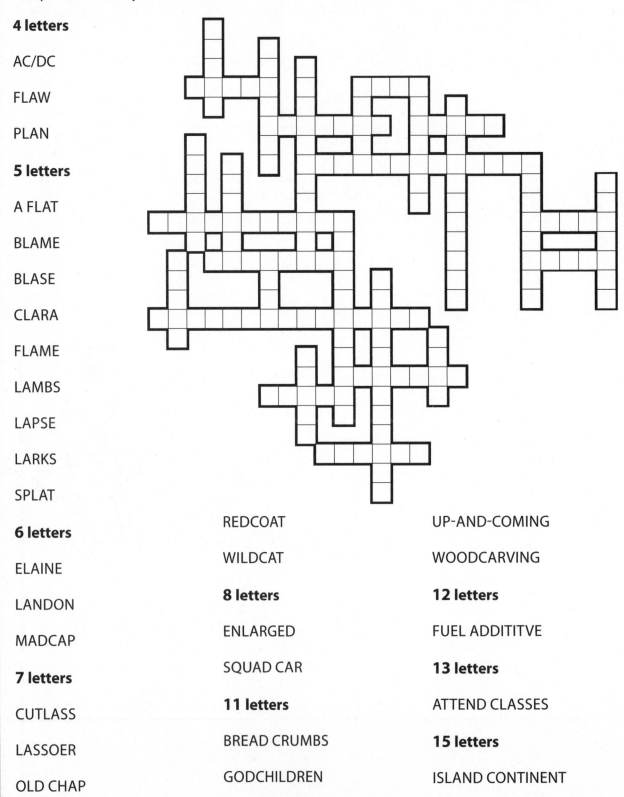

4 letters

AC/DC

FLAW

PLAN

5 letters

A FLAT

BLAME

BLASE

CLARA

FLAME

LAMBS

LAPSE

LARKS

SPLAT

6 letters

ELAINE

LANDON

MADCAP

7 letters

CUTLASS

LASSOER

OLD CHAP

REDCOAT

WILDCAT

8 letters

ENLARGED

SQUAD CAR

11 letters

BREAD CRUMBS

GODCHILDREN

UP-AND-COMING

WOODCARVING

12 letters

FUEL ADDITITVE

13 letters

ATTEND CLASSES

15 letters

ISLAND CONTINENT

Answer on page 359.

CAN YOU BE PICTURE-PERFECT?

These 2 illustrations may look the same, but there are some differences. Can you find all 4?

Answers on page 359.

NO TOUCHING!

In the word search below, none of the answers share any letters. Words can be found in a straight line horizontally, vertically, or diagonally. They may read either backward or forward. Just don't forget, no touching!

ADJACENT

ALONE

APART

DISTANT

FAR-FLUNG

INACCESSIBLE

INSULATED

ISOLATED

OFF

ONE

ONLY

PRIVATE

REMOTE

SCATTERED

SECLUDED

SEGREGATED

SEPARATE

SINGLE

SOLITARY

SOLO

UNCONNECTED

```
I  F  F  O  A  D  E  T  A  L  O  S  I
N  G  N  U  L  F  R  A  F  S  W  S  Q
S  D  E  R  E  T  T  A  C  S  D  E  R
U  S  E  E  D  Z  O  A  T  E  P  G  B
L  O  L  N  X  N  P  N  T  R  E  R  E
A  L  G  O  L  A  A  C  I  E  T  E  T
T  I  N  Y  R  T  E  V  N  O  O  G  A
E  T  I  T  S  N  A  O  H  L  M  A  R
D  A  S  I  N  T  L  Y  P  O  E  T  A
P  R  D  O  E  A  N  L  U  S  R  E  P
Z  Y  C  D  E  D  U  L  C  E  S  D  E
R  N  B  A  D  J  A  C  E  N  T  N  S
U  E  L  B  I  S  S  E  C  C  A  N  I
```

Answers on page 359.

FOOTBALL FEVER BY ALPHA SLEUTH™

Move each of the letters below into the grid to form common words. You will use each letter only once. The letters in the numbered cells of the grid correspond to the letters in the phrase below the grid. Completing the grid will help you complete the phrase and vice versa. When finished, the grid and phrase should be filled with valid words, and you will have used all the letters in the letter set. The letters already included in the grid will help get you started.

HINT: The numbered cells in the grid are arranged alphabetically, so the letter in the cell marked 1 will appear in the alphabet before the letter in the cell marked 2, and so on.

A B C D E F G H I J K L M N O P Q R S T U V W X Y Z

Answer on page 359.

QUIC-KROSS

This is a crossword puzzle with a twist. Use the clues to solve the puzzle. When complete, the circled letters will spell out a mystery word.

ACROSS

1. Tear (cloth)
2. Wager
3. Entreat

DOWN

4. Same type
5. Large Australian bird
6. Signal

Clue: Government system

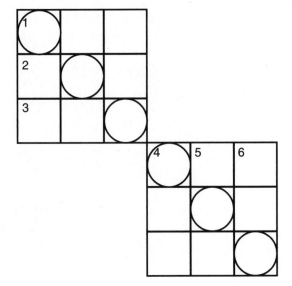

WACKY WORDY

Can you "read" the phrase below?

WAITC

Answers on page 359.

CODEWORD

The letters of the alphabet are hidden in code: They are represented by random numbers from 1 through 26. With the letters already given, complete the crossword puzzle and break the code.

A B C D E F G H I J K L M N O P Q R S T U V W X Y Z

1	2	3	4	5	6	7	8	9	10	11	12	13
U			N									

14	15	16	17	18	19	20	21	22	23	24	25	26
		C										

BEE-BOP JIVE

Only one bee looks the same in these 2 pictures after an hour of serious bee-bop. Can you find it?

Answer on page 359.

WORD-A-MAZE: ON THE GO

Travel in sequence through the puzzle from the left side to the right, using each numbered clue to determine the correct word. Connect adjacent words together with a common letter to proceed through the maze. Some letters are already given. The first and last words tie into the title.

1. Biography beginning
2. Business assn.
3. Choke
4. Trial answer
5. Look for
6. Type of roll
7. Amazon, for one
8. Spool
9. Quantity of bread
10. "Model T"
11. Draw parallel
12. _____ of corn
13. Spoil
14. One way to get there
15. Tell on
16. Haircut
17. Crib decoration

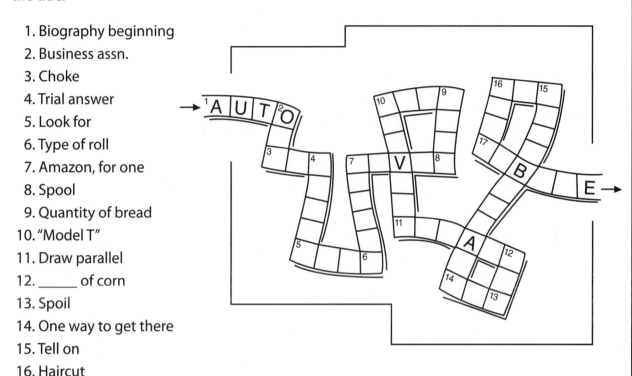

CROSS-MATH

Place the numbers 1 through 9 in the empty white squares so that the 3 horizontal and 3 vertical equations are true. Each digit will be used once. Calculations are done from left to right and from top to bottom.

	+		÷		=	9
+		÷		+		
	×		+		=	26
-		+		-		
	+		+		=	16
=		=		=		
8		10		4		

Answers on pages 359–360.

FLOCK OF F'S

This picture contains a flock of things beginning with the letter **F.** Can you find at least 9?

Answers on page 360.

WACKY WORDY

Can you "read" the phrase below?

PLAY
THERIM

COOL CAFÉ

In the Cool Café, the waiter has written down his orders incorrectly. Each item in the chart is in the correct column, but only one item in each column is correctly positioned. Using the clues below, can you correctly identify the surname, drink, and number of sugars for each order?

1. The latte or the coffee gets either 0 or 1 sugar.

2. Second to receive their order is Aviary, who has neither 1 nor 3 sugars and did not order a latte.

3. Just after Aviary is neither Bloggs nor Dribble, but whoever it is receives 0 sugar in either tea or mocha.

	Surname	Drink	Sugars
1	Aviary	tea	0
2	Bloggs	coffee	1
3	Crumple	latte	2
4	Dribble	mocha	3

Solve the clues below and then place the letters in their corresponding spots in the grid to reveal a historic quote. The letter in the upper-right corner of each grid square refers to the clue the letter comes from. A black square indicates the end of a word or the end of a row.

A. Author of quote: 2 wds.

‾‾ ‾‾ ‾‾ ‾‾ ‾‾ ‾‾ ‾‾ ‾‾ ‾‾ ‾‾ ‾‾
43 2 50 5 46 42 14 41 22 7 24

B. Surprise football tactic

‾‾ ‾‾ ‾‾ ‾‾ ‾‾
54 23 31 57 71

C. Resided

‾‾ ‾‾ ‾‾ ‾‾ ‾‾
12 1 55 11 15

D. 31st U.S. president (1929–33)

‾‾ ‾‾ ‾‾ ‾‾ ‾‾ ‾‾
65 27 48 21 3 19

E. Candid and straight to the point

‾‾ ‾‾ ‾‾ ‾‾ ‾‾ ‾‾ ‾‾ ‾‾ ‾‾ ‾‾
28 72 56 64 67 69 34 36 16 29

F. "King _____" (1933)

‾‾ ‾‾ ‾‾ ‾‾
33 68 35 25

G. Unfair circumstances

‾‾ ‾‾ ‾‾ ‾‾ ‾‾ ‾‾ ‾‾ ‾‾ ‾‾ ‾‾
20 73 17 59 60 9 37 53 26 44

H. Metropolis of northern India

‾‾ ‾‾ ‾‾ ‾‾ ‾‾
47 6 40 45 61

I. Sister's son

‾‾ ‾‾ ‾‾ ‾‾ ‾‾ ‾‾
4 39 18 30 66 49

J. Corpulent

‾‾ ‾‾ ‾‾ ‾‾ ‾‾ ‾‾
51 52 10 63 38 8

K. State of agreement

‾‾ ‾‾ ‾‾ ‾‾ ‾‾
13 32 70 62 58

1 C	2 A	3 D	4 I	■	5 A	6 H	7 A	■	8 J	9 G	10 J	11 C	12 C	■	13 K	14 A
15 C	16 E	17 G	■	18 I	19 D	20 G	21 D	22 A	23 B	24 A	25 F	26 G	■	27 D	28 E	■
29 E	30 I	31 B	32 K	33 F	34 E	35 F	36 E	■	37 G	38 J	39 I	■	40 H	41 A	42 A	43 A
44 G	45 H	46 A	47 H	48 D	49 I	■	50 A	51 J	■	52 J	53 G	54 B	55 C	56 E	57 B	58 K
59 G	60 G	61 H	62 K	63 J	■	64 E	65 D	66 I	■	67 E	68 F	69 E	70 K	71 B	72 E	73 G

Answers on page 360.

WHAT'S WRONG WITH THIS PICTURE?

This classroom is definitely crazy, but it's not just the kids who are out of control. There are 16 things wrong here that are helping to feed this room's 3 Rs—rowdy, rambunctious, and ridiculous. Can you find them all?

Answers on page 360.

STAR POWER

Fill in each empty square of the grid so that each star is surrounded by the numbers 1 through 8 with no repeats.

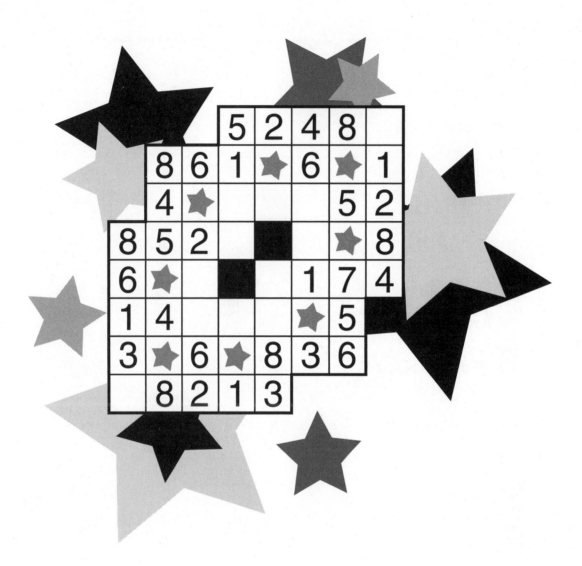

Answer on page 360.

SNACK TIME

Cryptograms are messages in substitution code. Break the code to read the brief biography and quote. For example, THE SMART CAT might become FVO QWGDF JGF if **F** is substituted for **T, V** for **H, O** for **E,** and so on.

OCQUBF O. OCINOBUV PB., WTDU NBURTJULF CLJUB SVLJML

PMOLRML, ML ZOKF DMLRFTFCFUJ OTR XKWMBTFU RKLJZTDO:

"NUKLCF QCFFUB, QMSMELK, DOUJJKB DOUUUBU, SUFFCDU

KLJ IKVMLLKTRU ML FMKRFUJ QBUKJ ZTFO SMFR MX

DKFRCN ML FOU RTJU."

CRYPTO-LOGIC

Each of the numbers in the 4-digit sequence below represents a letter. Use the mathematical clues to determine which number stands for which letter, and then reveal the encrypted word.

4 9 3 1

CLUES:

$S = 5$

$2S = I$

$I \div 10 = T$

$S - T = N$

$N - A = T$

$3A = E$

PASSPORT LETTERBOX

The letters in QATAR can be found in boxes 5, 8, 10, and 16, but not necessarily in that order. Similarly, the letters in all the other country names can be found in the boxes indicated. Your task is to insert all the letters of the alphabet into the boxes. If you do this correctly, the shaded cells will reveal the name of another country.

Hint: Compare PERU and JAPAN to get the value of **P,** then PERU and QATAR for the value of **R.**

1	2	3	4	5	6	7	8	9	10	11	12	13

14	15	16	17	18	19	20	21	22	23	24	25	26

BELGIUM: 1, 4, 7, 9, 18, 23, 24

CHILE: 4, 7, 9, 13, 21

DENMARK: 7, 8, 10, 11, 12, 17, 24

FRANCE: 7, 8, 10, 11, 21, 26

GERMANY: 1, 7, 8, 10, 11, 15, 24

HOLLAND: 9, 10, 11, 12, 13, 25

JAPAN: 10, 11, 14, 19

KUWAIT: 3, 4, 5, 10, 17, 18

LATVIA: 4, 5, 9, 10, 22

MEXICO: 4, 7, 20, 21, 24, 25

PERU: 7, 8, 14, 18

QATAR: 5, 8, 10, 16

SWEDEN: 2, 3, 7, 11, 12

ZIMBABWE: 3, 4, 6, 7, 10, 23, 24

Answer on page 360.

Can you "read" the phrase below?

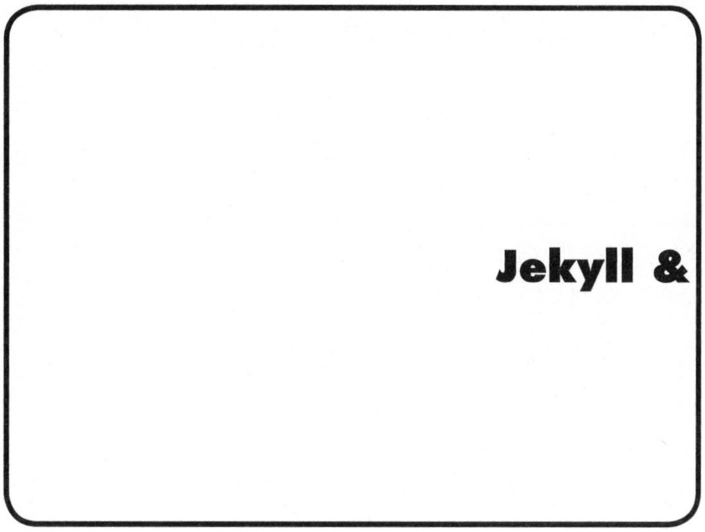

Jekyll &

WORD LADDER

Change just one letter on each line to go from the top word to the bottom word. Do not change the order of the letters. You must have a common English word or a name at each step.

FORD

_____

_____

_____

SOLO

CAN'T SEE THE TREES FOR THE FOREST?

Each set of words below contains the name of a tree. Can you find it? For example, the word "cloak" contains "oak," which is a type of tree.

1. Spine-tingling _____

2. Eyewitness _____

3. Clarence Darrow _____

4. Gospel music _____

5. Burma-Shave _____

6. Tea kettle _____

7. Shah of Iran _____

8. Naval architect _____

ELEVATOR WORDS

Like an elevator, words move up and down the "floors" of this puzzle. Starting with the first answer, the second word from each answer carries down to become the first word of the following answer. With the clues given, complete the puzzle.

1. Know _____	1. Expertise
2. _____ _____	2. "Why?"
3. _____ _____	3. Confess
4. _____ _____	4. Innocence
5. _____ _____	5. "Don't Touch!"
6. _____ _____	6. Mistaken
7. _____ Hit	7. Single, in baseball

Answers on page 360.

AUTO SHOWCASE BY ALPHA SLEUTH™

Move each of the letters below into the grid to form common words. You will use each letter once. The letters in the numbered cells of the grid correspond to the letters in the phrase at the bottom. Completing the grid will help you complete the phrase and vice versa. When finished, the grid and phrase should be filled with valid words, and you will have used all the letters in the letter set.

Hint: The numbered cells in the grid are arranged alphabetically, so the letter in the cell marked 1 will appear in the alphabet before the letter in the cell marked 2, and so on.

A B C D E F G H I J K L M N O P Q R S T U V W X Y Z

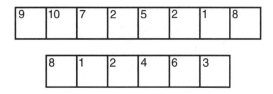

Answers on page 360.

ACROSTIC ANAGRAM

Unscramble the letters below to form words, then place the letters in their corresponding spots in the grid to reveal a quote from writer Denis Waitley. The letter in the upper-right corner of each grid square refers to the clue the letter comes from. A black square indicates the end of a word.

A. A T R A A N A M C
    — — — — — — — — —
    1 37 25 73 46 12 53 33 13

B. R B T E O E U T A H
    — — — — — — — — — —
    26 2 15 59 6 41 17 47 52 62

C. F T E L E L A
    — — — — — — —
    18 45 67 57 56 40 72

D. U B U C M S C
    — — — — — — —
    54 65 69 31 29 61 74

E. E C H B N
    — — — — —
    38 49 42 22 8

F. D A C E F A
    — — — — — —
    58 20 21 3 43 28

G. G A E H G L
    — — — — — —
    63 16 5 35 75 19

H. E E V N E N G C R C O
    — — — — — — — — — — —
    10 51 66 48 70 44 14 23 4 68 55

I. P O N H E E L T E
    — — — — — — — — —
    7 36 39 9 24 11 60 30 76

J. N Y E H H P
    — — — — — —
    27 50 71 32 64 34

1 A	2 B	3 F	4 H	5 G	6 B		7 I	8 E	9 I		10 H	11 I	12 A	13 A	14 H	15 B	16 G	17 B	18 C
19 G		20 F	21 F	22 E	23 H	24 I	25 A		26 B	27 L	28 F		29 D	30 I	31 D	32 L	33 A	34 L	35 G
36 I	37 A	38 E	39 I	40 C		41 B	42 E	43 F		44 H	45 C	46 A	47 B	48 H	49 E		50 L	51 H	52 B
53 A	54 D	55 H	56 C	57 C		58 F	59 B	60 I	61 D		62 B	63 G	64 L		65 D	66 H	67 C	68 H	69 D
70 H	71 L	72 C	73 A	74 D	75 G	76 I												

Answers on page 360.

NO SHOES, NO SHIRT, NO SERVICE

To protest other restaurants' "No shoes, no shirt, no service" policy, the sign on the door of the Hippy Dippy Vegetarian Restaurant reads: "Bare feet only." One Monday, 20 people showed up for dinner: 7 wearing socks, 5 wearing shoes, and 4 wearing both. How many people were allowed in?

QUIC-KROSS

This is a crossword puzzle with a twist. Use the clues to solve the puzzle. When complete, the circled letters will spell out a mystery word.

ACROSS

1. Floating craft
2. Metric weight measure
3. Thermal energy
4. Suspend

DOWN

5. Small, rough particle
6. Silicon oxide granule
7. Market place
8. Small pie

Clue: Boaster

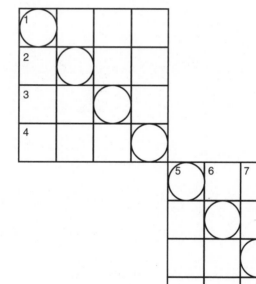

Answers on page 360.

SHOOTING STAR

Continue to fill in the alphabet moving clockwise around the wheel. Put one letter in every third space until you use all 26 letters of the alphabet. Then unscramble the letters at the 5 points of the star to form a common word.

THE BUT-NOT GAME

The object of the But-Not Game is to uncover the common element in each statement.

Carol likes felines but not cats.

Carol likes halibut but not flounder.

Carol likes palaces but not castles.

So...what does Carol like?

Answers on page 360.

ABCD

Every cell in this grid contains 1 of 4 letters: A, B, C, or D. No letter can be horizontally or vertically adjacent to itself. The tables above and to the left of the grid indicate how many times each letter appears in that column or row. Can you complete the grid?

				A	3	0	2	0	2	2
				B	1	2	0	2	2	2
				C	1	2	2	2	1	1
A	B	C	D	1	2	2	2	1	1
0	2	2	2							
3	0	2	1							
0	3	0	3							
2	0	2	2							
1	3	1	1							
3	1	2	0							

VEX-A-GON

Place the numbers 1 through 6 into the triangles of each hexagon. The numbers may be in any order, but they do not repeat within each hexagon shape.

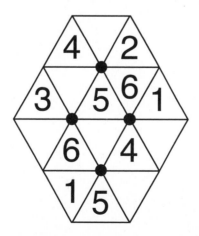

SUMMERTIME FUN

ACROSS

1. Give up, as a territory
5. Nautical assent
8. Scottish girl
12. Get-out-of-jail cash
13. Drink like a kitten
14. Director Kazan
15. Summertime warmer
17. Waiter's handout
18. "Gosh!"
19. "On the Road" writer Jack
21. Restaurant bill, informally
23. Wish undone
25. Loosen, as a shoelace
26. Pole or Czech
28. Vintage photograph shade
30. Flower features
32. Make beloved
36. Kitchen gadget
38. Major show, briefly
39. Capital of Jordan
42. It precedes Sept.
44. Teacher's favorite
45. Knitted baby shoes
47. Major ISP
49. Play opener: 2 wds.
50. Summertime destination
54. "Scat!"
55. Priest's robe
56. By mouth
57. Merit
58. Put into service
59. Egg layers

DOWN

1. Cronkite's former employer
2. _____ de Cologne
3. Nutcake
4. "What _____ is new?"
5. "The Greatest" prize-fighter
6. Northern Civil War soldier
7. Sporting blade
8. Summertime quaff
9. Native Alaskan
10. Mount in Exodus
11. Spaghetti topper
16. That girl
20. Wreck
21. Cookbook meas.
22. Pub offering
24. Cold War letters
27. Summertime respite from school
29. Lima's land
31. Unaccompanied
33. Emulate Christopher Columbus
34. Imitate
35. Deteriorate
37. Portrait painters' stands
39. Humiliate
40. Cocoa-flavored coffee
41. Car engine
43. Car fuel
46. Jacob's twin
48. "Yikes!": hyph.
51. Lincoln's nickname
52. Hightailed it
53. Golf legend Ernie

GRID FILL

To complete this puzzle, place the given letters and words into the shapes in this grid. Words and letters will run across, down, and wrap around each shape. When the grid is filled, each row will contain one of the following words: append, Boston, canary, Lipton, nickel, shiver, spices.

1. E, S

2. CA, ND, PP

3. SPIN, VARY

4. TONER

5. PICNIC

6. ABOLISH

7. SKELETON

ODD-EVEN LOGIDOKU

The numbers 1 to 9 are to appear once in every row, column, long diagonal, irregular shape, and 3 by 3 grid. Cells marked with the letter **E** contain even numbers. From the numbers given, can you complete the puzzle?

WACKY WORDY

Can you "read" the song title below?

N
O
O
M
D
A
B

102

Answers on page 361.

RHYME TIME

Each clue leads to a 2-word answer that rhymes, such as BIG PIG or STABLE TABLE. The numbers in parentheses after the clue give the number of letters in each word. For example, "cookware taken from the oven (3, 3)" would be "hot pot."

1. Substantial swine (3, 3): _____ _____

2. Purchase pastry dessert (3, 3): _____ _____

3. Look for mountaintop (4, 4): _____ _____

4. High-pitched dentist's tool (6, 5): _____ _____

5. Frighten grizzly (5, 4): _____ _____

6. Pony Express route (4, 5): _____ _____

7. Malicious monarch (4, 5): _____ _____

8. Too-cool young mare (6, 5): _____ _____

9. Polite request for cheddar (6, 6): _____ _____

10. Larger ship worker (6, 6): _____ _____

HOW'D HE DO IT?

Ivan was an extremely dangerous bank robber imprisoned at a maximum security prison. The warden wanted to make sure Ivan couldn't escape, so Ivan spent 24 hours a day 20 feet from the prison wall attached to one end of a 15-foot chain made from industrial-strength steel. In spite of this, Ivan still managed to climb the wall and go back to robbing banks. How did he escape?

PICNIC PUZZLE

Sally was preparing a picnic lunch for her hungry family. First, she covered the square table with a red-and-white checkerboard tablecloth that had 64 squares on its top surface. Then she put a pitcher of lemonade in each of 2 diagonal corner squares of the tablecloth. She had a plate of 31 hoagie sandwiches, each one big enough to cover 2 adjacent squares of the tablecloth. Sally wanted to put the hoagies on the tablecloth and cover the remaining 62 squares with no hoagies overlapping, none hanging over the edge of the table, and none standing on end. Was she able to figure out a way to do it before her hungry family showed up to eat them?

FITTING WORDS

In this miniature crossword, the clues are listed randomly and are numbered for convenience only. It is up to you to figure out the placement of the 9 answers. To help you, we've inserted one letter in the grid, and this is the only occurrence of that letter in the puzzle.

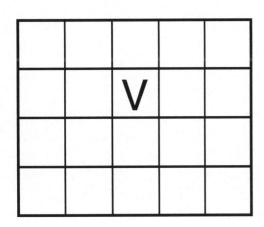

CLUES

1. Visibility problem

2. Peru's capital

3. Dumbfound

4. Track shape

5. Waikiki welcome

6. Bundles of hay

7. Show horse

8. Competitor

9. Pub quaffs

Answers on page 361.

FLOWERS LETTERBOX

The letters in ROSE can be found in boxes 6, 8, 16, and 23, but not necessarily in that order. Similarly, the letters in all the other flower names can be found in the boxes indicated. Your task is to insert all the letters of the alphabet into the boxes. If you do this correctly, the shaded squares will reveal the names of two more flowers.

Hint: Compare TULIP and AZALEA to get the value of **L,** then TULIP and SNOWDROP for the value of **P.**

AQUILEGIA: 5, 7, 8, 11, 12, 13, 21

AZALEA: 7, 8, 14, 21

BEGONIA: 5, 6, 8, 12, 21, 22, 25

CARNATION: 3, 5, 6, 9, 16, 21, 22

DAFFODIL: 5, 6, 7, 10, 19, 21

HONEYSUCKLE: 3, 6, 7, 8, 13, 18, 22, 23, 24, 26

JASMINE: 2, 5, 8, 17, 21, 22, 23

JONQUIL: 2, 5, 6, 7, 11, 13, 22

ORCHID: 3, 5, 6, 16, 19, 26

OXALIS: 1, 5, 6, 7, 21, 23

OXEYE: 1, 6, 8, 24

ROSE: 6, 8, 16, 23

SNOWDROP: 6, 15, 16, 19, 20, 22, 23

TULIP: 5, 7, 9, 13, 20

VERONICA: 3, 4, 5, 6, 8, 16, 21, 22

ZINNIA: 5, 14, 21, 22

1	2	3	4	5	6	7	8	9	10	11	12	13

14	15	16	17	18	19	20	21	22	23	24	25	26

CIRCUS TIME

Every word listed is contained within the group of letters below. Words can be found horizontally, vertically, or diagonally. They may read either backward or forward.

ACROBATS

AERIALISTS

BAREBACK RIDER

BARKER

BEARDED LADY

BEARS

BIG TOP

CALLIOPE

CLOWNS

ELEPHANTS

FAT MAN

FLYING TRAPEZE

KNIFE THROWER

LION TAMER

MAGIC

MIDWAY

PARADE

PEANUTS

POPCORN

RINGMASTER

RINGS

RUBES

SEALS

SIDESHOWS

TENTS

TIGERS

TIGHTROPE

```
S S T S I L A I R E A R E I R
T I G H T R O P E N G Z S I E
N I R E K R A B T L E I N R W
A N G N G R B R S P O G W E O
H R T E A L B E A R S H O D R
P O S D R I I R M F T M L I H
E C E I G S T O G E A E C R T
L P R T D G S B N G P T S K E
E O O M N E A T I T E T M C F
R P N I U M S C R A A N D A I
B A Y D L S S H I B N M L B N
Y L T W E L H E O E U G E E K
F R E A A T A R B W T E S R T
S H L Y O W C C O U S N E A A
R S T Y D A L D E D R A E B H
```

Answers on page 361.

TOTALLY CUBULAR!

As if he weren't diabolical enough, legend has it that the inventor of this cube has a dark side. Not content to produce a puzzle that can be solved only by bright 8-year-olds, his evil twin came up with a maze on top of a cube. Would you kindly come to the rescue of the black dot in the top square and help it get to the gray square at the bottom right?

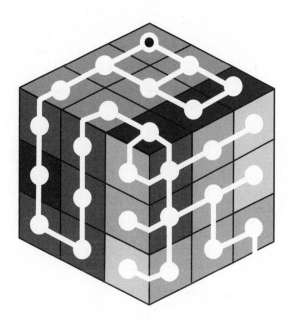

WORD LADDER

Use the clues to change just one letter on each line to go from the top word to the bottom word. Do not change the order of the letters. You must have a common English word at each step.

DINNER

_____ one who emerges victorious

_____ opposite of summer

_____ remote, or providing clues

_____ on the trail of his prey

HUNTED

Answers on page 361.

SUDOKU

Use deductive logic to complete the grid so that each row, each column, and each 3 by 3 box contains the numbers 1 through 9 in some order. The solution is unique.

6	4			3	8	9		
			2	9			6	
		5	1					
5	6			4	3	8		2
9		8	6	5			3	4
					9	3		
	7			6	2			
		6	7	1			4	9

THREE-LETTER ANAGRAMS

What 2 words, formed from different arrangements of the same 3 letters, can be used to complete the sentences below?

1. She _____ a trophy and _____ she is happy.

2. Dad gave me a _____ on my shoulder and a _____ on my head.

3. The queen sipped her _____ and _____ a scone.

4. We drove the _____ over an _____-shaped bridge.

5. The _____ gave birth to a _____ lamb.

Answers on page 361.

GRID FILL

To complete this puzzle, place the given letters and words into the shapes in this grid. Words and letters will run across, down, and wrap around each shape. When the grid is filled, each row will contain one of the following words: bat, batters, fly, glove, infield, peanuts, pitch.

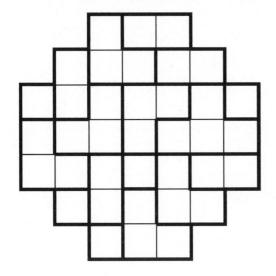

1. B, B, G, I, S

2. CH, FL, LD, LY, PA

3. EVE, FIT, OAT, PIN, TEA, TEN

4. RUTS

SIGN HERE, PLEASE

Carly is an autograph collector and sports fan who loves getting the autographs of baseball players but refuses to collect autographs from professional wrestlers because she has a sneaking suspicion the sport might be fake. Carly won a free ticket from her favorite morning radio program for a big local autograph show featuring a total of 100 baseball players and professional wrestlers. Carly didn't want any wrestlers to sign her autograph book. The DJ warned her that there would be at least one professional wrestler at the show, but out of every two people she approached for an autograph, at least one would be a baseball player. If every baseball player in attendance signed her book once, how many autographs would Carly get?

Answers on page 361.

WORD LADDERS

Change just one letter on each line to go from the top word to the bottom word. Do not change the order of the letters. You must have a common English word at each step.

1. DAWN

___
___
___

DUSK

2. JUMP

___
___
___

LAND

3. BOOT

___
___
___

KICK

4. BOAT

___
___
___

FISH

5. WAVE

___
___
___

SURF

6. KISS

___
___
___

LOVE

HASHI

③—②—③   ④ ②
 ③ ③   ②
    ④   ④ ③
③   ①
 ④   ⑥ ② ③
    ② ③ ④ ③
② ① ② ①
 ① ③ ② ② ③
② ③ ② ③ ①
 ① ② ③ ③ ③

Each circle represents an island, with the number inside indicating the number of bridges connected to it. Draw bridges between islands using the number given, but there can be no more than 2 bridges going in the same direction and there must be a continuous path connecting all islands. Bridges can only be vertical or horizontal and may not cross islands or other bridges. We've drawn some bridges to get you started.

Answers on page 361.

H IS FOR HELP!

Get from A to B as quickly as possible!

CUBE QUANDARY

In order for these 18 blocks to form a regular cube, an individual block must have a certain ratio of its height, length, and width. What is that ratio?

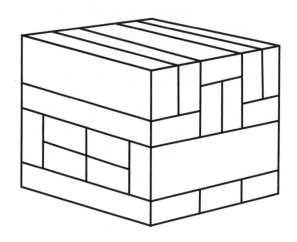

CODEWORD

The letters of the alphabet are hidden in code: They are represented by a random number from 1 through 26. With the letters already given, complete the crossword puzzle with English words and break the code.

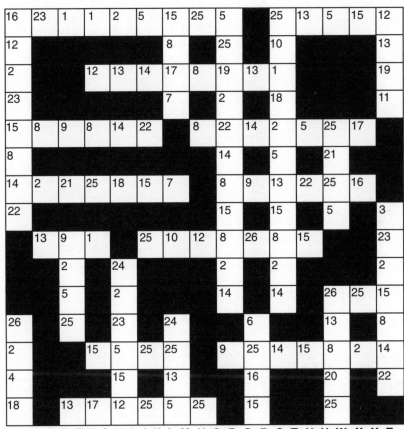

1	2	3	4	5	6	7	8	9	10	11	12	13
P								M				A

14	15	16	17	18	19	20	21	22	23	24	25	26

Answers on page 362.

RHYME TIME

Each clue leads to a 2-word answer that rhymes, such as BIG PIG or STABLE TABLE. The numbers in parentheses after the clue give the number of letters in each word. For example, "cookware taken from the oven (3, 3)" would be "hot pot."

1. Key to the poem's secret message (3, 4): _____ _____

2. Long-lasting winter ailment (3, 4): _____ _____

3. Stolen ship (3, 5): _____ _____

4. Prime fishing spot feature (4, 4): _____ _____

5. Dangerous place for a stroll (4, 4): _____ _____

6. Hardware store promo (4, 4): _____ _____

7. Scabbard hanger (5, 4): _____ _____

8. Little heist (5, 4): _____ _____

9. Missing color (4, 5): _____ _____

10. The fish always bite it (5, 4 or 4, 4): _____ _____

11. Gymnastic group (4, 4): _____ _____

12. Slugger's fast bat (5, 5): _____ _____

13. Short poem (5, 5): _____ _____

14. Disappointing dessert (4, 6): _____ _____

15. Some high-school swimmers practice here (6, 4): _____ _____

PRVRBS

Can you figure out these proverbs without their vowels?

1. S T T C H N T M S V S N N _____

2. B T T R L T T H N N V R _____

3. L L S W L L T H T N D S W L L _____

ANIMAL FARM

Welcome to the Mixed-Up Menagerie, a veritable zoo of friendly, if somewhat tangled, critters. You can't get in here unless you've found a suitable disguise. See that little SNEAK over there? Oops, he's really a SNAKE! How many other of our anagrammed beasts can you uncover?

Over there is the NE'ER RIDE, who thinks he's a caribou and doesn't like it when the tiny BALD GUY lands on his head. You wouldn't want to trifle with a GLARING BEET, a feline refugee from a circus act. The giant THE PLANE is about the only one who doesn't seem intimidated by the cat. The AMHERST and LEG RIB appear to enjoy running inside that little Ferris wheel, while GOLF DISH tend to prefer the safety of the pond. The EGO NIP flutters around dropping "presents" on everyone, even the graceful African PALE NOTE.

CROSS-MATH

Place the numbers 1 through 9 in the empty white squares so that the 3 horizontal and 3 vertical equations are true. Each digit will be used exactly once. Calculations are done from left to right or from top to bottom.

					=	2
×		+		+		
	+		+		=	21
×		-		×		
	+		+		=	12
=		=		=		
21		4		20		

Top row operators: + ÷ =

Answers on pages 362.

HITORI

The object of this puzzle is to have a number appear only once in each row and column. By shading a number cell, you are effectively removing that number from its row and column. There's a catch though: Shaded number cells are never adjacent to one another in a row or column.

6	4	4	4	7	6	2	1
5	8	7	6	4	1	2	2
6	4	2	2	5	8	7	3
3	1	3	8	8	4	5	7
7	7	1	2	3	5	6	8
8	2	6	4	1	3	2	5
8	7	5	8	6	2	1	1
8	3	2	1	2	7	8	4

THE FIRST LADY OF CINEMA

Cryptograms are messages in substitution code. For example, THE SMART CAT might become FVO QWGDF JGF if **F** is substituted for **T, V** for **H, O** for **E,** and so on. Break the code to read the quote from Katharine Hepburn.

"NPL JDUQ MPRC YS MPR NBKJM NKMP ORUMPRBJ NPRS LYZ EUS

TRDM MPRC YHRB MPR PRUX NKMP U JDRXWRPUCCRB?"

BAD WEATHER

ACROSS

1. Put into play
4. "_____ Blue" (TV show)
8. What a pumpkin grows on
12. Wrinkly dog
13. Honolulu's island
14. Wrinkle remover
15. San Diego Chargers logo: 2 wds.
18. Go after
19. Golfer Els
20. Drilling site?
21. Ore tester
23. Hosp. trauma units
24. "_____ to Avoid" (1965 Herman's Hermits hit)
25. Weather protection at the entrance
29. Tiny amounts
30. Occult ability
33. Female grouse
36. Ipso _____
38. Actor Davis
39. Suit maker
40. Suddenly astonished
43. "When you get right down _____…"
44. Beef or pork
45. Location of UFO sightings
46. Sgt. Snorkel's dog
47. Nimble
48. Road twist

DOWN

1. Missing one's bedtime
2. One seeking a mate
3. Picnic contest: 2 wds.
4. Tally mark
5. Pull quickly
6. Fraternity letter
7. Pester for payment
8. Violinist's asset
9. Subtle sarcasm
10. "It's the truth!"
11. Participate in
16. Cap
17. Painting surface
21. Jordan's capital
22. Brewskis
24. Comedian Johnson
26. Connect with
27. Partner of aahed
28. Howard Hughes became one
31. Part of a mutual fund
32. 1982 comedy about high schoolers
33. _____ voce
34. _____ in the dark
35. Astronaut's attire
36. Silent film comedian Arbuckle
37. Tire filler
39. Ruler mixed up in arts?
41. In typography-speak, more than one long dash
42. Account exec

CALCU-DOKU

Use arithmetic and deductive logic to complete the grid so that each row and each column contains the numbers 1 through 4 in some order. Numbers in each outlined set of squares combine to produce the number in the top corner using the mathematical sign indicated.

Answers on page 362.

GO FIGURE

Fill in each empty square with a number from 1 through 9. When the numbers in each row are added, you should arrive at the total on the bottom line. When the numbers in each column are added, you should arrive at the total on the bottom line. The numbers in each long diagonal must add up to the totals in the upper- and lower-right corners.

	4	4		1	20
3	2	6	7		25
9			1	6	25
8		9		5	33
		1		8	17

20

30 26 21 16 27 21

RHYME TIME

Each clue leads to a 2-word answer that rhymes, such as BIG PIG or STABLE TABLE. The numbers in parentheses after the clue give the number of letters in each word. For example, "cookware taken from the oven (3, 3)" would be "hot pot."

1. Order to appear before the boss (3, 2): _____ _____

2. Police chief (3, 3): _____ _____

3. Overweight belfry resident (3, 3): _____ _____

4. "Dinner, immediately!" (4, 3): _____ _____

5. Previous year's performers (4, 4): _____ _____

6. Despots on the Red Planet (4, 5): _____ _____

7. Incorrect flip-flop (5, 5): _____ _____

8. Small horse's pals (5, 7): _____ _____

Answers on page 362.

STAR POWER

Fill in each empty square of the grid so that each star is surrounded by the numbers 1 through 8 with no repeats.

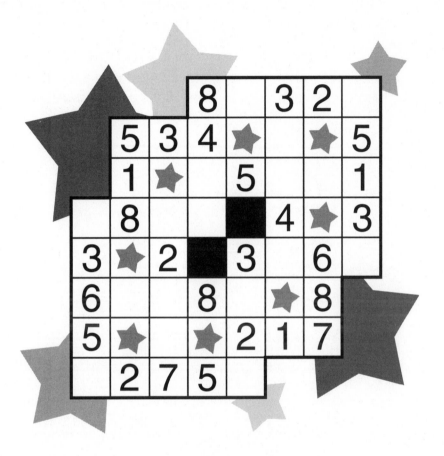

DESERT ISLAND QUIZ

While fishing for perch, Dean and Jerry accidentally hooked a killer whale that dragged their little boat to a deserted uncharted island where the boat crashed, stranding the unlucky fishermen. Having only a pencil and a puzzle book to pass the time, Dean and Jerry quickly solved every puzzle in the book and became bored. Jerry decided it was time to come up with his own puzzle. He handed Dean the puzzle book and asked him to secretly tear out a page. Jerry then told Dean to add up the remaining page numbers and tell him the total. When Dean said, "The total is 90," Jerry immediately knew the numbers on the page Dean tore out and how many pages were originally in the book. What were the answers?

Answers on page 362.

CHICK FLICK BY ALPHA SLEUTH™

Move each of the letters below into the grid to form common words. You will use each letter once. The letters in the numbered cells of the grid correspond to the letters in the phrase at the bottom. Completing the grid will help you complete the phrase and vice versa. When finished, the grid and phrase should be filled with valid words, and you will have used all the letters in the letter set.

Hint: The numbered cells in the grid are arranged alphabetically, so the letter in the cell marked 1 will appear in the alphabet before the letter in the cell marked 2, and so on.

A B C D E F G H I J K L M N O P Q R S T U V W X Y Z

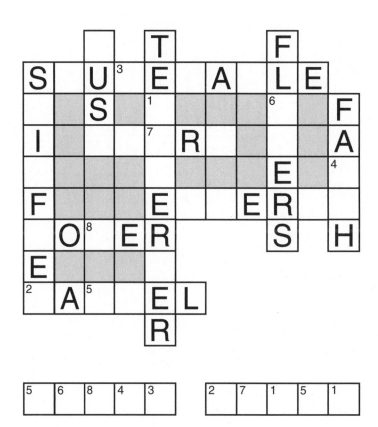

Answers on page 362.

FITTING WORDS

In this miniature crossword, the clues are listed randomly and are numbered for convenience only. It is up to you to figure out the placement of the 9 answers. To help you, we've inserted one letter in the grid, and this is the only occurrence of that letter in the puzzle.

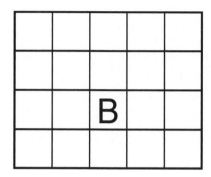

CLUES

1. Hindu sage

2. Accustom

3. Over again

4. Abominable Snowman

5. Credit's counterpart

6. Disencumbers

7. Tattered and torn

8. Quick haircut

9. Big horn

UNMISTAKABLE AROMA

Cryptograms are messages in substitution code. Break the code to read the humorous message. For example, THE SMART CAT might become FVO QWGDF JGF if **F** is substituted for **T, V** for **H, O** for **E,** and so on.

SDE YJU'V JYV WKRI J AREUR QKVGDEV

ADCIDUI MIVVKUM QKUT DL KV.

Answers on page 362.

HOW WILL YOU CONDUCT YOURSELF?

Every word listed below is contained within this group of letters. Words can be found horizontally, vertically, or diagonally. They may read either backward or forward.

ADAGIO

ALLEGRO

BEAT

BRASS

CANTATA

CHORD

CLASSICAL

CONCERTO

CONDUCTOR

ENCORE

ÉTUDE

FORTE

HARMONY

LEGATO

MOVEMENT

MUSIC

ORCHESTRA

PERCUSSION

REST

SCALE

SCORE

STRINGS

```
O Y T D P C L Y N O M R A H N
N I K L T I L A C I S S A L C
K R G Y N S T H C A N T A T A
D K M A R U W L D P A C L N N
H H G N D M N D M E L E R V R
P T F S S A R B B B G D S O K
E C O N C E R T O A N C T T M
R N O R C H E S T R A C X O E
C O Q L R S E O W L U D V K D
U R R E S T T F E D T E G C U
S G N S R Q K R N R M B H H T
S E C O C F H O I E O F J O E
I L F N L O C D N N H C B R M
O L F Q R T R T N K G M N D R
N A L K T L V E G L F S T E D
```

Answers on page 362.

SMART SCRAMBLEGRAM

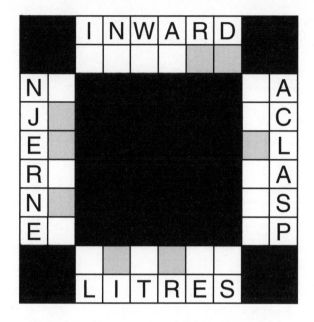

Four 6-letter words, all of which revolve around the same theme, have been jumbled. Unscramble each word, and write the answer in the accompanying space. Next, transfer the letters in the shaded boxes into the shaded keyword space, and unscramble the 8-letter word that goes with the theme. The theme for this puzzle is scientists.

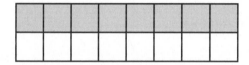

QUIC-KROSS

This is a crossword puzzle with a twist. Use the clues to solve the puzzle. When complete, the circled letters will spell out a mystery word.

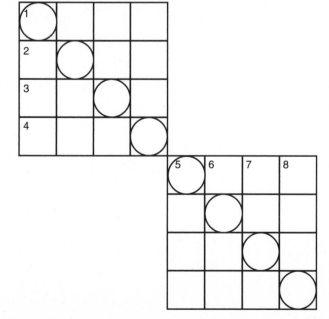

ACROSS

1. Relaxation
2. Large brown N.A. mammal
3. Final
4. After expected time

DOWN

5. Cost per unit
6. On top of
7. Small leak
8. Expired

Clue: quiet, conservative

Answers on page 363.

SUDOKU

Use deductive logic to complete the grid so that each row, each column, and each 3 by 3 box contains the numbers 1 through 9 in some order. The solution is unique.

		9	7	2				
1	4		6	5				
7		6	8		9			
2	9					7	8	
	6						4	
	1	4					2	9
			3		6	9		8
				8	7		3	6
				9	5	1		

WISE WORDS

Determine the next letter in this progression.

A P S I A P ___

Answers on page 363.

CIRCULAR REASONING

To solve this maze, just imagine you're on a survival-type TV show. Your team and the rival team have been led, blindfolded, to the center. Now the blindfolds are off, and you have to find your way out. The team that negotiates this puzzle fastest wins the challenge. How quickly can you get out?

RHYME TIME

Each clue leads to a 2-word answer that rhymes, such as BIG PIG or STABLE TABLE. The numbers in parentheses after the clue give the number of letters in each word. For example, "cookware taken from the oven (3, 3)" would be "hot pot." As a bonus, can you figure out the theme of this puzzle?

1. Microsoft mogul Bill glides across the ice (5, 6): _____ _____

2. Course of study taught by fashion designer Bill (5, 5): _____ _____

3. Cause "Groundhog Day" star Bill to fret (5, 6): _____ _____

4. "Shake, Rattle and Roll" singer Bill's Sunday through Saturday newspapers (6, 7): _____ _____

5. Former U.S. President Bill droppin' a clue (7, 6): _____ _____

Theme: _____

STAR POWER

Fill in each empty square of the grid so that each star is surrounded by the numbers 1 through 8 with no repeats.

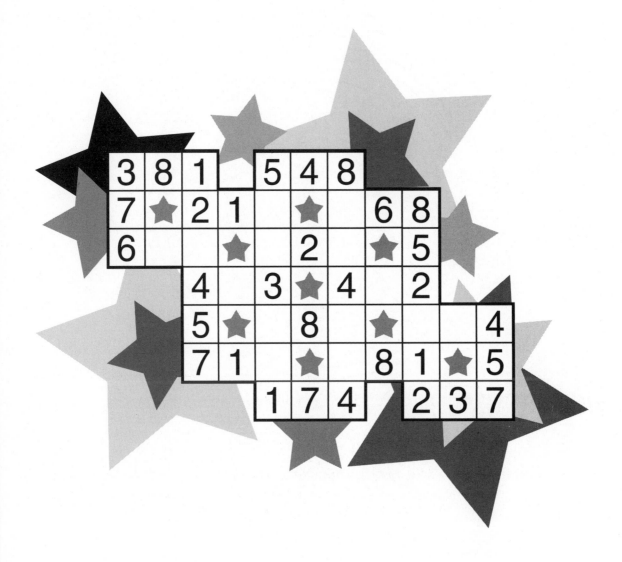

Answer on page 363.

BOYS' NAMES LETTERBOX

The letters in BILL can be found in boxes 2, 8, and 18, but not necessarily in that order. Similarly, the letters in all the other boys' names can be found in the boxes indicated. Your task is to insert all the letters of the alphabet into the boxes. If you do this correctly, the shaded squares will reveal two more names.

Hint: Compare PAUL and STEPHEN to get the value of **P,** then PAUL and MAX for the value of **A.**

BARRY: 6, 7, 18, 24

BILL: 2, 8, 18

CARL: 4, 6, 7, 8

DAVID: 2, 6, 16, 26

FRED: 7, 9, 12, 16

GREGORY: 7, 9, 22, 24, 25

JIM: 2, 3, 14

JOHN: 3, 5, 22, 23

MARK: 6, 7, 14, 19

MAX: 6, 14, 15

PAUL: 1, 6, 8, 11

QUENTIN: 2, 9, 11, 17, 21, 23

ROWAN: 6, 7, 13, 22, 23

STEPHEN: 1, 5, 9, 10, 21, 23

ZAK: 6, 19, 20

1	2	3	4	5	6	7	8	9	10	11	12	13

14	15	16	17	18	19	20	21	22	23	24	25	26

DEGREES OF CONFUSION

In order to graduate with a prestigious degree from Existential University, philosophy majors have to answer one simple question on the final exam: "What is at the end of time?"

What is the correct answer to this one simple question that will give the philosophy majors their coveted degrees from old E.U.?

Answers on page 363.

ACROSTIC CLUES

Solve the clues below and then place the letters in their corresponding spots in the grid to reveal a quote from John Lennon. The letter in the upper-right corner of each grid square refers to the clue the letter comes from. A black square indicates the end of a word.

A. John Lennon's first son

— — — — — —
68 3 86 61 30 43

B. The most-recorded song in pop history

— — — — — — — — —
58 83 70 6 20 72 5 46 78

C. Time restriction

— — — — — —
21 69 40 57 77 1

D. "_____ Submarine"

— — — — — —
37 51 76 4 2 84

E. Beatles 1968 chart-topper: 2 wds.

— — — — — — —
22 29 13 82 80 44 10

F. "I'm _____ Just to Dance with You"

— — — — —
7 42 36 25 88

G. Beatles lead guitarist

— — — — — — — —
41 35 27 81 16 28 38 47

H. Numerical data

— — — — —
45 75 73 71 32

I. Like many a Beatles concert: 2 wds.

— — — — — — — — —
12 65 34 67 50 79 39 9 26

J. "The _____ Hill": 3 wds.

— — — — — — — — —
62 64 56 66 14 17 55 19 23

K. Original Beatles bassist, _____ Sutcliffe

— — — — — —
54 18 60 24 52 74

L. Performed in various locations

— — — — — —
49 59 15 87 85 48

M. Wile E. _____

— — — — — —
33 8 63 11 31 53

1 C	2 D	3 A	4 D	5 B		6 B	7 F	8 M	9 I	10 E		11 M	12 I		13 E	14 J
15 L		16 G	17 J		18 K	19 J	20 B		21 C	22 E	23 J	24 K	25 F	26 I	27 G
28 G	29 E	30 A	31 M	32 H		33 M	34 I	35 G	36 F		37 D	38 G	39 I	40 C		41 G
42 F	43 A	44 E	45 H		46 B	47 G	48 L		49 L	50 I	51 D		52 K	53 M	54 K	55 J
	56 J	57 C		58 B	59 L	60 K		61 A	62 J		63 M	64 J	65 I	66 J	67 I
68 A	69 C	70 B	71 H		72 B	73 H	74 K	75 H	76 D	77 C		78 B	79 I	80 E	81 G
82 E	83 B	84 D	85 L	86 A	87 L	88 F								

Answers on page 363.

FINDING A DIGIT

In the grid, find a stylized number exactly like that shown next to the grid. The digit may be rotated but not mirrored.

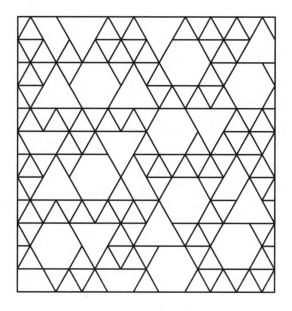 

WACKY WORDY

Can you "read" the phrase below?

INNING

INNING

INNING

INNING

INNING

INNING

I N N I N G

PRESIDENTIAL PUZZLE

Use each of the names below to complete the clue-less crossword grid on the next page. The puzzle has only one solution.

4 letters

FORD

5 letters

NIXON

TYLER

6 letters

HOOVER

WILSON

7 letters

CLINTON

LINCOLN

9 letters

CLEVELAND

10 letters

EISENHOWER

GEORGE BUSH

JAMES K. POLK

11 letters

JAMES MONROE

12 letters

RONALD REAGAN

13 letters

ULYSSES S. GRANT

ZACHARY TAYLOR

14 letters

CALVIN COOLIDGE

WARREN G. HARDING

15 letters

JAMES EARL CARTER

JOHN QUINCY ADAMS

MILLARD FILLMORE

THOMAS JEFFERSON

16 letters

BENJAMIN HARRISON

GEORGE WASHINGTON

17 letters

CHESTER ALAN ARTHUR

THEODORE ROOSEVELT

WILLIAM HOWARD TAFT

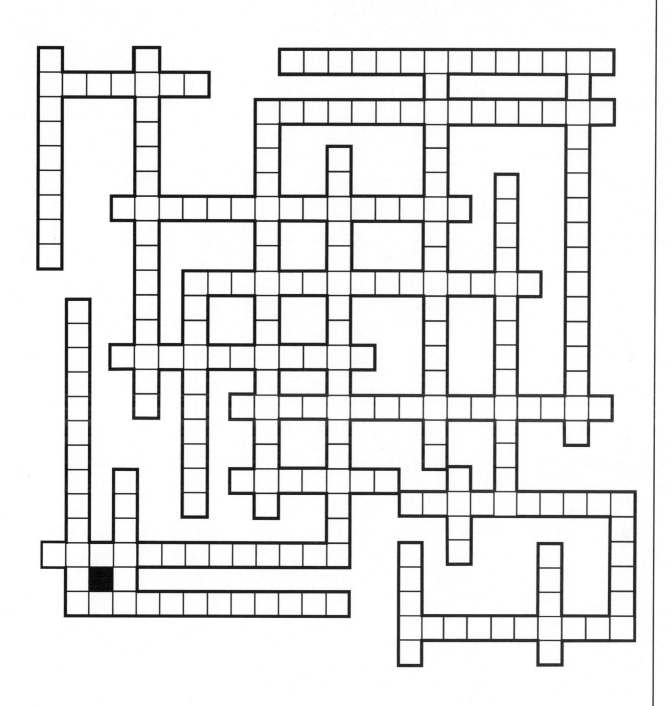

Answer on page 363.

ODD-EVEN LOGIDOKU

The numbers 1 to 9 are to appear once in every row, column, long diagonal, irregular shape, and 3 by 3 grid. Cells marked with the letter **E** contain even numbers. From the numbers given, can you complete the puzzle?

GO FIGURE

Fill in each empty square with a number from 1 through 9. The numbers in each row must add up to the numbers in the right-hand column. The numbers in each column must add up to the numbers on the bottom line. The numbers in each diagonal must add up to the numbers in the upper- and lower-right corners.

	4	6		2	4	26
1			7	9	1	26
4	6	8		4		30
9		5	3		9	34
2	4		8	1		24
	3	5	7		1	26

25

19 27 35 35 26 24 18

Answers on page 363.

VOWEL PLAY

In the freeform crossword below, each word or phrase of the answer contains the vowels **A, E, I, O,** and **U,** though not necessarily in that order. Numbers in parentheses indicate the number of letters in each word of the answer. When you solve a clue, its letters may help you figure out intersecting words.

ACROSS

2. Holding fast; persistent (9)
5. Entree (4, 6)
7. Giant tree of California (7)
9. State of extreme fatigue (9)
10. Limits (10)

DOWN

1. French farewell (2, 6)
3. Warned (9)
4. Playground challenge (1, 4, 3)
6. Broccoli relative (11)
8. Jesting; not meant to be taken seriously (9)

HONEYCOMB

Answer each clue with a 6-letter word. Write the words in a clockwise direction around the numbers in the grid. Words overlap each other and may start in any of the spaces around the numbers. To assist you, some letters have already been placed.

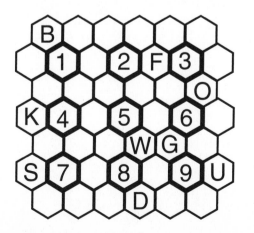

1. Incorporate
2. Envelop
3. Blundered
4. Servile follower
5. Luxuriate
6. Courting
7. Climbed
8. Seized with fingernails
9. Spice

Answers on pages 363–364.

GESUNDHEIT! BY ALPHA SLEUTH™

Move each of the letters below into the grid to form common words. You will use each letter once. The letters in the numbered cells of the grid correspond to the letters in the phrase at the bottom. Completing the grid will help you complete the phrase and vice versa. When finished, the grid and phrase should be filled with valid words, and you will have used all the letters in the letter set.

Hint: The numbered cells in the grid are arranged alphabetically, so the letter in the cell marked 1 will appear in the alphabet before the letter in the cell marked 2, and so on.

A B C D E F G H I J K L M N O P Q R S T U V W X Y Z

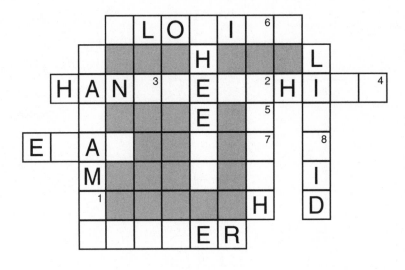

WACKY WORDY

Can you "read" the phrase below?

HAND
SERVE

Answers on page 364.

DOWNTOWN

Every word listed below is contained within this group of letters. Words can be found horizontally vertically, or diagonally. They may read either backward or forward. The leftover letters reveal the first two lines of a song describing the downtown area.

ARCADE

BANK

CHURCH

CITY HALL

COURTHOUSE

EMPORIUM

GROCERY

LIBRARY

MALL

MUSEUM

POLICE STATION

SCHOOL

STORE

THEATERS

```
            T C H
            E O G
          B M U R R
          I U R O S
          G I T C H
        T E R H E A R
        R R O O R A Y
        O O P U Y M L
      F E L T M S U C L B Y
      I D T S E E Y L A I R
      G A H T S S A N H S A
      H C R U H C K F Y A R
      R R M A M A L L T S B
    T H E A T E R S I C I A I N S
    E E N O I T A T S E C I L O P
```

Leftover letters: _____

_____

Answers on page 364.

IT'S ALL RELATIVE

Cryptograms are messages in substitution code. Break the code to read the humorous quote and its author. For example, THE SMART CAT might become FVO QWGDF JGF if **F** is substituted for **T, V** for **H, O** for **E,** and so on.

"XJNE V CVE OFQO XFQJ V IMNQQZ HFMA LGM VE JGSM, FQ

ONNCO AFBN V CFESQN. TSQ ANQ JFC OFQ GE V JGQ OQGUN

LGM V CFESQN—VEP FQ'O AGEHNM QJVE VE JGSM. QJVQ'O

MNAVQFUFQZ."

—VATNMQ NFEOQNFE

WORD LADDER

Use the clues to change just one letter on each line to go from the top word to the bottom word. Do not change the order of the letters. You must have a common English word at each step.

RANGER

_____ look-alike

_____ stick around

_____ more extended

_____ roomer

_____ The Artful _____

_____ walk unsteadily

_____ silo holdings

_____ file holder

_____ electrician's alloy

_____ you, when you complete this

SILVER

Answers on page 364.

SUDOKU

Use deductive logic to complete the grid so that each row, each column, and each 3 by 3 box contains the numbers 1 through 9 in some order. The solution is unique.

	3	7					9	
5			9	3			1	2
			1			9		
8			2	7	4			3
		3			5			
3	7			6	2		8	
	6					1	5	

BOTTOM OF THE DICE

You can't see the bottoms of the dice below, but can you determine the total number of dots on them anyway?

Hint: Opposite sides of standard dice always add up to the same number.

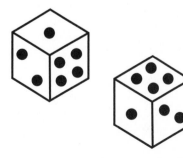

Answers on page 364.

GRID FILL

To complete this puzzle, place the given letters and words into the shapes in this grid. Words and letters will run across, down, and wrap around each shape. When the grid is filled, each row will contain one of the following words: almond, arrest, chains, firsts, golden, smacks, worker.

1. F, S

2. AC, SS, ST, TS

3. KIN

4. ENDS, GOAL, KERN, MORE

5. WORLD

6. ARMCHAIR

MAXIMS TO PONDER

Cryptograms are messages in substitution code. Break the code to read the humorous pieces of advice. For example, THE SMART CAT might become FVO QWGDF JGF if **F** is substituted for **T, V** for **H, O** for **E,** and so on. The code is the same for each of these cryptograms.

1. RHDKRQ FHJ QYHO TVC ZRHQRKQ WYP'C DRC QVLIRW MPCY SRC RPDMPRQ.

2. PRNRO HODVR ZMCX H QBYVQR ZXY MQ BHLIMPD JYVO BHOHLXVCR.

3. PRNRO FYYP H ZRORZYKE.

Answers on page 364.

HATS OFF

Can you find the 12 differences between the windows of this stylish hat shop?

Answers on page 364.

TRAINING EXERCISE

Run your train through the maze entering and exiting with the arrows. You can't back up, and you can't jump track at the crossovers—you must go straight through them.

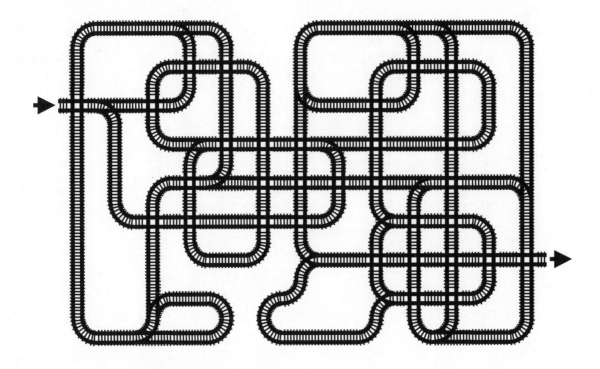

CALCU-DOKU

Use arithmetic and deductive logic to complete the grid so that each row and each column contains the numbers 1 through 4 in some order. Numbers in each outlined set of squares combine to produce the number in the top corner using the mathematical sign indicated.

4×	8×	3	4+
		2	
9+		4×	
		6+	

Answers on page 364.

CAN YOU CONJUGATE A BEATLE?

While on a round-the-world solo sailing trip, Maggie Ellen thought she had packed everything she needed. When an unexpected tropical storm blew her tiny boat aground on the small Pacific island of Uma-Uma, she realized she forgot to bring the 1 thing that would help her there: an Uma-Uma-to-English translation guide. The only thing she could remember was that the Uma-Uma language was made up entirely of the first names of famous rock stars. By listening carefully to the Uma-Umas speak while pointing to different things, she figured out that "John Paul George" meant large apple tree, "George Ringo" meant small tree, and "Paul Chubby" meant large coconut. What name did Maggie Ellen have to say to tell the Uma-Umas she wanted an apple?

SUPERFLUITY

Only 9 of the 12 boxes on the right are usable in this puzzle. Your mission is to find the 9 boxes that, when properly arranged, form a capital letter. Try to do this with your eyes only.

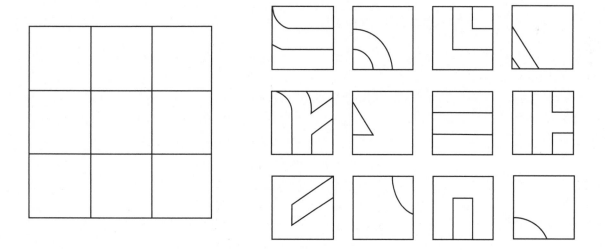

Answers on page 364.

ACROSTIC ANAGRAM

Unscramble the letters below to form words, then place the letters in their corresponding spots in the grid to reveal a quote from Will Rogers. The letter in the upper-right corner of each grid square refers to the clue the letter comes from. A black square indicates the end of a word.

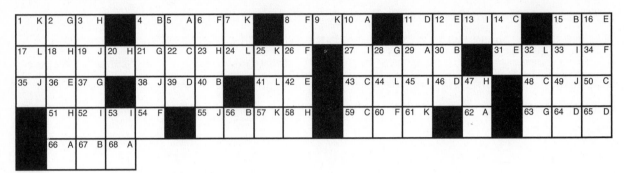

A. Y A Y N W A
___ ___ ___ ___ ___ ___
62 29 68 66 5   10

B. T C R I A C
___ ___ ___ ___ ___ ___
67 40 4   30 56 15

C. Y W T E A R
___ ___ ___ ___ ___ ___
48 22 14 43 50 59

D. E W R T O
___ ___ ___ ___ ___
11 39 65 64 46

E. I C A N H
___ ___ ___ ___ ___
36 12 31 16 42

F. N Y A N S O
___ ___ ___ ___ ___ ___
34 6   26 60 54 8

G. Z O E O N
___ ___ ___ ___ ___
28 21 2   63 37

H. Y I U T I L T
___ ___ ___ ___ ___ ___ ___
3   23 18 58 20 51 47

I. E D H A E V
___ ___ ___ ___ ___ ___
52 53 13 33 45 27

J. A N K L F
___ ___ ___ ___ ___
38 19 49 35 55

K. U O A Y T L
___ ___ ___ ___ ___ ___
57 9   1   25 61 7

L. D I V V I
___ ___ ___ ___ ___
44 41 17 24 32

Answers on page 364.

CODE-DOKU

Solve this puzzle just as you would a sudoku. Use deductive logic to complete the grid so that each row, each column, and both diagonals contain each of the letters of the word MOUTH in some order. The solution is unique. We've filled in 6 letters to get you started.

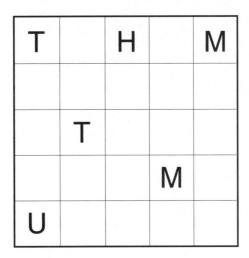

NAME SEARCH

Bob and Rob had a contest to see who could hide their name more times in this grid. One of the boys was victorious over his friend by only one! Reading their 3-letter names forward, backward, up, down, and diagonally, can you figure out the winner?

Each of them has also hidden the same 3-letter spherical object in the grid. Can you find both places where it appears?

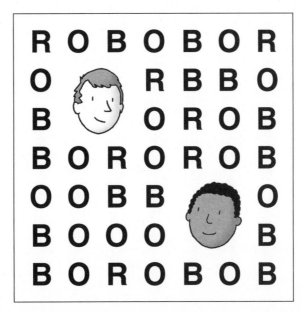

Answers on page 364.

HELLOO

Only one hand appears multiple times in an even number. Can you find it?

CALCU-DOKU

Use arithmetic and deductive logic to complete the grid so that each row and each column contains the numbers 1 through 4 in some order. Numbers in each outlined set of squares combine to produce the number in the top corner using the mathematical sign indicated.

10+		16×	
2/			
	3+	7+	3×
4			

Answers on page 365.

DECEMBER THE WHAT?

You are cordially invited to attend the annual Festival of Games. The contest will be in December, but competition begins the moment you read this invitation. Hope to see you there!

1. The date of the contest is not a multiple of 5.

2. The date is not the eve of a major holiday.

3. Neither of the digits of the date are the same, nor is the second digit equal to 1 more than the first.

4. The sum of the digits in the date is less than 7.

5. The contest is not on a Monday.

DECEMBER

SUN	MON	TUE	WED	THU	FRI	SAT
		1	2	3	4	5
6	7	8	9	10	11	12
13	14	15	16	17	18	19
20	21	22	23	24	25	26
27	28	29	30	31		

WHAT'S FLIPPED IN VEGAS, STAYS IN VEGAS

Vivian loved Las Vegas. After seeing all the hottest shows, eating at all the hottest buffets, and walking down all the hottest sidewalks, Vivian was ready to try and get hot at gambling. Unfortunately, the only game she knew was flipping coins. Luckily, she found Caesar's Shack, a tiny casino that catered to coin flippers. The croupier—or in this case, flippier—invited her to play the house game. He would let her flip a coin 20 times. Each time the coin landed on heads, he would pay her $2. Each time the coin landed on tails, she had to pay him $3. Vivian was on the edge but decided to give it a try. She flipped the coin 20 times and left Caesar's Shack with the same amount of money she came in with. How many times did the coin come up heads?

TOTALLY CUBULAR!

Which of the shapes below (A through D) can be folded to form the cube in the center? Hint: There may be more than one answer.

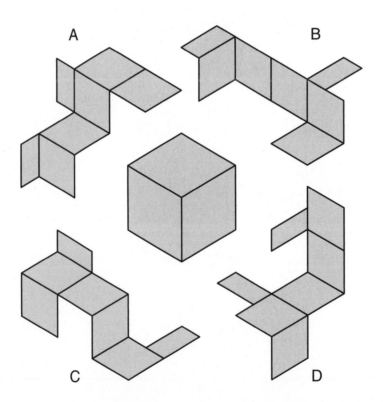

Answers on page 365.

GO FOR THE GOURD

Ignoring spaces, capitalization, and punctuation, how many occurrences of the consecutive letters **GO** can you find in the following paragraph?

Gomer got the urge to drag out an orange gourd even though it wasn't Halloween. He carved his own face (which shows that his ego was a big one!). Gomer got more gourds and carved a goose with gout, an egg on a wall, and a gang of gorillas going ape. He showed them to his gal Gloria, a former go-go dancer who was now a big old gourd grower from Georgia. She gave Gomer a bag of seeds to grow more gourds and go whole-hog out on his porch carving them.

DON'T MISS THE BOAT ON THIS ONE

Study these numbers carefully.

3 7 8 2

1 2 6 3 4 4

9 7 4

5 3 7 5

2 1 2 2 3 4 3 3

7 1 1 3 4 2 2

Based on your observations, what number should replace the question mark the sequence below?

3 3 5 5 ? 2 1

"EASY" DOES IT

ACROSS

1. "I'm glad that's over!"
5. Edit from the tape
10. Non-Gentile
13. Mae West's invite, in part: 2 wds.
14. "Superman" star
15. Baaed girl
16. Circe and Lorelei
18. Shirt kind
19. Incessantly
20. Excited, with "up"
21. Insignificant sort
23. Misplayed at bridge
25. Worthless?
27. Bishopric
28. Unmatched
32. French seaport
35. 14-Across's role
36. "Death and Fire" artist
37. Potent wriggler
38. Princess Di's family name
41. Mrs.: Fr., abbr.
42. "Holy cow!"
44. Oceanbound flier
45. a.k.a. Barnaby Jones
47. Unexpected successes
49. Spelldown
50. Oculist's creation
51. Establishes
55. Pup
58. Game, _____, match
59. SOS
60. "A mouse!"
61. Legendary ballplayer: 3 wds.
65. Churchillean gesture
66. Completed
67. Fouled up
68. Chicago trains, for short
69. Rushes
70. Admit, with "up"

DOWN

1. Annoy
2. Muscle Beach denizens: hyph.
3. Josephine, e.g.
4. Soppy
5. Poodle or Peke
6. "_____ we forget"
7. Undergoers of: suff.
8. Garden gal
9. See 1-Down
10. "_____ plumerai": Fr., 2 wds.
11. Pitcher
12. Turn on the waterworks
13. Gag or gang ending
17. Name in Korea's history
22. Bubbly bandmaster
24. Understands
25. Mugwump's perch
26. Network
28. William's kin
29. O'Neill's "Desire" site
30. Dotted, coat-of-arms-wise
31. Spotted
32. Entreats
33. Tackle-box item
34. Robert _____: 2 wds.
35. Jean and Deborah
39. Hammerhead part
40. "_____ pleat," zoot suit feature
43. Former governor and senator Miller
46. Show up: 2 wds.
48. Mill contents
49. _____ noire
51. Burpee's wares
52. Lascivious looks
53. "It's nobody _____ business"
54. Drove 80
55. "_____ Only Just Begun"
56. Scoundrel
57. Barely makes it
58. Garbo's home: abbr.
62. Compass point
63. Town near Arhem
64. Zebra on the field, for short

WORD JIGSAW

Fit the pieces into the frame to form common words reading across and down. There's no need to rotate the pieces; they'll fit as shown, with each piece used once.

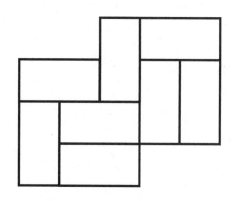

Answers on page 365.

LET IT SHINE BY ALPHA SLEUTH™

Move each of the letters below into the grid to form common words. You will use each letter once. The letters in the numbered cells of the grid correspond to the letters in the song title at the bottom. Completing the grid will help you complete the song title and vice versa. When finished, both should be filled with valid words, and you will have used all the letters in the letter set.

Hint: The numbered cells in the grid are arranged alphabetically, so the letter in the cell marked 1 will appear in the alphabet before the letter in the cell marked 2, and so on.

A B C D E F G H I J K L M N O P Q R S T U V W X Y Z

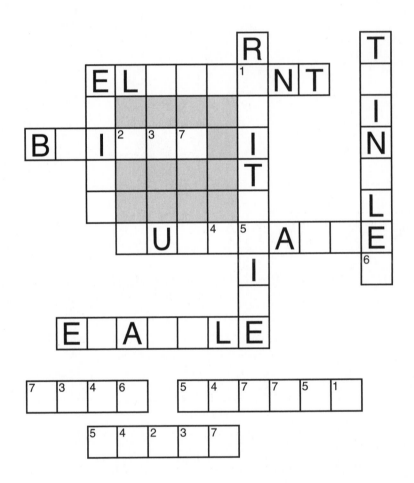

Answers on page 365.

WACKY WORDY

Can you "read" the phrase below?

L
O
A
D
S
O
N
G
S

NAME CALLING

Decipher the encoded words in the humorous quips below using the numbers and letters on the phone pad. Remember that each number can stand for 3 or 4 possible letters.

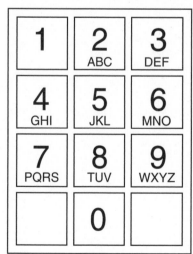

1	2 ABC	3 DEF
4 GHI	5 JKL	6 MNO
7 PQRS	8 TUV	9 WXYZ
	0	

1. So easy to use a child can do it. Child sold 7–3–7–2–7–2–8–3–5–9.

2. Common sense 2–4–6'–8.

3. A king's castle is 4–4–7 4–6–6–3.

4. Length, width, height, and cost are the four 3–4–6–3–6–7–4–6–6–7.

AT THE MOVIES

Every word listed below is contained within this group of letters. Words can be found horizontally, vertically, or diagonally. They may read either backward or forward.

ACADEMY AWARD

ACTION

ACTOR

ACTRESS

AISLES

ARCADE

BALCONY

BOX OFFICE

CAMERA

CANDY

CAST

CLASSIC

COMEDY

CO-STAR

DIRECTOR

DOCUMENTARY

EGRESS

EPIC

FEATURE

FILM NOIR

GENRE

INDIE

MULTIPLEX

MUSICAL

OPENING

PREQUEL

PREVIEW

PRODUCER

REVIEWER

SCI-FI

SCREEN

SCRIPT

SEATS

SEQUEL

SODA

SOUND

STUBS

USHER

WRITER

```
Y C W A C A D E M Y A W A R D
N A Z F E A T U R E P I C O I
O N C G F I L M N O I R C Z R
C D M T L T P I R C S U A M E
L Y S C I F I R S W M Y S U C
A O J P R O T C A E S S T S T
B P L E I D N I N L Q O Y I O
O E E R X Y S T U B S U D C R
X N U E C L A S S I C N E A E
O I Q W R R Z S S E W D M L C
F N E E Y N C O S T A R O U U
F G R I A R E M A C Z T C S D
I Y P V E T E G R E S S S H O
C S S E R T C A I S L E S E R
E V N R E T I R W E I V E R P
```

Answers on page 365.

BARBERSHOP DUET

Something has gone drastically wrong in this barbershop. We count 7 things that are wrong. Can you find them all?

QUIC-KROSS

This is a crossword puzzle with a twist. Use the clues to solve the puzzle. When complete, the circled letters will spell out a mystery word.

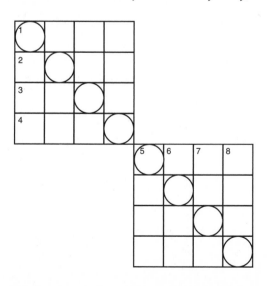

ACROSS

1. Medieval poet
2. Heavy, cheap metal
3. Rant
4. Satisfy

DOWN

5. Wander
6. Columbus: "I see _____"
7. Wire enclosure
8. Become dim

Clue: Drink

Answers on page 365.

TRIPLE-JOINTED

Use each of the words and phrases below to complete this clue-less crossword grid. The puzzle has only one solution.

7 letters

WELL-LIT

9 letters

CHESS SETS

CLIFF FACE

FREE E-MAIL

STILL LIFE

10 letters

DRESS SHIRT

FULL-LENGTH

GRASS SKIRT

SCOTT TUROW

SQUALL LINE

STIFF FINES

SWISS STEAK

YOU'LL LAUGH

11 letters

CROSS SWORDS

MISS SCARLET

SEE EYE TO EYE

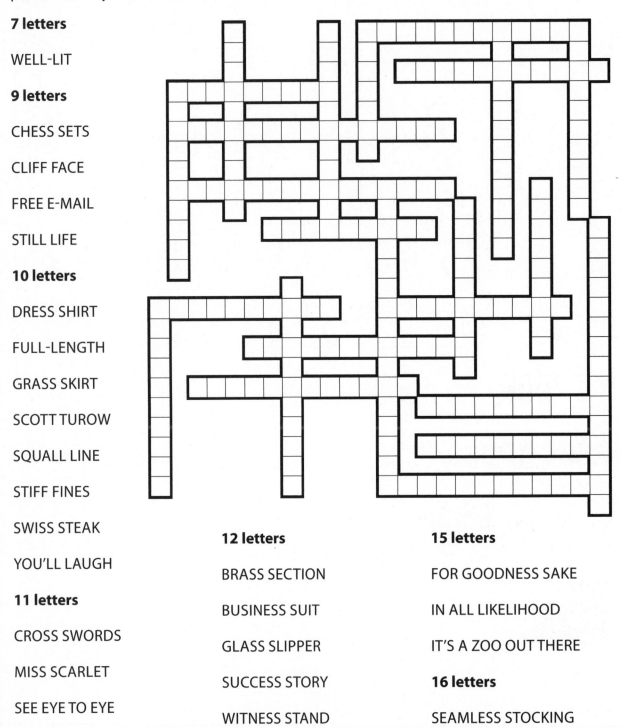

12 letters

BRASS SECTION

BUSINESS SUIT

GLASS SLIPPER

SUCCESS STORY

WITNESS STAND

15 letters

FOR GOODNESS SAKE

IN ALL LIKELIHOOD

IT'S A ZOO OUT THERE

16 letters

SEAMLESS STOCKING

Answer on page 365.

SUDOKU

Use deductive logic to complete the grid so that each row, each column, and each 3 by 3 box contains the numbers 1 through 9 in some order. The solution is unique.

4			7					
	3	8		4				
9				8			3	
2			8			4	5	
		4	6		5	8		
	8	6			9			1
	6			9				8
				6		3	1	
					8			7

NUMBER CROSSWORD

Fill in this crossword with numbers instead of letters. Use the clues to determine which of the numbers 1 through 9 belongs in each square. No zeros are used.

ACROSS
1. Consecutive digits, ascending
4. A number of the form abab
6. A palindrome
8. Consecutive digits, ascending

DOWN
1. A square
2. A palindrome
3. Consecutive digits, ascending
5. Its third digit is the sum of its first 2 digits
7. Both of its digits are odd

Answers on pages 365–366.

WORD LADDERS

Change just one letter on each line to go from the top word to the bottom word. Do not change the order of the letters. You must have a common English word at each step.

1. GRAY
   _____
   _____
   _____
   _____
   GOLD

2. BLUE
   _____
   _____
   _____
   _____
   GRAY

3. BLACK
   _____
   _____
   _____
   _____
   GREEN

4. ROSE
   _____
   _____
   JADE

5. TEAL
   _____
   _____
   _____
   LIME

1-2-3

Place the numbers 1, 2, or 3 in the circles below. The challenge is to have only these 3 numbers in each connected row and column—no number should repeat. Any combination is allowed.

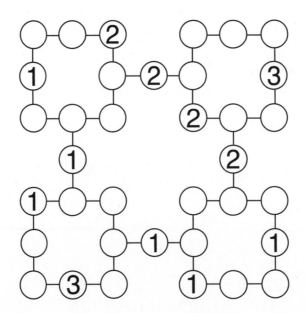

156

Answers on page 366.

MATCH-UP TWINS

The 10 hexagons below may look identical at first glance, but they're not. They can actually be divided into 5 pairs of identical designs. Can you match them up?

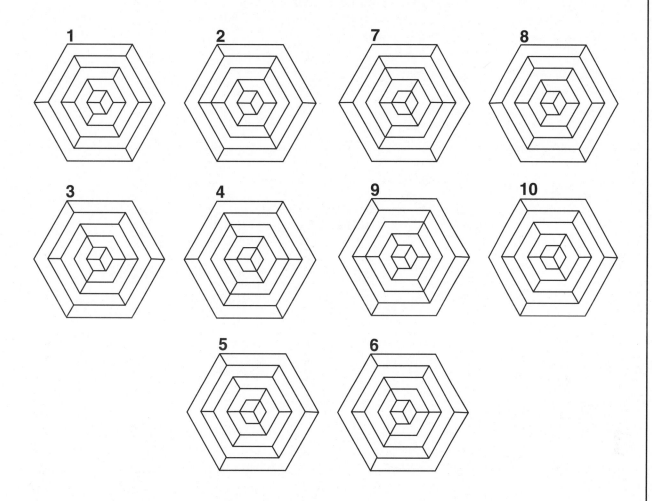

WACKY WORDY

Can you "read" the phrase below?

CHIMADENA

TALK SHOW

On *The Jock Letterbox Show,* the producer has written down the guest list incorrectly. Although each entry is in the correct column only one entry in each column is correctly positioned. The following facts are true about the correct order:

1. Ponds is one place below book.

2. Bruce is one place above movie.

3. The discussion of a movie is not second.

4. Hal is one place above Wells.

Can you give the guest's name, surname, and topic for each position?

	Name	Surname	Topic
1	Hal	Bore	politics
2	Jackie	Rawlings	book
3	Bruce	Wells	movie
4	Gary	Ponds	baseball

CODE-DOKU

B		D				A		
A		I			E		R	
G	R		I		B			M
			A	R				E
	M	B	E		D		G	
A			B	M			R	
E		G		A			B	
B		M			I	C		
	I					D		

Solve this puzzle just as you would a sudoku. Use deductive logic to complete the grid so that each row, each column, and each 3 by 3 box contains each of the letters ABCDEGIMR in some order. The solution is unique.

When you have completed the puzzle, unscramble those 9 letters to reveal a university town in England.

Answer: _____

Answers on page 366.

STAR POWER

Fill in each empty square of the grid so that each star is surrounded by the numbers 1 through 8 with no repeats.

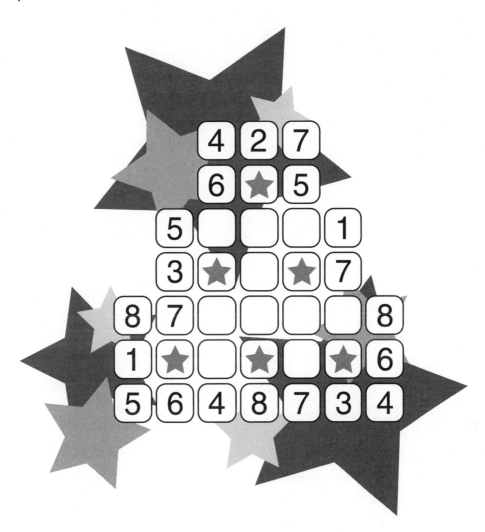

WACKY WORDY

Can you "read" the phrase below?

C(AKE)

Answers on page 366.

COLOR-CODED

ACROSS

1. Mud, dust, and grime
6. Blackthorn
10. Resistance units
14. "The Tempest" prankster
15. Rate
16. Free-for-all
17. "Jealousy consumes me!": 4 wds.
20. Lipped off
21. Roman emperor of unsavory repute
22. Gaming cube
23. It's a long story
25. Alliances
27. Benevolent Order member
30. Wild guess
32. Slip up
33. Superman's Lane
35. Heavy obligation
37. Sordid
41. Sudden turn of events: 4 wds.
44. Snorer's problem
45. Sporting sword
46. Send out
47. Bird's beak
49. Wine label datum
51. _____ Lanka
52. Soft felt hats
56. "Aw, heck!"
58. Boston Bruins legend
59. Ancient Peruvian
61. Has faith in
65. "Coward!": 3 wds.
68. Competitive advantage
69. Butter substitute
70. Andes beast of burden
71. What's left over, with "the"
72. Reaction to a pass, maybe
73. Aden's land

DOWN

1. Honoree's spot
2. 1963 film "_____ la Douce"
3. Fixes illegally, as an election
4. Concise
5. Gets some shuteye
6. D.C. bigwig
7. Green frontage
8. Bay window
9. Main course
10. Galena, e.g.
11. Bombay believer
12. Hollywood release
13. Eyelid afflictions
18. Newspaper employee
19. Suffering from laryngitis, maybe
24. River conveyance
26. Diving bird
27. Napoleon's home, once
28. Buttonhole alternative
29. Pottery oven
31. Like a ride on a rough road
34. Court reporter, briefly
36. Spirited mount
38. Poor box contents
39. Sierra Club co-founder John
40. Abominable Snowman
42. Spenser's "The _____ Queene"
43. Like an exuberant welcome
48. Bluegrass instruments
50. Hardly ever
52. Vestibule
53. Wear away
54. Pharmaceutical output
55. Rower's craft
57. Bridal veil material
60. Between ports
62. Bridge coup
63. Hefty volume
64. Graceful swimmer
66. Eligible for a pension, maybe: Abbr.
67. Spinning toy

HASHI

Each circle represents an island, with the number inside indicating the number of bridges connected to it. Draw bridges between islands using the number given, but there can be no more than 2 bridges going in the same direction and there must be a continuous path connecting all islands. Bridges can only be vertical or horizontal and may not cross islands or other bridges. We've drawn some bridges to get you started.

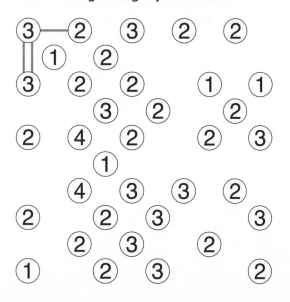

Answers on page 366.

SUDOKU

Use deductive logic to complete the grid so that each row, each column, and each 3 by 3 box contains the numbers 1 through 9 in some order. The solution is unique.

						1		
	5			4				3
9	6		8					
3	4			7				9
		9		1		2		
7				2			3	8
					1		4	6
1				3			5	
		5						

TO THE LETTER

Each letter represents a number between 1 and 9. No zeros are used. Can you determine the set of letter values that will make all of the equations work?

Hint: Start by listing all of the combinations of 3 different digits that add up to 9.

$$A + B + C = 9$$

$$B + D + E = 11$$

$$A + B + B = 13$$

$$E + E + F = 15$$

Answers on page 366.

Unscramble the letters below to form words, then place the letters in their spots in the grid to reveal a quote from James Thomson. The letter in the upper-right corner of each grid square refers to the clue the letter comes from. A black square indicates the end of a word.

A. T S S A R E L E B H

— — — — — — — — — —
46 7 31 20 16 40 60 61 38 12

B. E O E M R E R M T H T

— — — — — — — — — — —
50 51 41 28 1 26 8 47 69 37 14

C. E O E R O G S F

— — — — — — — —
58 71 3 52 30 23 63 49

D. O Y F I R F T

— — — — — — —
24 45 34 44 70 65 48

E. S I A N H A U T E A

— — — — — — — — — —
18 27 55 57 29 42 9 32 6 67

F. C I F A O T N

— — — — — — —
5 54 66 33 43 2 21

G. H U U C E N

— — — — — —
15 68 10 59 56 17

H. N U K H C Y

— — — — — —
25 19 13 72 36 62

I. O I D E D W W

— — — — — — —
53 35 11 64 39 4 22

1 B	2 F	3 C	4 I		5 F	6 E	7 A	8 B		9 E	10 G	11 I		12 A	13 H	14 B	15 G		16 A
17 G	18 E		19 H	20 A	21 F	22 I		23 C	24 D		25 H	26 B	27 E	28 B	29 E	30 C	31 A		32 E
33 F	34 D	35 I	36 H	37 B	38 A		39 I	40 A	41 B	42 E		43 F	44 D		45 D	46 A	47 B	48 D	49 C
	50 B	51 B	52 C		53 I	54 F	55 E	56 G	57 E	58 C	59 G	60 A		61 A	62 H	63 C		64 I	65 D
	66 F	67 E	68 G	69 B	70 D	71 C	72 H											

Answers on page 366.

WHAT'S FOR DINNER?

There are 18 differences between the top and the bottom scenes of this family dinner. Can you find all of them?

Answers on page 366.

ANAGRAMMATICALLY CORRECT

Fill in the blanks in each sentence below with 4-letter words that are anagrams (rearrangements) of one another.

1. Use _____ baseball bat if you want to get more _____.

2. Male cats are called _____ by _____ people.

3. The man _____ his _____ hat on the bus.

4. The old man related his _____ until _____ in the evening.

5. An _____ of land was the prize promised to the winner of the _____.

6. My finger is still _____ where I pricked it on the thorn of a _____.

7. It rained _____ and dogs on the _____ during the last 2 _____ of the play when it was performed in the park.

8. It was a _____ to clean the pots and _____ while the kids were taking their _____.

TIMES SQUARE

Fill each square in the grid with a digit from 1 through 9. When the numbers in each row are multiplied, you should arrive at the total in the right-hand column. When the numbers in each column are multiplied, you should arrive at the total on the bottom line. Important: The number 1 can only be used once in any row or column; other numbers can be repeated.

Hint: Some squares contain 5s or 7s. Identify these first.

				27
				225
				175
				28
147	50	75	54	

Answers on page 366.

SPIRAL: CLASSIC MOVIES

Spirals offer a novel twist on crossword puzzles. Instead of words crossing, they overlap. The last letters of one word form the first letters of the next word. Words bend around corners as necessary—always heading inward toward the center of the spiral.

1. Greta _____

2. Humphrey _____

3. Actor, musician, or painter

4. _____ Laurel

5. "The Blue _____" (Marlene Dietrich movie)

6. _____ Burstyn

7. Bring enjoyment to audiences

8. Cowboy's traditional foe

9. _____ Bancroft

10. Patricia _____

11. Alan _____

12. _____ O. Selznick

13. _____ Lupino

14. Blythe _____

15. _____ Borgnine

16. _____ Parsons

17. Jack _____

18. Yves _____

19. _____ Warhol

20. _____ Cannon

21. _____ Lansbury

22. _____ Turner

23. 1968 Luis Buñuel film

24. _____ Starr

Answers on page 366.

CRUISING ALONG

Every word listed below is contained within the group of letters below. Words can be found horizontally, vertically, or diagonally. They may read either backward or forward.

ACTIVITIES

BINGO

BUFFETS

CABIN

CAPTAIN

CASINO

CHEF

CLASSES

COUNSELOR

DANCING

DECK

DRINKS

GAMES

GIFTS

```
S  K  C  A  N  S  E  S  S  A  L  C  K  Y  T
K  C  A  C  T  I  V  I  T  I  E  S  A  H  H
N  E  P  R  O  M  E  N  A  D  E  W  R  C  S
I  D  T  M  X  G  E  S  E  M  A  G  A  N  T
R  R  A  A  Z  O  N  S  H  G  N  B  O  U  E
D  A  I  S  S  I  N  I  R  I  Z  A  K  L  F
Y  W  N  S  B  T  I  I  B  U  G  C  E  O  F
R  E  W  A  W  S  F  M  S  O  N  H  Y  O  U
A  T  C  G  L  F  I  I  Y  A  I  E  T  P  B
R  S  M  E  A  L  S  Z  G  G  C  F  G  E  S
B  D  S  T  C  R  O  L  E  S  N  U  O  C  A
I  S  S  K  M  O  O  R  E  T  A  T  S  Y  U
L  E  C  T  U  R  E  S  V  I  D  E  O  S  N
L  O  U  N  G  E  S  O  L  A  R  I  U  M  A
R  E  T  A  E  H  T  O  U  R  S  A  L  O  N
```

GOLF	MASSAGE	SOLARIUM
GYM	MEALS	STAFF
HIGH TEA	NURSE	STATEROOM
ISLES	POOL	STEWARD
KARAOKE	PROMENADE	THEATER
LECTURES	ROCK CLIMBING	TOURS
LIBRARY	SALON	VIDEOS
LOUNGES	SAUNA	YOGA
LUNCH	SNACKS	

Answers on page 367.

HAVE A TASTE, BUD

An independent research company decided to recreate a famous "taste test" commercial between Cola A and Cola B. Students would be blindfolded, given sips of each, and asked to identify the soda. Since it meant a day off from school, 100 students applied to be participants. In order to be selected, a student had to have tasted both Cola A and Cola B. Thirteen students admitted their moms wouldn't let them drink anything but juice. Sixty-five of the students had tasted Cola A, and 78 had tasted Cola B. How many of the students had tasted both and would spend the rest of the day blindfolded, sipping, and burping?

Hint: Start by eliminating students who have tasted neither.

ANIMAL SAFARI

How many names of animals can you find here? We count 18. To spell out an animal, keep moving from one letter to the next in any direction—up, down, across, or diagonally. You may move in several different directions for each word, but no letter can be used more than once in any one word.

C	H	T	P	L
O	A	D	I	O
E	R	O	G	N
B	S	E	O	M
T	A	U	L	U

Answers on page 367.

STAR POWER

Fill in each of the empty squares in the grid so that each star is surrounded by the numbers 1 through 8 with no repeats.

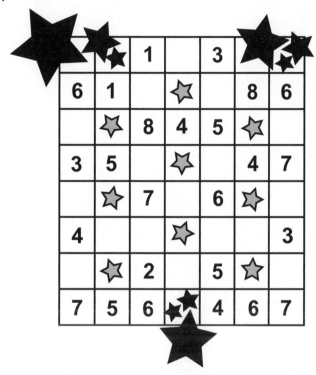

WORD JIGSAW

Fit the pieces into the frame to form common words reading across and down. There's no need to rotate the pieces; they'll fit as shown, with each piece used once.

E A S E

B E T E

R R R W

M A I E

Answers on page 367.

AWFULLY NICE

ACROSS

1. Korea's continent
5. Napoleon's isle of exile
9. Wedding party transports
14. Shellac ingredients
15. Refrigerate
16. "_____ a Parade"
17. Fill-in for a talk show, e.g.: 2 wds.
19. Chimney channels
20. Dress, as a judge
21. "Ditto": 2 wds.
23. Imp
24. Got up
25. Decompose
27. London cathedral: 2 wds.
31. Mexican money
35. Forty winks
37. Bisects
38. Strong glue
40. Teacher's favorite
42. Explosive experiment, for short
43. Colored anew
45. Hit with a stun gun
47. Panamas and boaters
48. Joins forces (with)
50. Practical joke
52. "_____ mio!"
54. Search parties, in the Old West
59. Retaliation
62. Geritol target
63. Mistake
64. "Heavens!": 2 wds.
66. Skirt style
67. Until: 2 wds.
68. "I cannot tell _____"
69. Singer/actress Della
70. Fair hiring org.
71. Big wigs in biz

DOWN

1. Horatio of inspirational books
2. Spa spot
3. Bakery employees
4. Org.
5. Level of authority
6. Toilet, in London
7. "Blame It on the _____ Nova"
8. Sanctuary centerpieces
9. Threescore and 10, maybe: 2 wds.
10. Sickness: 2 wds.
11. Pout
12. Finished
13. Ousted Zaire ruler Mobuto _____ Seko
18. Way up the ski slope
22. Wool-eating insect
26. Faucet
28. Middle layer of the eye
29. "_____ we forget"
30. Grounded sound breakers: abbr.
31. Saucy, as a young lass
32. Pointless fencing sword
33. Fountain treat
34. What 17-Across, 64-Across, 10-Down, and this puzzle's title are
36. Dispenser candy
39. "You betcha!"
41. "You're it!" chasing game
44. Performing twosomes
46. One time Haitian dictator, informally: 2 wds.
49. One of 10 in Exodus
51. Bell hit with a hammer
53. Wed on the run
55. Glacial ridge
56. Photographer's request
57. Old MacDonald's refrain
58. Bank vaults
59. Back side
60. _____ Stanley Gardner
61. _____-dieu (prayer bench)
65. Oklahoma Native American

WORD LADDER

Change just one letter on each line to go from the top word to the bottom word. Do not change the order of the letters. You must have a common English word at each step.

READ

_____

_____

_____

BOOK

Answers on page 367.

GIRLFRIENDS

Four women's names are hiding in this grid. Each name contains the letter **N** twice. The number of times each name appears is indicated in the circles in the 4 corners. The blanks next to the circles indicate the number of letters in each name. Can you fill in the 4 correct names? Names read across, down, backward, forward, and diagonally.

FOUR-LETTER ANAGRAMS

Fill in the blanks in each sentence below with 4-letter words that are anagrams (rearrangements) of one another.

1. We could smell the foul _____ as soon as we opened the barn _____.

2. When the chef tried to carry a stack of _____, one _____ off and made a terrible clang.

3. The _____ of the litter waited for his _____ at the food dish.

4. The actor portrayed his _____ so well that he had the _____ attention of the audience.

5. When Sally's boyfriend gave her a _____, she had a happy _____ on her face.

6. The street _____ cast strange shadows through the leaves of the _____ tree.

7. The _____ letter was _____ an insurance company.

8. As the woman tried to keep _____ with her friend, the wind blew her _____ around her.

Answers on page 367.

WORD LADDERS

Change just one letter on each line to go from the top word to the bottom word. Do not change the order of the letters. You must have a common English word at each step.

1. CALF

   _____

   _____

   BULL

2. WORK

   _____

   _____

   _____

   REST

3. MOON

   _____

   _____

   _____

   BEAM

4. TRAIN

   _____

   _____

   _____

   _____

   WRECK

5. HARD

   _____

   _____

   _____

   _____

   _____

   SOFT

6. FOOL

   _____

   _____

   _____

   _____

   _____

   WISE

SAY WHAT?

Below are a group of words that, when properly arranged in the blanks, reveal a quote from Leo Tolstoy.

own   unhappy   way   families   happy   one   family   in

All _____ _____ resemble _____ another, each _____ _____ is unhappy _____ its _____ _____.

PYRAMID

To build this pyramid, begin by placing the answer to the first clue at the very top of the pyramid. To find the answer to each consecutive clue and fill in the remaining lines in the pyramid, add a letter to the previous answer and rearrange the letters.

1. East: abbr.
2. Olivia _____ Havilland
3. Lair
4. Tear apart
5. Beneath
6. Put up with
7. Set of false teeth
8. Made a daring attempt
9. Exciting incident
10. Not visited by tourists

GO FIGURE

Fill each square in the grid with a digit from 1 through 9. When the numbers in each row are added, you should arrive at the total in the right-hand column. When the numbers in each column are added, you should arrive at the total on the bottom line. The numbers in each long diagonal must add up to the totals in the upper- and lower-right corners.

29

6		4	9		2	27
	4	3				23
2		7	1	6	4	22
1	6			5		27
	9		3	3	1	28
7		3	4	4	5	27

27 30 26 26 24 21   32

Answers on page 367.

SQUARE THE CIRCLE

All you have to do to solve this puzzle is move in a single, unbroken path from the circle in the upper-left corner to the circle in the lower right. Your path must alternate between circles and squares, and you can only move vertically and horizontally (not diagonally). There are two ways to do it—can you find both?

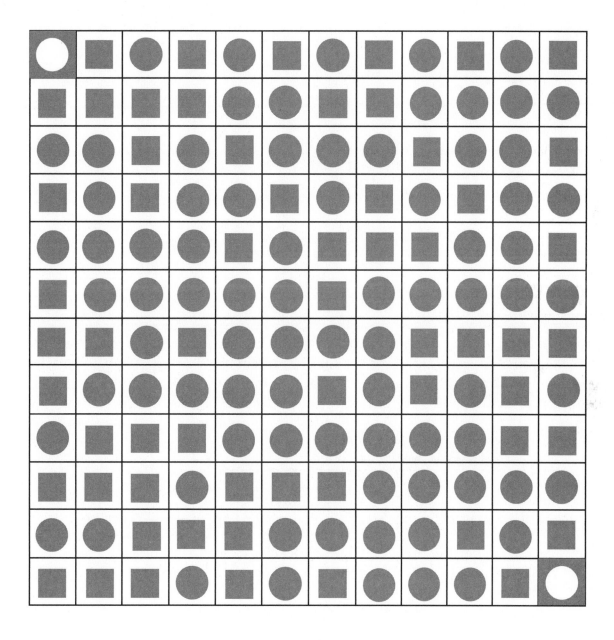

Answers on page 367.

IT'S A WRAP!

Which folded cube correctly represents the center pattern?

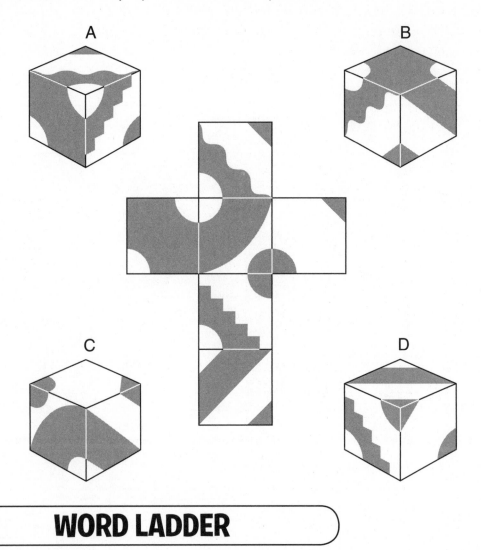

A

B

C

D

WORD LADDER

Change just one letter on each line to go from the top word to the bottom word. Do not change the order of the letters. You must have a common English word at each step.

SLEEP

———

———

———

———

DREAM

Answers on page 367.

QUIC-KROSS

This is a crossword puzzle with a twist. Use the clues to solve the puzzle. When complete, the circled letters will spell out a mystery word.

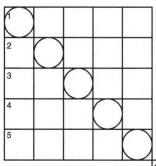

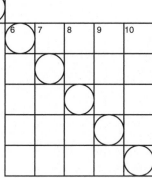

ACROSS

1. Teach
2. Overbearing person
3. Homo sapien
4. Started
5. Sum

DOWN

6. Instantly (Old English)
7. Fortunate
8. Solitary
9. Nearly
10. Government fees

Clue: Noisy and disorderly

INITIALLY YOURS

We hope you don't come up short trying to figure out what these famous abbreviations stand for!

1. AKA, in a police report _____

2. BART, in San Francisco _____

3. FAQ, on a website _____

4. IBM _____

5. "M*A*S*H" _____

6. MSG, in food preparation _____

7. POTUS, in American government _____

8. PVC, the plastic used in some household pipes _____

9. SST, as in the Concorde SST _____

10. VCR _____

Answers on page 367.

SUDOKU

Use deductive logic to complete the grid so that each row, each column, and each 3 by 3 box contains the numbers 1 through 9 in some order. The solution is unique.

	3		5					2
5		9	3			8		
4	6							
		5			9		1	
				6				
	1		4			7		
							7	5
		6			7	3		9
8					5		6	

BREAK THIS COLOR'S COVER

What is the next color in this familiar progression of colors?

Yellow, blue, red, purple, orange, green, maroon, _____

Answers on pages 367–368.

CRYPTO-QUOTE

A cryptogram is a message in substitution code. Break the code to read the quote and its source. For example, THE SMART CAT might become FVP QWGDF JGF if **F** is substituted for **T,** **V** for **H, O** for **E,** and so on. Hint: In the cryptogram below, **N** equals **G.**

"BFS JDD QHFW KNNM RZ HZK EJMYKS—JZP OJSGA SAJS

EJMYKS."

—UJWY SOJRZ

FAMOUS ADDRESS

Complete the horizontal phrase by finding the merging phrases.

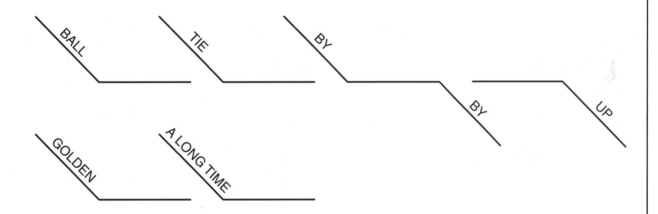

ACROSTIC ANAGRAM

Unscramble the letters below, then transfer the corresponding letters to the grid. When the grid is complete, you'll be rewarded with a quote from George F. Will.

A.　C　A　R　B　E　C　I

　　 — — — — — — —
　　61 49 69 21 55 63 52

B.　V　R　T　E　E　I　I　P　E　T

　　 — — — — — — — — — —
　　6 59 47 37 62 29 12 43 17 39

C.　S　E　H　G　U　S

　　 — — — — — —
　　70 5 11 36 73 46

D.　T　E　N　I　T　Y

　　 — — — — — —
　　18 24 50 10 42 3

E.　O　R　V　O　Y　J　S　E

　　 — — — — — — — —
　　71 40 48 67 7 20 27 32

F.　L　O　I　A　G　A　N　A　N　T　I　V

　　 — — — — — — — — — — — —
　　64 16 30 23 45 41 35 1 4 44 51 14

G.　B　E　I　L　N　V　E　A

　　 — — — — — — — —
　　54 72 60 34 25 9 28 31

H.　N　E　O　B　G　E　D　L

　　 — — — — — — — —
　　68 15 53 8 19 65 57 22

I.　L　W　E　L　O　R　F　O

　　 — — — — — — — —
　　2 13 58 38 66 33 56 26

1 F	2 I		3 D	4 F	5 C	6 B		7 E	8 H	9 G		10 D	11 C		12 B	13 I	
14 F	15 H	16 F	17 B	18 D	19 H		20 E	21 A	22 H	23 F	24 D	25 G	26 I	27 E			
28 G	29 B	30 F	31 G	32 E			33 I	34 G	35 F	36 C		37 B	38 I	39 B	40 E	41 F	42 D	43 B	44 D	45 F
	46 C	47 B	48 E	49 A	50 D	51 F	52 A	53 H	54 G		55 A	56 I					
57 H	58 I	59 B	60 G	61 A	62 B	63 A	64 F	65 H		66 I	67 E		68 H	69 A		70 C	71 E	72 G	73 C

Answers on page 368.

20-SIDED TRIANGLE

Arrange the numbers 1 through 9—using each number once—in the squares below so that the numbers on each side add up to 20. There are several possible solutions.

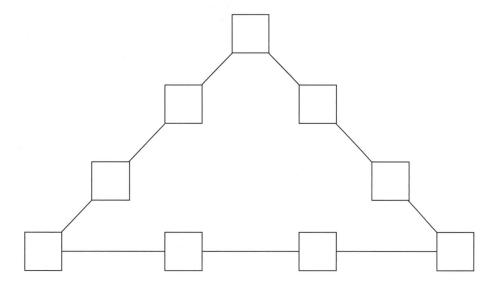

B NICE

Bea's favorite words begin with the letter **B,** and she loves to use them in word games, especially with her snooty neighbor, a tan gent named Matt, the high school math teacher. Matt bragged he could never be fooled by numbers, so Bea decided to test him. She told him that if you say the number "10" after saying the letter **B,** you get the word "beaten." She challenged Matt to find three quantities other than 10 that, when said after saying the letter **B,** phonetically make three common English words. Matt made a beeline for a dictionary and his calculator and quickly came up with the first two, but didn't get the third word until Bea asked him if he took anything in his coffee. What are the three words?

WORD COLUMNS

Find the hidden humorous observation by using the letters directly below each of the blank squares. Each letter is used only once. A black square indicates the end of a word.

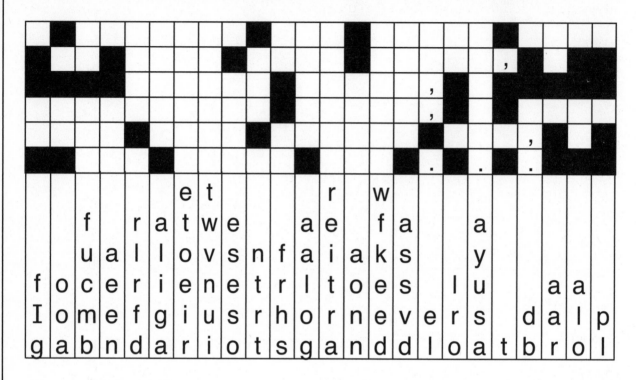

SAGE ADVICE

Can you determine the next letter in this progression?

A F A H M A S ___

Answers on page 368.

ALL THE COLORS OF THE RAINBOW

Every word listed below is contained within the group of letters below. Words can be found horizontally, vertically, or diagonally. They may read either backward or forward. Leftover letters spell a hidden message related to the puzzle's topic.

AMBER

AQUA

AZURE

BISTER

BLUE

BUFF

CARMINE

CHARTREUSE

CINNABAR

COPPER

CREAM

CRIMSON

EMERALD

```
C R R E D N E V A L E R O S E
R R C D O N V R A A U Q A I N
E U I G I E U Y T M Y R T L E
P L E M E R A L D E I E N V L
P L R M S Z M N O N L W E E G
O A G A U O R O D E E R G R R
C T N R E E N I R E G N A T E
B E E O R P G L N W L Y M C T
U L G O T O A I E P H A I E S
E O I N R N W M U Z Y I S N I
C I N N A B A R B R A S T E B
N V D I H R P E O E U H G E L
M A E R C L O V O R R C V R U
I O V L E S I O U Q R U T G E
R U B Y E L L O W E T F F U B
```

FUCHSIA	MAROON	RED	TURQUOISE
GRAY	MAUVE	ROSE	VERMILION
GREEN	MYRTLE	RUBY	VIOLET
HAZEL	NAVY	RUSSET	WHITE
ICE (BLUE)	ORANGE	SCARLET	WINE
INDIGO	PEARL	SILVER	YELLOW
IVORY	PUCE	TAN	
LAVENDER	PURPLE	TANGERINE	
MAGENTA			

Hidden message: _____

Answers on page 368.

MOTEL HIDEOUT

A thief hides out in one of the 45 motel rooms listed in the chart below. The motel's in-house detective received a sheet of four clues, signed "The Holiday Thief." Using these clues, the detective found the room number within 15 minutes—but by that time, the thief had fled. Can you find the thief faster?

1. Of the two digits in the room number, one of them is an odd number and the other is even.

2. The second digit in the room number is more than twice as large as the first digit.

3. The room number cannot be evenly divided by 7.

4. If the two digits in the room number exchanged positions, it would still be a room number in the motel as listed in the chart.

51	52	53	54	55	56	57	58	59
41	42	43	44	45	46	47	48	49
31	32	33	34	35	36	37	38	39
21	22	23	24	25	26	27	28	29
11	12	13	14	15	16	17	18	19

NUMBERS GAME

Which 4-figure number that consists of 4 different digits meets the following criteria?

1. The first digit is twice the value of the fourth digit and 2 more than the second digit.

2. The third digit is one more than the first digit and 5 more than the fourth digit.

Answers on page 368.

TRIANGLE CUT

If this triangle is cut along the dotted lines, can the 4 sections be arranged to form a perfect square? No need to use a protractor to solve this puzzle. We think you can do it with just your eyes.

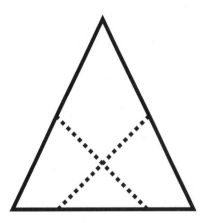

FIND THE BOOTY!

Fill in the blanks below using the clues given; we've added a few letters to help out. Then take the middle 3 letters of each word, put them together, and rearrange them to make a word that means "booty." Or is that "booties"? Either way, the answer is something you'd be glad to find.

1. Amuse an audience: __ __ T __ __ __ __ I __

2. "And a cast of _____ !": __ H __ __ __ __ __ __ S

3. Major celeb: __ __ P __ __ __ T __ __

What you'd be glad to find: _____

THINGS ARE HEATING UP

ACROSS

1. Pottery class gunk
4. Drain the energy from
7. Actresses Evans and Hamilton
13. Opp. of WSW
14. President's time in office
16. Tiny critter seen on a slide
17. U.S. spy org.
18. Nobel winner Harold who discovered heavy hydrogen
19. Suggested indirectly
20. Little consolation: 2 wds.
23. Summer in Paris
24. Clownish action
25. Western Hemisphere org.
26. Mo. after Mar.
28. One who stays calm during a tense situation: 2 wds.
33. Game with Professor Plum
36. "_____ to Joy"
37. Common way to fortify table salt
38. Fled
39. Chant sounds
40. Hockey great Bobby
41. Org. that sticks to its guns
42. Pay what is owed: 2 wds.
44. Bullring cheer
45. Walrus relative
46. Not be a first-string player: 3 wds.
49. "_____ about time!"
50. _____ glance
51. Partner of "aahed"
55. Unit of electrical resistance
57. Passionate: 3 wds.
60. Realm
62. Prefix for -logy or -gram
63. First U.S. st.
64. _____ million
65. CNN offering
66. Pitcher's stat.
67. Turn the color of a beet
68. Queue after Q
69. Happy for glad: abbr.

DOWN

1. Holy city of Islam
2. Teamsters, e.g.
3. Did a poker task
4. Wall plaster
5. Early plane prefix
6. Casts a shape in advance
7. Cowardly Lion portrayer Bert
8. One who mimics
9. "Smoking or _____?"
10. Decide conclusively
11. Help in a crime
12. Marquis de _____
15. "Get outta _____!" ("Stop hassling me!")
21. Craps cubes
22. Big Ten sch.
27. Pea holder
29. Energy or enthusiasm
30. Ambulance wail
31. Poet Pound
32. Actual
33. Gullet
34. Actress Turner
35. Like some beards or Christmas trees
39. Do better than
40. Shrub also known as a rose bay
43. Paramedic: abbr.
44. Get
45. Loafer, e.g.
47. Dine
48. Kelly to Regis
52. Lord of the underworld
53. Each
54. Raspy singer Bob
55. Smell
56. Sharpen, as a knife
58. Put _____ act (pretend)
59. Mountain drinks?
61. Help

MATH GRID

Fill each square of the grid with a digit from 1 through 9. When the numbers in each row are multiplied, you should arrive at the total in the right-hand column. When the numbers in each column are multiplied, you should arrive at the total on the bottom line. The numbers in each diagonal must multiply to the totals in the upper- and lower-right corners.

Important: The number 1 can only be used once in any row or column; other numbers can be repeated.

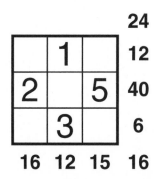

TWO RULES

Cryptograms are messages in substitution code. Break the code to read the humorous advice. For example, THE SMART CAT might be FVO QWGDF JGF if **F** is substituted for **T, V** for **H, O** for **E,** and so on.

HNMFM TFM HIG FPQMK WGF PQHCJTHM KPAAMKK CO QCWM

OMSMF HMQQ MSMFLHNCOY LGP EOGI.

HASHI

Each circle represents an island, with the number inside indicating the number of bridges connected to it. Draw bridges between islands using the number given, but there can be no more than 2 bridges going in the same direction and there must be a continuous path connecting all islands. Bridges can only be vertical or horizontal and may not cross islands or other bridges.

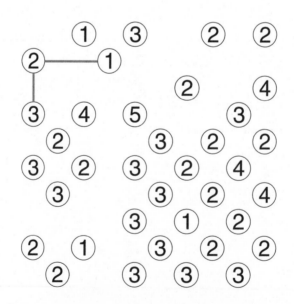

Answers on page 368.

CAR CHASE

These people have had a great day shopping in the city! One problem: They can't find the parking garage to get their car. Can you help?

Answer on page 368.

FIT IT

Use each of the city names found below to complete the clue-less crossword grid on the next page. The puzzle has only one solution.

4 letters

CALI

GIZA

KIEV

LIMA

ROMA

5 letters

BOGOR

CAIRO

DELHI

DHAKA

OSAKA

PARIS

PUSAN

TOKYO

6 letters

ANKARA

BOGOTA

BOMBAY

INCHON

LAHORE

LONDON

MADRID

MALANG

MOSCOW

SYDNEY

TAIPEI

TEHRAN

7 letters

BAGHDAD

BANGKOK

CHICAGO

JAKARTA

KARACHI

NEW YORK

TORONTO

8 letters

BRASILIA

BUDAPEST

HONG KONG

ISTANBUL

KINSHASA

SANTIAGO

SAO PAULO

SHANGHAI

YOKOHAMA

9 letters

BANGALORE

SINGAPORE

10 letters

ADDIS ABABA

ALEXANDRIA

CASABLANCA

LOS ANGELES

MEXICO CITY

11 letters

BUENOS AIRES

12 letters

RIO DE JANEIRO

ST. PETERSBURG

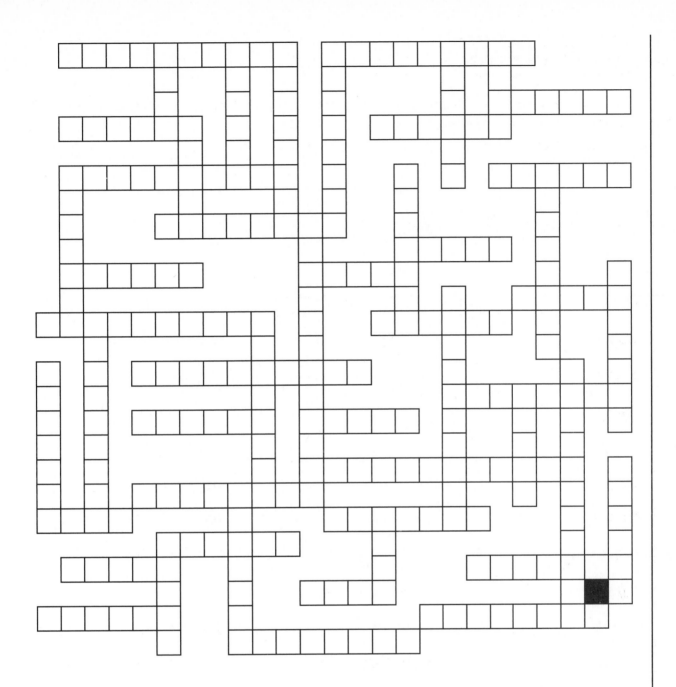

Answer on page 368.

STAR POWER

Fill in each of the empty squares in the grid so that each star is surrounded by numbers 1 through 8 with no repeats.

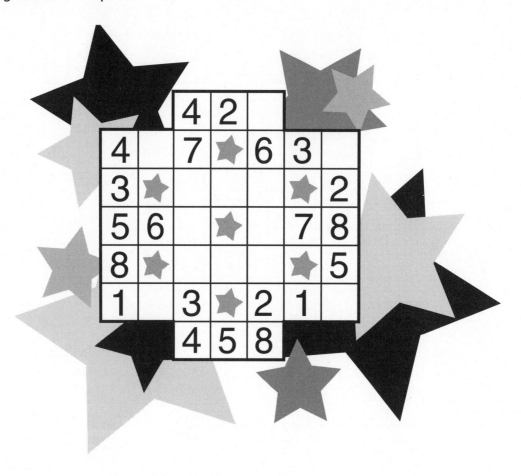

WACKY WORDY

Find the one letter that, when placed in each of the five spaces below, completes a common phrase.

___AT___H AS ___AT___H ___AN

Answers on page 369.

RHYME TIME

Each clue leads to a 2-word answer that rhymes, such as BIG PIG or STABLE TABLE. The numbers in parentheses after the clue give the number of letters in each word. For example, "cookware taken from the oven (3, 3) would be "hot pot."

1. Hay-filled upper barn area (4, 4): _____ _____

2. NFL training camp defense exercise (4, 5): _____ _____

3. Have too light of a color (4, 5): _____ _____

4. It's right at the bottom (4, 5): _____ _____

5. Praise a seasoning (5, 4): _____ _____

6. It's wiped off after gluing (5, 5): _____ _____

7. Where a blackbird is safe (5, 5): _____ _____

8. Bakery byproduct (5, 5): _____ _____

9. A rag for cleaning up soup spills (5, 5): _____ _____

10. Thrive as an inventor (6, 5): _____ _____

11. Move the cattle to a new pasture (6, 5): _____ _____

12. He's using the middle of the mall (6, 6): _____ _____

13. Holding place for some jewelry (6, 6): _____ _____

14. A leash made from animal skin (7, 6): _____ _____

15. Buyer born in 1950 (6, 8): _____ _____

Answers on page 369.

DIGITAL SUDOKU

Fill in the grid so that each row, column, and 2 by 3 block contains the numbers 1 through 6 exactly once. Numbers are in digital form and some segments have already been filled in.

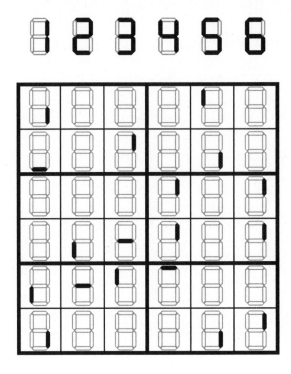

SEASON'S GREETINGS

Can you determine the missing letter in this logical progression?

D D P V C ___ D B

Answers on page 369.

FINDING A DIGIT

In the grid, find a stylized digit exactly like that shown next to the grid. The digit can be rotated but not mirrored.

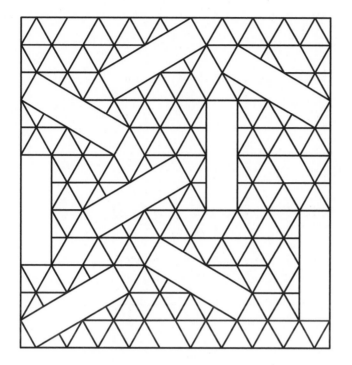 

PORK PUZZLER

At the county fair hog competition, best friends Gomer, Homer, Romer, and Domer entered the 4 different breeds of hogs they had raised during the past year. While the friends ate deep-fried Twinkies and awaited the results, the judge hung the award ribbons in each hog pen. Unfortunately, the smell of the Twinkies made the hogs hungry, and they ate the ribbons. When the friends returned, the judge told them what he could remember about the awards. Homer's Hampshire did not finish last. Romer's hog came in third. The Berkshire hog came in first. Gomer's hog finished ahead of the Chester White, and the Duroc finished ahead of Domer's hog. Which hog was raised by which friend, and in which order did they finish?

Answers on page 369.

CUBE FOLD

Which of the 12 figures below would not form a perfect cube if it were folded along the dotted lines?

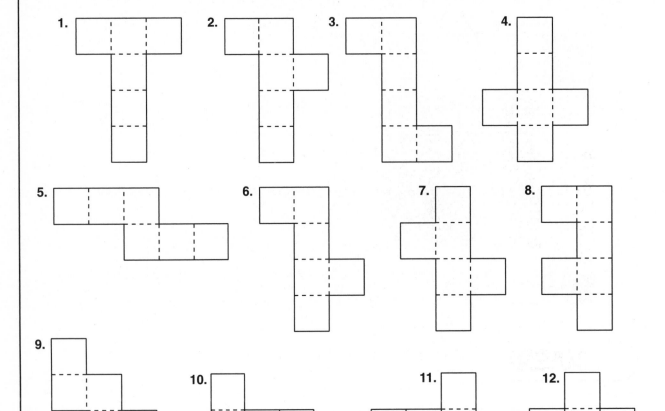

NEXT LETTER?

Determine the next letter in this progression,

O, T, T, F, F, S, S, _____

Answers on page 369.

MATH SCRAMBLEGRAM

Four 6-letter words, all of which revolve around the same theme, have been jumbled. Unscramble each word, and write the answer in the accompanying space. Next, transfer the letters in the shaded boxes into the shaded keyword space, and unscramble the 8-letter word that goes with the theme. The theme for this puzzle is mathematics.

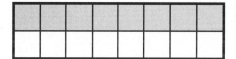

HASHI

Each circle represents an island, with the number inside indicating the number of bridges connected to it. Draw bridges between islands using the number given, but there can be no more than 2 bridges going in the same direction, and there must be a continuous path connecting all islands. Bridges can only be vertical or horizontal and may not cross islands or other bridges. We've drawn some bridges to get you started.

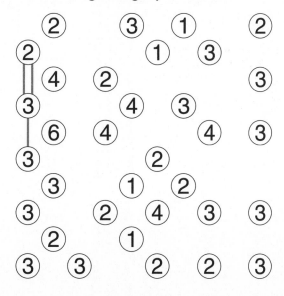

LOGIDOKU

The numbers 1 through 8 should appear once in every row, column, long diagonal, irregular shape (indicated by marked borders), and 2 by 4 grid (indicated by shaded or white blocks). With the help of the provided numbers in this square, can you complete the puzzle?

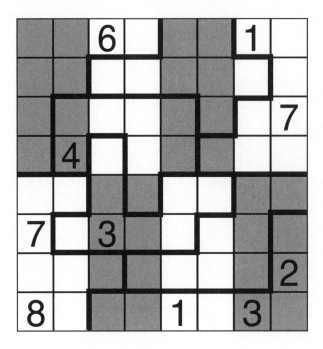

LAND OF THE FREE

Determine the next letter in this progression.

O, S C Y _____

Answers on page 369.

HORSING AROUND

Every phrase listed is contained within the group of letters below. The words can be found in a straight line diagonally. They may read either backward or forward.

As an added challenge, see if you can figure out the theme of this puzzle.

CLOTHES CLOSET

CRAZY QUILT

DARK SHADOWS

DEAD RINGER

GIFT OF GAB

HIGH AND LOW

HOBBY SHOP

IRON MAIDEN

ONE AT A TIME

PACK RAT

RACE RELATIONS

RIVER PHOENIX

ROCKING CHAIR

SAW EYE TO EYE

SEA CHANGE

STUD POKER

WAR AND PEACE

WILD WEST

WORK OF ART

```
            S  E  R  X  P  S  W  E  R  E  S
            S  A  I  O  T  G  C  I  O  N  S
         T  R  H  W  U  C  A  I  A  L  T  B  E
      R  G  N  I  I  D  E  E  K  H  F  N  D  O  W  C  I
      T  A  H  E  P  V  P  Y  O  I  E  T  N  W  L  W  S
      O  R  C  O  D  D  E  B  E  G  N  E  O  O  E  W  D
      S  R  K  E  N  I  B  R  N  T  A  G  T  F  O  S  T
      H  E  E  A  R  Y  A  A  P  T  O  H  C  D  G  L  T
      R  I  R  G  S  E  H  M  A  H  E  E  A  H  I  A  T
      T  A  G  H  N  C  L  T  N  S  O  H  Y  U  A  R  B
      W  H  O  H  A  I  I  A  C  O  S  E  Q  E  A  I  P
      A  P  T  E  A  M  R  L  T  K  R  Y  N  F  C  A  R
      O  M  S  E  E  N  O  D  R  I  Z  I  O  I  C  B  E
      F  O  R  E  T  S  D  A  A  A  O  K  H  K  X  E  W
         O  R  E  D  D  L  R  E  R  N  R  H  O
         T  R  S  E  C  O  O  D  A  S  I
         N  A  P  H  R  W  W  T  A  S  E
```

Puzzle theme: _____

Answers on page 369.

DAY AT THE ZOO

Can you spot the 24 differences between these two pictures?

Answers on pages 369.

GO FIGURE

Fill each square in the grid with a digit from 1 through 9. When the numbers in each row are added, you should arrive at the total in the right-hand column. When the numbers in each column are added, you should arrive at the total on the bottom line. The numbers in each diagonal must add up to the totals in the upper- and lower-right corners.

							26
2	3		8		3	5	34
3		3	9	1		7	31
	2	7		3	6	8	39
9		2	6	7	3		42
1	3		9		2	1	22
3	5	4	7		8		34
2	4	9			2	4	34
28	27	32	49	32	28	40	36

COSTARRING

Two of these star fragments can be put together to form a perfect 5-pointed star like the one at left. Can you figure out which 2 pieces they are?

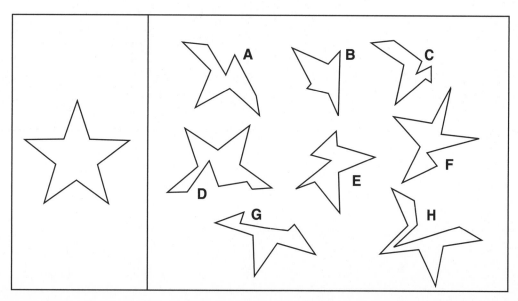

Answers on pages 369–370.

HIGH TIMES

ACROSS

1. Constellation's second brightest star
5. Exponent
10. For men only
14. Sacred image
15. Early adding machines
16. Arizona native
17. Biblical structure: 4 wds.
20. Pain
21. Of gulls
22. Challenge
23. Goes over a book again
24. Scrawny fellows
27. Moronic
28. Hearten
29. Actor and photographer Lollobrigida
30. Ashen
33. Noted disaster movie, with "The": 2 wds.
37. Wall, State, et al: abbr.
38. "Mildred Pierce" author
39. Stradivarius's teacher
40. Suit piece
41. Repast
42. Testy
46. Casserole ingredient
47. Antiaircraft fire: hyph.
48. Produce
52. Famous campanile: 3 wds.
54. Labor
55. Sample
56. Asian princess
57. Male offspring
58. Go in
59. "Auld Lang _____"

DOWN

1. Pieces' partner
2. Alpine answer
3. Rule follower
4. Come before
5. Rough handlers
6. Chubby
7. "Star _____"
8. Environmental: pref.
9. '50s TV show, with "The"
10. Extra
11. Leg bone
12. Make corrections
13. Strong winds
18. Old-time catapult
19. Biting remark
23. Quarrel: hyph.
24. Hardens
25. Solidify
26. Edges that aren't hemmed
27. Finger
29. Grind one's teeth
30. Stole
31. Pot starter
32. Black: Fr.
34. Emulate Kwan: hyph.
35. Tap
36. Napoleon and Hirohito
40. Squad's target
41. "Shosha" author
42. Bulb units
43. "Gesundheit" elicitor
44. Yarn bundle
45. Loses strength
46. Budget item: Fr.
48. Main point
49. Removed
50. Neighbor of MO
51. Ontario's neighbor
53. "No No" girl, for short

RHYME TIME

Each clue leads to a 2-word answer that rhymes, such as BIG PIG or STABLE TABLE. The numbers in parentheses after the clue give the number of letters in each word. For example, "cookware taken from the oven (3, 3) would be "hot pot."

1. Heap in a pathway inside a plane (5, 4): _____ _____

2. Rough duplicate (6, 4): _____ _____

3. Yarn about an escargot (5, 4): _____ _____

4. Successful oil wells of one who seats people in pews (6, 7): _____ _____

5. Beach footwear of defacers of public property (7, 7): _____ _____

Answers on page 370.

THE LOGIC OF CRAYONS

Sabrina, Jill, Kelly, and Kris are 4 teen girls. They like to get together occasionally for a "color therapy" session, which consists of gossiping, eating pizza, comparing lip gloss, and coloring with crayons. They especially love the jazzy names that Creative Colors has come up with for some of their crayons. The girls also like to check out the latest lip glosses.

One of the girls loves the crayon color Neon Carrot. Another adores Vivid Tangerine.

One can't resist Tickle Me Pink, and the fourth one can't wait to try to color inside the lines with Mauvelous.

Their lip-gloss flavors are Strawberry Smackers, Hard Candy Lollipop, Bubble Gum, and Plum Wicked.

Using the clues below, see if you can figure out each girl's favorite crayon color and lip gloss flavor. Write your answers in the graph on the opposite page. Here are your clues:

1. Sabrina is a health-food nut (no pizza, thanks), so she likes crayons and lip gloss flavors that remind her of fruits and vegetables.

2. Kelly borrowed the Vivid Tangerine crayon one day from one of the other girls. She also felt like borrowing the Bubble Gum lip gloss just once.

3. Jill tends to favor anything that reminds her of her Elmo doll, so she picked a crayon that did just that.

4. Kris is trying to cultivate a pouty, seductive look, so she picked a lip gloss that sounded promising and just a bit devilish—in a totally wholesome way, of course. She also likes fruity flavors.

5. Kelly likes to color with various shades of violets and purples, especially when they sound "wunnerful"!

6. One of Kris's favorite crayon colors is pink, but someone else had already chosen that color.

7. Kris is not a big fan of vegetables, but she does like fruits.

8. The girl who likes violet shades also likes suckers—the "all-day" candy kind, that is.

9. Sabrina has always been partial to the only fruit that has its seeds on the outside, so she chose that for her lip gloss.

Girl	Crayon Color	Lip Gloss
Sabrina		
Jill		
Kelly		
Kris		

FITTING WORDS

In this miniature crossword, the clues are listed randomly and are numbered for convenience only. It is up to you to figure out the placement of the 9 answers. To help you, we've inserted one letter in the grid, and this is the only occurrence of that letter in the completed puzzle.

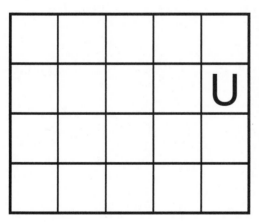

CLUES

1. "Quiet!"
2. Heavy books
3. Domino on the piano
4. "Goodbye, Pierre!"
5. Golf supporters
6. Screen star
7. Foul matter
8. Spill clumsily
9. Prom ride

Answers on page 370.

TAKE 30

Alf was the 93rd caller to a radio-station contest and was told he would win a free car if he could go into a room and come out exactly 30 minutes later. The room had no clock, and Alf was not allowed to wear a watch or bring in anything else that tells time. The only thing he could take into the room was a lighter and a candle in a candle holder (supplied by the radio station) that was guaranteed to burn completely in exactly one hour. Alf was not allowed to use a ruler to measure exactly halfway down the candle. Alf went into the room and emerged exactly 30 minutes later to win the car. How did he do it?

HIDDEN CRITTERS

The sentences below are crawling with hidden critters. Look carefully. Can you find an animal name in each sentence?

1. She epitomizes elegance. _____

2. Soap is anti-germ. _____

3. He made errors. _____

4. Urban renewal rushes on. _____

5. He did the task unknowingly. _____

6. Her badge revealed her mission. _____

7. I went to a dandy party. _____

8. Smell new olfactory sensations. _____

9. Would you rebuff a local swain? _____

10. Yes, if Roger will. _____

Answers on page 370.

SAY IT AGAIN, SAM

Homophones are words that sound the same but are spelled differently. Solve each clue below with a pair of homophones. For example, "a breezy eagle's nest" is an "airy aerie."

1. Consumed $^2/_3$ of a dozen: _____

2. Insert commercial: _____

3. Whitish bucket: _____

4. Composition on tranquility: _____

5. Twin to a fruit: _____

6. Jurist on a wharf: _____

7. Unadorned aircraft: _____

8. Entire cavity: _____

9. Completely sacred: _____

10. Henry Clay or Daniel Webster's toupee: _____

11. Somebody was victorious: _____

12. Sea animal's groan: _____

13. Egotistical blood vessel: _____

14. A pull with a certain digit: _____

15. Compose correctly: _____

16. Sardonic grain: _____

17. Only spirit: _____

18. A contract stowed in a suitcase: _____

19. A seer's bottom line: _____

20. High-ranking maize unit: _____

Answers on page 370.

ACROSTIC CLUES

Solve the clues below and then place the letters in their corresponding spots in the grid to reveal a quote about the brain. The letter in the upper-right corner of each grid square refers to the clue the letter comes from.

A. Renaissance artist, inventor, and author of quote: 3 wds.

___ ___ ___ ___ ___ ___ ___ ___ ___ ___ ___ ___ ___ ___ ___
25 49 28 17 72 6   8   20 59 53 10 79 73 63 41

B. Absent-minded fantasies

___ ___ ___ ___ ___ ___ ___ ___ ___
14 1   33 74 32 13 23 21 62

C. Plunged

___ ___ ___ ___ ___
70 11 40 3   19

D. Fully owned, as in stock options

___ ___ ___ ___ ___ ___
30 5   27 47 46 37

E. Type of computer

___ ___ ___ ___ ___ ___ ___
42 50 2   15 80 64 77

F. Mushroom, e.g.

___ ___ ___ ___ ___ ___
84 58 51 18 68 71

G. Breaks up

___ ___ ___ ___ ___ ___ ___ ___
12 39 78 45 76 54 44 75

H. Most breezy

___ ___ ___ ___ ___ ___ ___ ___
48 16 69 38 9   29 26 57

I. In an obnoxious manner

___ ___ ___ ___ ___ ___ ___ ___ ___ ___ ___
67 66 22 82 36 81 35 4   31 24 55

J. To a great extent

___ ___ ___ ___ ___ ___ ___ ___ ___
60 52 34 61 65 56 43 83 7

1 B	2 E			3 C	4 I	5 D	6 A	7 J		8 A	9 H	10 A	11 C	12 G	13 B	14 B		15 E	16 H	17 A
18 F	19 C	20 A	21 B		22 I	23 B	24 I	25 A	26 H		27 D	28 A		29 H	30 D	31 I	32 B	33 B	
34 J	35 I	36 I	37 D		38 H	39 G	40 C	41 A	42 E	43 J	44 G		45 G	46 D	47 D	48 H	49 A	50 E	51 F
	52 J	53 A	54 G	55 I		56 J	57 H	58 F	59 A	60 J	61 J	62 B		63 A	64 E	65 J	66 I	67 I	68 F
69 H	70 C	71 F		72 A	73 A	74 B		75 G	76 G	77 E	78 G		79 A	80 E	81 I	82 I	83 J	84 F

Answers on page 370.

LOGIDOKU

To solve the puzzle, place the numbers 1 through 8 only once in every row, column, long diagonal, irregular shape, and 2 by 4 grid. From the starters given, can you complete the puzzle?

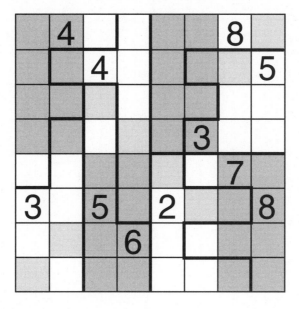

QUILT QUEST

The small, tricolored pattern below appears exactly 3 times in the quilt at left. Find all 3 instances. Note that the pattern might be rotated but not overlapped and/or mirrored in any of the instances.

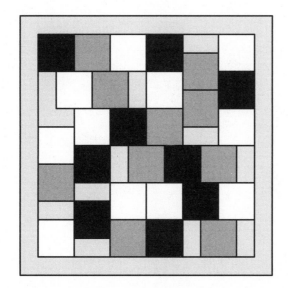

Answers on page 370.

SUDOKU

Use deductive logic to complete the grid so that each row, each column, and each 3 by 3 box contains the numbers 1 through 9 in some order. The solution is unique.

	5			9			6	
8		3			6			1
				7			2	
	7							
6		4				8		2
							5	
	3			5				
7			8			5		6
	2			3			4	

WACKY WORDY

Can you "read" the phrase below?

IIIIIIIIIIIIIITTTTTTTTTT

i t

Answers on page 370.

RED, WHITE, AND BLUE

Each row, column, and long diagonal contains 2 reds, 2 whites, and 2 blues. From the clues given, can you complete the grid?

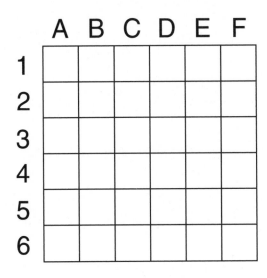

1. The blues are adjacent.
2. One white is between the reds and the other is between the blues.
3. The blues are somewhere to the right of the rightmost red.
4. The whites are adjacent.
5. The blues are adjacent and bounded by the whites.
6. The whites are adjacent and bounded by the reds.

A. One red is bounded by the whites.
B. The blues are adjacent and bounded by the reds.
C. There are no adjacent squares of the same color.
D. The reds are adjacent and bounded by the blues.
E. The reds are adjacent.
F. The pattern of the first 3 cells is repeated in the second 3.

QUIC-KROSS

This is a crossword puzzle with a twist. Use the clues to solve the puzzle. When complete, the circled letters will spell out a mystery word.

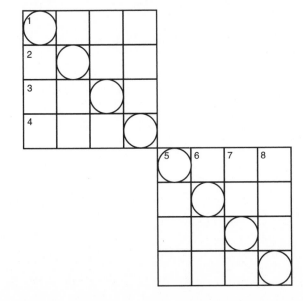

ACROSS

1. Bleed (past tense)
2. Say (past tense)
3. Decorative edging
4. Storage display

DOWN

5. Sleigh
6. Spherical adornment
7. A type of moss
8. Precise

Clue: Rear position

Answers on pages 370–371.

FOR THE FELLAS

Four 8-letter words, all of which revolve around the same theme, have been jumbled. Unscramble each word, and write the answer in the accompanying space. Next, transfer the letters in the shaded boxes into the shaded keyword space, and unscramble the 9-letter word that goes with the theme. The theme for this puzzle is men's names.

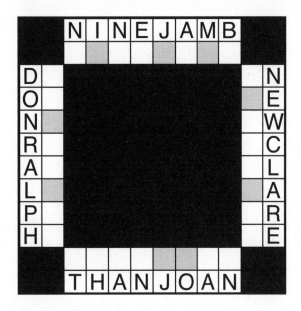

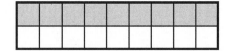

NUMBER CROSSWORD

Fill in this crossword with numbers instead of letters. Use the clues to determine which number from 1 through 9 belongs in each square. No zeros are used.

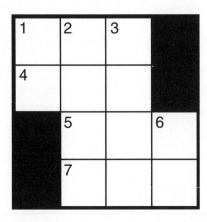

ACROSS
1. A perfect cube that is a palindrome (reads the same backward as it does forward)
4. A multiple of 9
5. Its digits add up to 16
7. Its middle digit is the sum of its two outside digits

DOWN
1. A multiple of 17
2. A palindrome
3. A number of the form abab
6. Its first digit is twice its last digit

Answers on page 371.

WACKY WORDY

Can you "read" the phrase below?

TTTTACRES+MULE

WHAT A WHISTLE (PART I)

Read the story that follows. Then turn the page for a quiz on what you've read.

When I was 14, I used to hang out at a nature center in Connecticut, where I grew up.

One day a man brought in a sparrow hawk with a busted wing. These days the official name of the bird is the American kestrel, but they will always be sparrow hawks to me. Anyway, it was a little beauty, a small falcon about the size of a jay, with beautiful colors—blue-gray wings, rufous tail and back—and that piercing gaze of hawks.

One of the curators, Les, took care of the sparrow hawk for a few months, feeding it small strips of raw meat. As the bird's wing grew stronger, Les started retraining it to fly indoors, holding a piece of meat in a gloved hand. He'd stand close at first, so the bird could practically jump to his hand, but then he'd stand farther and farther away. Soon the little hawk was flying to him for the food.

Each time Les held out the food, he'd do this remarkable whistle, which he said was the sound of a screech owl. It had a slightly eerie, tremulous sound. You do the whistle by fluttering the back of your tongue loosely against your palate. It's hard to explain. I practiced a lot, and soon I could do it too. People always seem surprised at the sound—it's not a typical whistle. You can vary the pitch to high or low by how you flutter your tongue. I don't have a lot of talents, but I can do the screech-owl whistle!

Answer on page 371.

WHAT A WHISTLE (PART II)

Do not read this until you have read the previous page!

1. In which state did the author grow up?

2. Another name for the "sparrow hawk" is:
   a) blue grouse
   b) American kestrel
   c) purple finch

3. How old is the author at the time of the story?

4. True or false: The sparrow hawk has greenish wings.

5. Sparrow hawks in captivity can be fed:
   a) celery
   b) potatoes
   c) raw meat

6. The sparrow hawk in the story had:
   a) a bad wing
   b) a broken leg
   c) missing tail feathers

7. The sparrow hawk, or kestrel, is a type of:
   a) shore bird
   b) falcon
   c) jay

8. As the bird healed, the curator:
   a) let it go
   b) retrained it to fly
   c) took it home

9. The curator trained the bird by using:
   a) a certain whistle
   b) a clucking sound
   c) a duck decoy

10. The sound the curator made was that of:
    a) a bald eagle
    b) a screech owl
    c) a barn owl

LOGICAL HATS

Each of three logicians A, B, and C wears a hat with a positive whole number on it. The number on one hat is the sum of the numbers on the other two. Each logician can see the numbers on the other two hats but not on their own. They have this information and are asked in turn to identify their own number.

A: "I don't know my number."

B: "My number is 15."

What numbers are on A and C?

Answers on page 371.

WORD COLUMNS

Find the hidden humorous statement by using the letters directly below each of the blank squares. Each letter is used only once. A black square indicates the end of a word.

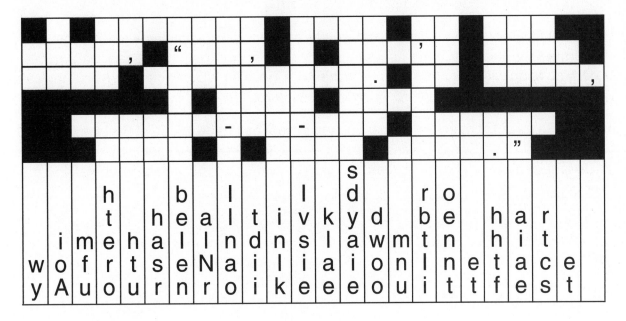

HASHI

Each circle represents an island, with the number inside indicating the number of bridges connected to it. Draw bridges between islands using the number given, but there can be no more than 2 bridges going in the same direction, and there must be a continuous path connecting all islands. Bridges can only be vertical or horizontal and may not cross islands or other bridges. We've drawn some bridges to get you started.

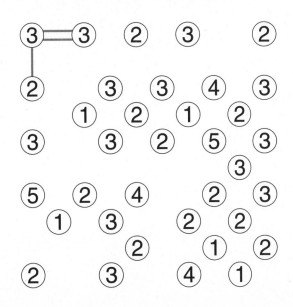

COLOR SCHEME WORD SEARCH

The color-full grid on the next page contains 20 words and phrases that each contain at least one color or hue. However, you'll start out color-blind because the word list isn't anywhere to be seen. Use the clues below to determine what's what and *hue's hue*.

Every answer will begin with a color, and 2 of the answers will also end with a color. Some answers use the color words in a direct, literal way; the meanings of other answers have little or nothing to do with color and so may surprise you. No color is ever repeated. Blanks indicate the number of letters in each word. Answers are in alphabetical order.

After you've solved as many answers as you can in your first run-through of the clues, go to the grid and circle those hidden answer words. Other words that you spot in the grid will help you to answer clues you haven't figured out yet. Grid words will run either horizontally, vertically, or diagonally.

After you've circled all the answers in the grid, write down and read the leftover letters in order from left to right, top to bottom to spell out a hidden message. The hidden message is a silly sentence about a superhero, a super-fit human, and a TV show. It contains 3 more colors.

CLUES

1. Illicit trade in goods or commodities __ __ __ __ __ __ __ __ __ __ __

2. Popular denim pants __ __ __ __ __ __ __ __ __

3. Dessert square, or a young Girl Scout __ __ __ __ __ __ __

4. Paul McCartney/Stevie Wonder hit, or colors of piano keys __ __ __ __ __ __ __ __
__ __ __ __ __

5. Bond villain __ __ __ __ __ __ __ __ __ __

6. Post cereal, with or without flakes __ __ __ __ __-__ __ __ __

7. Work I.D. for a non-U.S. resident __ __ __ __ __ __ __ __ __

8. World-weary __ __ __ __ __ __

9. Popeye's gal __ __ __ __ __ __ __ __

10. Mimosa ingredient __ __ __ __ __ __ __ __ __ __ __

11. Jim-dandy __ __ __ __ __ __

12. Little digit __ __ __ __ __ __

Answers on page 371.

```
E B O N Y A N D I V O R Y
N O O P S R E V L I S B A
I Q U A M L Y O E V I L O
R E G N I F D L O G A A N
A R A H O T T E L R A C S
M P E A C H Y B D A N K D
B R S S T H E L N A A M S
U E D V T Y S U E A J A N
S B E C I U J E G N A R O
W M R L E N N J J O Y K W
O U E O R O S E B U D E W
L L D G W R E A P Y S T H
L P A N G N I N N A T A I
E I K N I P I S T O R M T
Y D R A C N E E R G Y G E
```

13. Bathroom pipe fixer __ __ __ __ __ __ __ __

14. What Moses parted __ __ __   __ __ __

15. Citizen Kane's dying word __ __ __ __ __ __ __ __

16. Tara belle __ __ __ __ __ __ __ __   __'__ __ __

17. What a rich person is proverbially born with in his mouth __ __ __ __ __ __ __

__ __ __ __ __

18. Woman with 7 dwarfs __ __ __ __   __ __ __ __ __

19. Type of salon __ __ __ __ __ __ __

20. Underwater vehicle for the Beatles __ __ __ __ __ __   __ __ __ __ __ __ __ __ __

Answers on page 371.

PANAGRAM

In this crossword puzzle, every letter of the alphabet is used at least once.

ACROSS

1. Is apparently
6. Teen's "Yeah, right!": 2 wds.
10. Apparel
14. " . . . who _____ heaven"
15. Swiss hero William
16. Skin moisturizer
17. Proof of car ownership
18. Ward of "Sisters"
19. Techie workplaces, often
20. Applied pressure to
22. Moon stages
24. Kind of code or rug
25. Comet alternative
26. Barely burned
29. Animal with a duck bill
33. Shout of encouragement
34. Streisand's "Funny Girl" role
35. One-million link
36. Tattered attire
37. Disreputable doctor
38. Move like a hummingbird
39. Fruit drink suffix
40. "I Remember Mama" actress Irene
41. Plundered treasure
42. Nonconformist
44. Intermediate weight boxer, for short
45. Corleone's creator
46. Notorious pirate captain
47. Wings it: 2 wds.
50. Alluded to
54. Swamp reptile, for short
55. Burglar's take
57. Tater state
58. Simba's love, in "The Lion King"
59. Hershiser of baseball
60. Wrapped movie monster
61. Series ending
62. Money rolls
63. Fencing blades

DOWN

1. College entrance exams
2. "ER" actor La Salle
3. Words to Brutus
4. Odometer readings
5. Scoffing sort
6. Totally befuddled: 2 wds.
7. Sunflower edible
8. Not in the pink
9. Pancake
10. Large collection of stars
11. Wistful word
12. Dressing gown
13. Porgy's lady
21. Last letter, in Britain
23. Despise
25. Wonderland visitor
26. "Beat it!"
27. "If _____ nickel for every time…"
28. Israeli desert
29. Shenanigan
30. Light in the furnace
31. Link Up
32. Mythical reveler
34. Con game
37. "The $64,000 Question," e.g.: 2 wds.
38. Went out of business: 2 wds.
40. Defeat decisively
41. "Nighty-night" hour
43. Grand in scope
44. Finish first
46. Stops, as a story
47. Teen outbreak
48. Doggone!
49. Whatever she wants, she gets
50. Shaded
51. Title for Judi Dench
52. Sigh words
53. Playthings
56. Coach Parseghian of Notre Dame fame

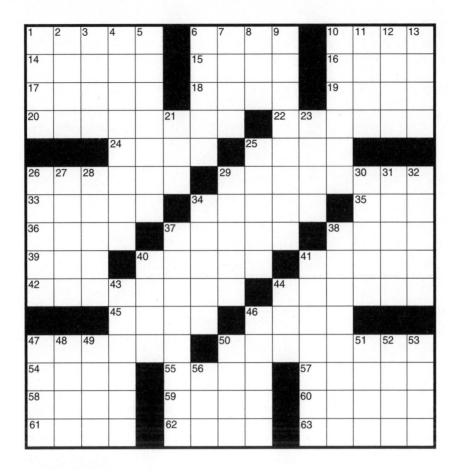

TIMES SQUARE

Fill each square in the grid with a digit from 1 through 6. When the numbers in each row are multiplied, you should arrive at the total in the right-hand column. When the numbers in each column are multiplied, you should arrive at the total on the bottom line. The numbers in each corner-to-corner diagonal must multiply to the totals in the upper- and lower-right corners.

					768
2				6	720
	5		4		120
	3	4		1	120
3		4	3		144
	5			3	120
48	450	384	300	72	360

Answers on page 371.

FITTING WORDS

In this miniature crossword, the clues are listed randomly and are numbered for convenience only. It is up to you to figure out the placement of the 9 answers. To help you, we've inserted one letter in the grid, and this is the only occurrence of that letter in the completed puzzle.

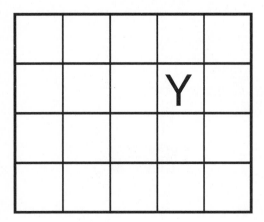

CLUES
1. Choice
2. Police officers
3. Between ports
4. Taco topping
5. Cajun cookery vegetable
6. Latin line dance
7. Big high-school rooms
8. Hardware store item
9. Green-lights

MORE TIMES THE FUN

Enter the digits 1 through 6 into the grid so each row and each column contains each digit only once. The number inside each circle is the product of the 4 digits that surround it.

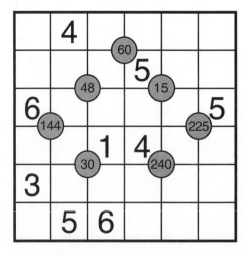

Answers on page 371.

TIMES SQUARE

Fill each square of the grid with the a number from 1 through 5. When the numbers in each row are multiplied, you should arrive at the total in the right-hand column. When the numbers in each column are multiplied, you should arrive at the total on the bottom line. The numbers in each long diagonal must multiply to the totals in the upper- and lower-right corners.

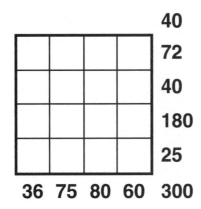

RHYME TIME

Each clue leads to a 2-word answer that rhymes, such as BIG PIG or STABLE TABLE. The numbers in parentheses after the clue give the number of letters in each word. For example, "cookware taken from the oven (3, 3) would be "hot pot."

1. Order to the miners (4, 3): _____ _____

2. Cruel college head (4, 4): _____ _____

3. Ten-story shopping center (4, 4): _____ _____

4. Plumber's duty (4, 4): _____ _____

5. Essential household task (4, 5): _____ _____

6. Neutral colored brimless hat (4, 5): _____ _____

7. Ancient Egyptian card game (5, 5): _____ _____

8. She gets better rest (6, 7): _____ _____

9. Zoo employee who works for less (7, 6): _____ _____

10. TV series finale (4, 9): _____ _____

Answers on page 372.

FOLD-O-RAMA

Follow the twists and turns of this edgy maze to get to the finish!

Answer on page 372.

Every cell in this grid contains 1 of 4 letters: A, B, C, or D. No letter can be horizontally or vertically adjacent to itself. The tables above and to the left of the grid indicate how many times each letter appears in that column or row. Can you complete the grid?

CAST-A-WORD

There are 4 dice, and there are different letters of the alphabet on the 6 faces of each of them (each letter appears only once). Random throws of the dice produced the words in this list. Can you figure out which letters appear on each of the 4 dice?

BONY	GRIM	QUIP
CHIT	HARE	SOAR
COVE	JOKE	TURN
DROP	MOCK	WEAR
FLAB	PONY	WIFE

Answers on page 372.

STAR POWER

Fill in each of the empty squares in the grid so that each starred square is surrounded by the numbers 1 through 8 with no repeats.

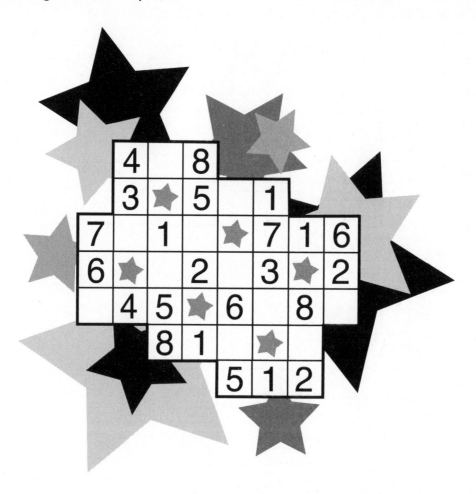

WORK IT!

Fill in the blanks in the sentence below with 8-letter words that are anagrams (rearrangements of the same letters) of one another.

The clothing _____ was _____ to the fact that his work wasn't good enough, so he decided to _____ the entire fall collection.

Answers on page 372.

FITTING WORDS

In this miniature crossword, the clues are listed randomly and are numbered for convenience only. It is up to you to figure out the placement of the 9 answers. To help you, we've inserted one letter in the grid, and this is the only occurrence of that letter in the puzzle.

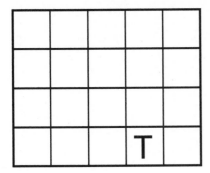

CLUES

1. Awaken
2. Sky-hued
3. Mollify
4. Track events
5. The "windows to the soul"
6. Aesop creation
7. Skin cream ingredient
8. Endure
9. Old MacDonald's place

CODE-DOKU

Use deductive logic to complete the grid so that each row, each column, and each 3 by 3 box contains the letters in the words FINAL VOTE. When you have completed the puzzle, read the shaded squares to find something you might sip.

			O					V
	E		I		F			O
		F				A		
E	A			N		I		F
			E			V		
V								E
		E			L		N	
	L		N			E		
	F	I		V		L		

Hidden message: _____

SUDOKU

Use deductive logic to complete the grid so that each row, each column, and each 3 by 3 box contains the numbers 1 through 9 in some order. The solution is unique.

	5		7		4	8		
						2	7	
	3			5				
				8			5	
1		5	6		2	3		4
	9		5					
				4			8	
	6	8						
		2	8		6		4	

WACKY WORDY

Can you "read" the phrase below?

> P O L I C E
>
>   N
>
>   I
>
>   L

Answers on page 372.

FOURTH ASSEMBLING

Each of the 16 square tiles shown in the illustration contains some part of the number 4. Select the four tiles that can create a 2 by 2 square so that a full "4" character appears on it. Tiles should not be rotated, flipped, or overlapped.

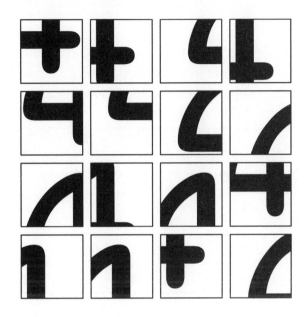

RED, WHITE, AND BLUE

Each row, column, and long diagonal contains 2 reds, 2 whites, and 2 blues. From the clues given below can you complete the grid?

A B C D E F

1
2
3
4
5
6

ROWS

1. The whites are adjacent.

2. The pattern of colors takes the form abcabc.

3. The whites and the reds are between the blues.

4. The whites are somewhere between the blues.

5. The pattern of colors takes the form abccba.

6. The blues are somewhere between the whites.

COLUMNS

A. Each red is directly above each white.

C. Each red is directly above each white.

F. The reds are somewhere between the whites.

Answers on page 372.

CAT LOGIC

When Ken the cat walker came down with a case of congestion, he asked his girlfriend Carla to fill in for him. He gave Carla a list of the names of the owners and their cats and warned her not to lose the list because the cats were identical except for the nametags on their collars. Coincidentally, the cats had the same names as his customers, but no customer owned a cat with his own name.

Carla made the mistake of putting the list in a lunch bag with her tuna sandwich, both of which were eaten when she wasn't looking by a very hungry cat named Stripes. Carla frantically tried to remember which cat belonged to which owner. She was sure that Mr. Puddles did not own Rusty. She knew that the cat owned by Mr. Rusty did not have the same name as the owner of Rusty. She was confident that Mr. Tommy's cat did not have the same name as the man who owned Puddles. She was certain that the cat owned by Mr. Stripes did not have the same name as the owner of Tommy. Help Carla deliver the right cat to the right owner so Ken doesn't lose his customers!

APHORISM CODE-DOKU

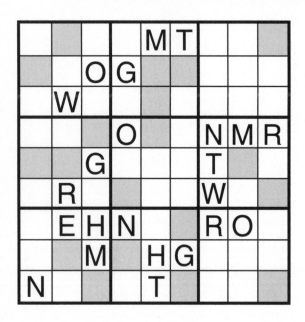

Solve this puzzle just as you would a sudoku. Use deductive logic to complete the grid so that each row, each column, and each 3 by 3 box contains each of the letters WRONG THEM in some order. The solution is unique. When you have completed the puzzle, read the shaded squares to reveal a hidden message.

Hidden message: _____

START YOUR DAY BY ALPHA SLEUTH™

Move each of the letters below into the grid to form common words. You will use each letter once. The letters in the numbered cells of the grid correspond to the letters in the phrase at the bottom. Completing the grid will help you complete the phrase and vice versa. When finished, the grid and phrase will be filled with valid words and you will have used all the letters in the letter set.

Hint: The numbered cells in the grid are arranged alphabetically, so the letter in the cell marked 1 will appear in the alphabet before the letter in the cell marked 2, and so on.

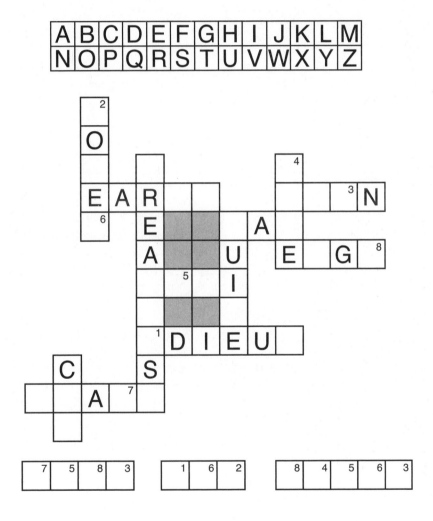

GET IT STRAIGHT

Don't get too caught up in all the twists and turns as you negotiate your way to the center of this intricate labyrinth.

Answer on page 373.

HASHI

Each circle represents an island, with the number inside indicating the number of bridges connected to it. Draw bridges between islands using the number given, but there can be no more than 2 bridges going in the same direction, and there must be a continuous path connecting all islands. Bridges can only be vertical or horizontal and may not cross islands or other bridges. We've drawn some bridges to get you started.

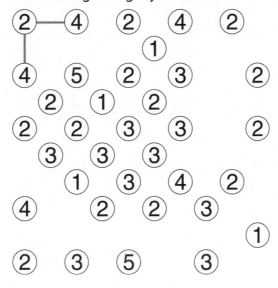

THINGS THAT SMELL GOOD (PART I)

Look at the crossword grid for two minutes. Then turn the page to see how many words you can remember.

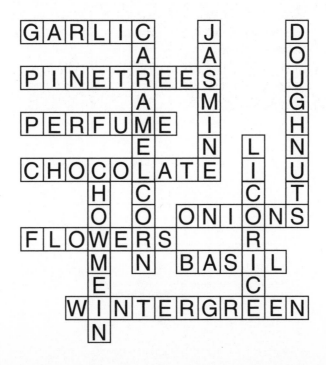

Answer on page 373.

Do not read this until you have read the previous page!

Check off the words you saw on the preceding page:

_____ GARLIC   _____ CARAMEL CORN

_____ LILAC   _____ DAISY

_____ JASMINE   _____ FORGET-ME-NOT

_____ ONIONS   _____ DOUGHNUTS

_____ LAVENDER   _____ PERIWINKLE

_____ CHOW MEIN   _____ CHOCOLATE

_____ LICORICE

STAR POWER

Fill in each of the empty squares in the grid so that every star is surrounded by the numbers 1 through 8 with no repeats.

Answers on page 373.

LAST LAUGH DEPARTMENT

What makes a bestseller? How publishers wish they knew! Below, you'll find 6 reasons why a writer should never give up. But you'll have to break the code first! The code is the same for each cryptogram.

1. XZXFJX UJBOWFOS'W GOBWF TVVR, "FJS PEWFSBOVMW XGGXOB XF WFENSW," DJOUJ OKFBVHMUSH JSB TSNZOXK HSFSUFOYS JSBUMNS LVOBVF, DXW BSQSUFSH TE FJS GOBWF WOC LMTNOWJSBW WJS WMTPOFFSH OF FV.

2. QVJK ZBOWJXP'W GOBWF KVYSN, "X FOPS FV RONN," DXW BSQSUFSH TE FDSKFE-SOZJF LMTNOWJSBW.

3. BVTSBF D. LOBWOZ'W "ISK XKH FJS XBF VG PVFVBUEUNS PXOKFSKXKUS" DXW BSQSUFSH—VMUJ!—VKS JMKHBSH XKH FDSKFE-VKS FOPSW TSGVBS OF TSUXPS X TSWFWSNNSB GVB PVBBVD OK KOKSFSSK WSYSKFE-GVMB.

4. XEK BXKH'W "FJS GVMKFXOKJSXH" DXW BSQSUFSH TE FJS GOBWF FDSNYS LMTNOWJSBW WJS XLLBVXUJSH.

5. Q. R. BVDNOKZ'W GOBWF TVVR, "JXBBE LVFFSB XKH FJS LJONVWVLJSB'W WFVKS," DXW FMBKSH HVDK TE KOKS LMTNOWJSBW, OKUNMHOKZ JXBLSBUVNNOKW XKH LSKZMOK, TSGVBS TNVVPWTMBE WOZKSH OF ML.*

6. HB. WSMWW'W GOBWF UJONHBSK'W TVVR, "XKH FV FJOKR FJXF O WXD OF VK PMNTSBBE WFBSSF," DXW BSQSUFSH TE FDSKFE-WOC LMTNOWJSBW TSGVBS OF DXW LMTNOWJSH OK KOKSFSSK FJOBFE-WSYSK

SPRING HAS SPRUNG!

ACROSS

1. Barbecue fare
5. Swelled head
8. Pound the keyboard
12. Not quite round
13. Like sushi dishes
14. Horse color
15. In spring, this sport goes into training
17. "_____ Lang Syne"
18. Follow
19. Twirl
21. Golf gadgets
24. Michael, Gabriel, or Raphael
27. Foot part
30. Poor box offerings
32. China's Chairman _____
33. Zero
34. Forest units
35. Perissodactyl mammal
36. Foot digit
37. Ersatz butter
38. Chip in chips
39. Ringo the drummer
41. Baby branch
43. Zero
45. Gymnast Comaneci
49. Etcher's fluid
51. In spring, this is a farmer's chore
54. Solo
55. 007 creator Fleming
56. Despise
57. Corporate symbol
58. IRS 1040 pro
59. Soothing plant

DOWN

1. Judge's garb
2. "Terrible" czar
3. Lowest male singing voice
4. Detective
5. Important time period
6. Guy's date
7. Nocturnal hooters
8. Railroad vehicle
9. In spring, his fancy turns to love: 2 wds.
10. Buddy
11. Terminate
16. Hive dweller
20. ". . . do not _____ Go, do not collect . . ."
22. British nobleman
23. Icy rain
25. Whence the sun rises
26. Be an also-ran
27. Industrious insects
28. Civil insurrection
29. In spring, a big task
31. Catty remark?
34. Ripped
38. Christie of mysteries
40. Cowboy show
42. Traveler's haven
44. Saga
46. Old telephone feature
47. Division word
48. "The African Queen" screenwriter James
49. The whole shebang
50. What lovebirds do
52. Place for a grandchild, maybe
53. Santa _____ winds

Answers on pages 373.

GREEDY SCRAMBLEGRAM

NOITEMTOPIC

P O O R A R T I C O N

H I D M E N A C E R S

ROCKTOKERBS

Four 11-letter words, all of which revolve around the same theme, have been jumbled. Unscramble each word, and write the answer in the accompanying space. Next, transfer the letters in the shaded boxes into the shaded keyword space, and unscramble the 9-letter word that goes with the theme. The theme for this puzzle is money.

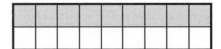

WORD JIGSAW

Fit the pieces into the frame to form common words reading across and down. There's no need to rotate the pieces; they'll fit as shown, with each piece used once.

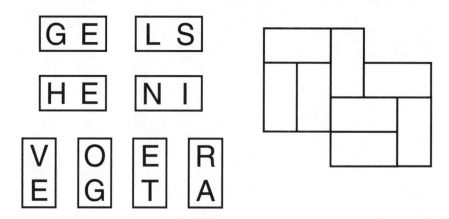

AMAZING BOUT WITH A TROUT

Help reel in this catch! Work your way from start to finish.

236

RHYME TIME

Each clue leads to a 2-word answer that rhymes, such as BIG PIG or STABLE TABLE. The numbers in parentheses after the clue give the number of letters in each word. For example, "cookware taken from the oven (3, 3) would be "hot pot."

1. Plumbing problem (4, 4): _____ _____

2. Entrée option (4, 4): _____ _____

3. Go on a road trip (4, 4): _____ _____

4. Obsessive one's objective (4, 4): _____ _____

5. Bovine that just ate (4, 4): _____ _____

6. "Jack and Jill" (4, 4): _____ _____

7. Trumpeter's oldest instrument (4, 4): _____ _____

8. Base stealer's maneuver (4, 5): _____ _____

9. Spectral party giver (5, 4): _____ _____

10. The "and" after "Four score" (5, 4): _____ _____

11. Equine army (5, 5): _____ _____

12. Pronouncement by U.S. Customs (6, 5): _____ _____

13. More irate snake (6, 5): _____ _____

14. Writer's advance (6, 6): _____ _____

15. Stronger snub (6, 8): _____ _____

Answers on page 373.

NUMBER WEB

It's a crossword without clues—or words! Place all the numbers into the grid to complete the puzzle. There's only one solution.

3 digits

101

103

290

444

827

838

999

4 digits

0023

0120

1002

5 digits

02933

11029

15243

28732

77762

90292

91821

98238

7 digits

0951411

0992882

0998821

4231725

5144256

9541880

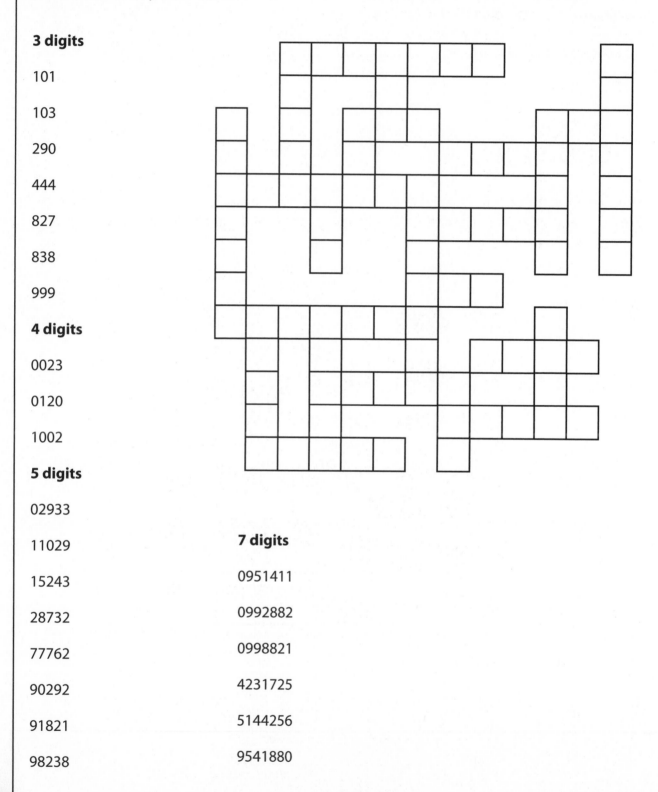

Answer on page 373.

Not wanting to be embarrassed by revealing her age on her birthday, Grandma instead told the grandkids that if they multiplied her age in five years by 5, then multiplied her age in six years by 6, and added the totals together, they would get a number that is 12 times her current age. When she saw the large wax forest fire atop her birthday cake, Grandma knew they had figured it out. How old is she?

CODEWORD

The letters of the alphabet are hidden in code: They are represented by a random number from 1 through 26. With the letters already given, complete the crossword puzzle with English words and break the code.

15	10	17	11	11	18	■	12	■	6	2	12
■	17	■	17	■	16	5	4	24	23	■	2
12	17	5	17	3	3	17	■	12	■	5	15
■	15	■	19	■	4	■	4	10	21	17	15
11	23	5	12	23	4	21	23	■	2	■	2
■	13	■	21	■	15	■	17	■	16	■	10
2	15	15	7	23	15	■	23	13	3	17	22	23
13	■	21	■	22	■	26	■	21	■	23	■
1	■	5	■	8	17	21	26	23	5	23	22
23	14	2	21	15	■	21	■	23	■	11	■
5	■	6	■	21	■	23	13	9	17	18	23	22
13	■	23	25	7	4	10	■	17	■	13	■
17	20	13	■	8	■	17	8	21	7	15	23

A B C D E F G H I J K L M N O P Q R S T U V W X Y Z

1	2	3	4	5	6	7	8	9	10	11	12	13

14	15	16	17	18	19	20	21	22	23	24	25	26
	S		O		K							

Answers on page 373.

WORD CIRCLE

Complete each 6-letter word so the last 2 letters of the first word are the first 2 letters of the second word, and the last 2 letters of the second word are the first 2 letters of the third word, etc. The last 2 letters of the final word are the first 2 letters of the first word, thus completing the circle.

__ __ L L __ __

__ __ O U __ __

__ __ Q U __ __

__ __ E V __ __

__ __ T I __ __

NUMBER CROSSWORD

Fill in this crossword with numbers instead of letters. Use the clues to determine which number from 1 through 9 belongs in each square. No zeros are used.

ACROSS

1. A power of 2
4. Consecutive digits, descending
5. The sum of its digits is 15
6. An even number
7. Its digits are in descending order
9. A square number

DOWN

1. Two different digits
2. A palindrome
3. A power of 2
4. Four identical digits
5. Its middle digit is the sum of its two outside digits
8. A square number

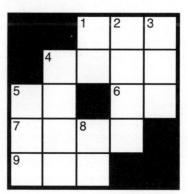

Answers on page 374.

ZOO LETTERBOX

The letters in IBEX can be found in boxes 4, 8, 10, and 20, but not necessarily in that order. Similarly, the letters in all the other animals' names can be found in the boxes indicated. Your task is to insert all the letters of the alphabet into the boxes. If you do this correctly, the shaded cells will reveal the names of two more critters.

Hint: Look for words that share a single letter. For example, IBEX shares a **B** with BUFFALO and an **E** with MOOSE. By comparing the number lists, you can then deduce the values of these letters.

1	2	3	4	5	6	7	8	9	10	11	12	13

14	15	16	17	18	19	20	21	22	23	24	25	26

AARDVARK: 5, 6, 9, 11, 17

BUFFALO: 4, 5, 14, 18, 19, 26

CHEETAH: 1, 5, 8, 23, 25

DONKEY: 6, 8, 11, 16, 19, 21

GIRAFFE: 5, 7, 8, 9, 10, 18

HORSE: 1, 2, 8, 9, 19

IBEX: 4, 8, 10, 20

JAGUAR: 5, 7, 9, 14, 24

MOOSE: 2, 8, 15, 19

SPRINGBOK: 2, 4, 7, 9, 10, 11, 12, 19, 21

SQUIRREL: 2, 8, 9, 10, 14, 22, 26

TIGER: 7, 8, 9, 10, 25

WEASEL: 2, 3, 5, 8, 26

ZEBRA: 4, 5, 8, 9, 13

MRS. SMITH'S DAUGHTERS

Jane, Anna, Kate, and Sarah are Mrs. Smith's 4 daughters. Each daughter has a different hair color (black, blond, brown, or red) and a different eye color (blue, brown, green, or hazel). Using the information given, try to determine not only each daughter's hair and eye color but also whether she is 1, 2, 3, or 4 years old.

1. The girl with black hair is younger than Sarah.

2. Of Jane and Anna, one has brown hair and the other has brown eyes but neither is the oldest or youngest.

3. Kate does not have hazel eyes.

4. The blond is younger than the girl with green eyes but older than Anna.

| | | JANE | ANNA | KATE | SARAH | HAIR | | | | EYES | | | |
						BLACK	BLOND	BROWN	RED	BLUE	BROWN	GREEN	HAZEL
4 YEARS OLD													
3 YEARS OLD													
2 YEARS OLD													
1 YEAR OLD													
EYES	BLUE												
	BROWN												
	GREEN												
	HAZEL												
HAIR	BLACK												
	BLOND												
	BROWN												
	RED												

Answers on page 374.

THE PERFECT CUBE

Fill in this crossword with numbers instead of letters. Use the clues to determine which of the numbers 1 through 9 belongs in each square. No zeros are used.

Hint: The complete list of three-digit cubes is: 125, 287, 512, 729.

ACROSS
1. A multiple of 41
4. A number with the pattern aabc whose digits add up to 13
5. Consecutive odd digits, ascending
6. The sum of the first three digits is equal to the last digit
7. A cube

DOWN
1. A palindrome
2. Consecutive digits out of order
3. A cube that's also a square
4. A cube that's also a palindrome
5. A cube

PARTY DRESS

Magenta, Teal, and Hazel were invited to the same party, not knowing the others would also be there. When they arrived, they were wearing magenta, teal, and hazel dresses. The woman in the teal dress said, "Isn't it funny that our dress colors are the same as our names, but not one of us is wearing the dress that matches her name?" Magenta looked at the other two women and agreed. What color dress was each woman wearing?

STAR POWER

Fill in each of the empty squares in the grid so that each star is surrounded by the numbers 1 through 8 with no repeats.

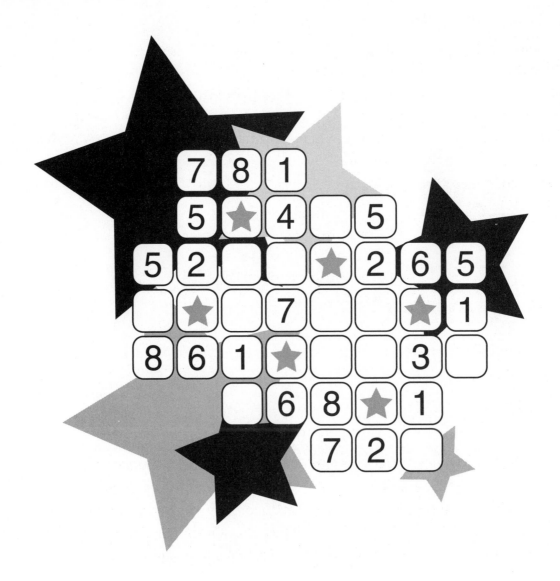

Answer on page 374.

FIND THE WORD

Ignoring spaces, capitalization, and punctuation, how many occurrences of the consecutive letters **ROOF** can you find in the paragraph below?

Rufus was a kangaroo fanatic, and the proof was the kangaroo frescoes he painted on his roof. Rufus owned a bistro, often bringing home food for his pet kangaroo, Fido. Fido, a boxing kangaroo, was a semipro, often fighting large wallabies. His win total was zero, officially, although he once defeated a koala in an unofficial match when the smaller koala pulled a switcheroo, falling to throw the fight. Rufus kept Fido in a leakproof hut with shatterproof windows and read him stories of the jackaroo, fantastic creatures that were part rabbit and part kangaroo. Fido didn't believe the stories but played along because he had no proof and wanted Rufus to keep bringing foods from the bistro, of which the rooster fondue was his favorite.

A PUZZLING PERSPECTIVE

Mentally arrange the lettered balls from large to small in the correct order to spell an 11-letter word.

Clue: Myopic

What letter completes this group of 4?

J, P, G, _____

MATH GRID

Fill each square in the grid with a digit from 1 through 9. When the numbers in each row are added, you should arrive at the total in the right-hand column. When the numbers in each column are added, you should arrive at the total on the bottom line. The numbers in each corner-to-corner diagonal must add up to the totals in the upper- and lower-right corners.

							51
6	3	2		2	6	5	33
	2	8	4		9	6	38
4		3	7	5	7		37
2	8	4	8			5	31
7			2	9		8	43
9		5	1	3	2	2	30
	5	6		4	6	3	40
42	39	35	38	28	37	33	33

Answers on page 374.

TESSELLATED FLOOR

Rearrange the 7 pieces to form the mosaic shape. Pieces can be rotated but not overlapped or mirrored.

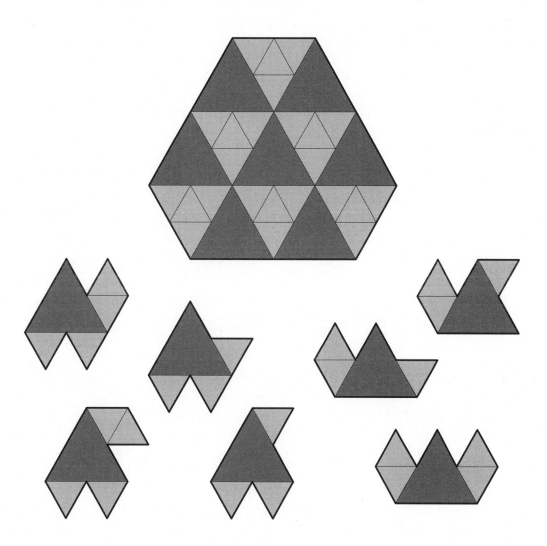

Answer on page 374.

FRENCH CONNECTION

The Eiffel Tower is usually filled with tourists, but here it's filled with words and phrases—all of them connected to France and interconnected with each other in the word search grid on the opposite page.

We've built the tower—but it's up to you to build the word list. First, take our written Tour de France and fill in the blanks. These answers will be the words and phrases you'll be looking for in the Eiffel Tower grid. Fill in as many words as you can, then search for and circle those words in the grid. Grid words and phrases will run horizontally, vertically, or diagonally.

After you've found everything in the grid, read the leftover letters in order from left to right, top to bottom. The letters will spell out a great way to enjoy French toast.

Your Personal Tour de France

Hello! Or as we say in Paris " _ _ _   _ _ _ _ !" High up here in our city's most recognizable landmark, the _ _ _ _ _ _   _ _ _ _ _ , you can see for miles. Look over there across the river _ _ _ _ _ and you'll spot that grand boulevard the _ _ _ _ _ _ - _ _ _ _ _ _ _ _ , literally the Elysian Fields. Perhaps you've seen the old Leslie Caron movie " _ _ _ _ ," where she strolls along this avenue and stops at a sidewalk _ _ _ _ (the French word for "coffee") to sip some bubbly _ _ _ _ _ _ _ _ _ , devour just one _ _ _ _ _ _ _ _ (a snail, you know), sample some soft _ _ _ _ cheese, and finish with a _ _ _ _ _ _ _ _ , a pastry named for our short general who conquered Europe in the early 1800s. (That was soon after the French Revolution, when our King _ _ _ _ _ XVI got his head chopped off by the _ _ _ _ _ _ _ _ _ _ . Bad for him, but now we get to celebrate _ _ _ _ _ _ _ _   _ _ _ every July 14th.)

Ah, so many famous people we have, both real and fictional: _ _ _ _ of Arc; that dashing trio, the _ _ _ _ _   _ _ _ _ _ _ _ _ _ _ , who were "All for one and one for all"; Louis _ _ _ _ _ _ _ , whose name is forever linked to his milk-preserving process; and Victor _ _ _ _ , who wrote about a hunchback named _ _ _ _ _ _ _ _ _ _ , the bell ringer at _ _ _ _ _   _ _ _ _ Cathedral. He also wrote _ _ _   _ _ _ , the abbreviated title of a book turned into a hit musical about the French Revolution.

If you like art, hop on the _ _ _ _ _ (the Paris subway) to get to the _ _ _ _ _ _ , where you can view the "Mona Lisa," and the works of _ _ _ _ _ (those water lilies!) and Toulouse-Lautrec, who might have gushed " _ _ _ - _ _ - _ _ !" as he painted the Moulin Rouge's naughty _ _ _ _ _ _ dancers. If you like to shop, I know a place to buy a sporty _ _ _ _ _ _ for your father's head and some lovely lavender-scented _ _ _ _ _ _ _ for your mother. If you'd like to attend a real French party, I can get you in, but you'll need to _ _ _ _ , which is, of course, short for "répondez s'il vous plaît."

For a different French experience, vacation in the resort city of _ _ _ _ . It's on the French _ _ _ _ _ _ _ (also the name of a Buick). Or visit the Canadian province of _ _ _ _ _ _ , where a different brand of French is spoken.

But "thank you" there is the same as it is here. For coming on tour, we say " _ _ _ _ _ !"

Answers on page 374.

```
                              E
                              M
                         T    F    E
                         H    R    I
                         R    E    F
                         E    P    F
                         E    A    E
                         M    S    L
                         U    T    T
                         S    E    O
                         K    U    W
                    B    E    R    E    T
                    A    T    M    R    R
                    S    E    I    N    E
               A    T    E    I    S    M    Q
          E    R    I    R    A    U    A    U    P
          O    Y    L    S    O    R    D    A    L
     O    O    H    L    A    L    A    E    S    O    U
          C    R    E                   R    I    U
          H    I    D                   T    M    V
     U    A    C    A                   O    O    R    I
G    G    M    R    Y                   N    D    E    L    R
O    A    S    P    E                   O    C    A    F    E
     C    H    A    M    P    S    E    L    Y    S    E    E    S
     T    O    G    R    A    C    S    E    O    S    C    L    B
A    N    E    N    I    T    O    L    L    I    U    G    A    O    E
S    I    M    S    E    L                   G    I    N    N    P    U
D    C    J    O    A    N                   I    S    J    C    A    Q
E    S    A    N    Y                        G    O    C    A    N
B    R    I    E                             U    H    E    N
E    R    S    T                             R    S    V    P
```

Hidden message: _____

CARRYING ON

ACROSS

1. Ring
5. Mardi _____
9. Do a Thanksgiving dinner job
14. Bear constellation
15. River past Buckingham
16. Foreign
17. Competitions with forwards and guards: 2 wds.
20. SASE, e.g.
21. "For shame!"
22. Cookie-selling org.
25. "Tommy" rock opera group: 2 wds.
27. "I _____ Little Prayer for You": 2 wds.
31. Holler
33. Quite pale
34. Retired prof's title: abbr.
35. Actress Normand of the silents
37. Brunch time, maybe: 2 wds.
39. Saint Patrick's Day parade participant, likely: 2 wds.
42. Provided funds for, as a car loan
43. Facial features
45. _____ the Red
46. China's Zhou _____
49. Alternative magazine founded in 1984
50. 6/6/44
51. The highest volcano in Eur.: 2 wds.
53. Gridiron gains: abbr.
54. Poetic meadow
55. Gambler's figures
57. Facially expressing disapproval, perhaps: 3 wds.
65. Small musical combos
66. "The Virginian" author Wister
67. State settled by Brigham Young
68. Apprehension
69. Tree house?
70. Like many a horror film

DOWN

1. Place to get a Guinness
2. Memorable period
3. Ninny
4. Fresh body of water
5. "Aha!"
6. Russian coins
7. Botanist Gray
8. Bookstore section, hyph., 2 wds.
9. Parakeet's place
10. _____ mode: 2 wds.
11. Edge
12. Churchill's sign
13. Coast Guard rank: abbr.
18. Treebeard in "The Lord of the Rings," e.g.
19. Big name in model trains
22. Phys. ed. class locale
23. Gull or tern
24. Tirane's country
26. Cajole
27. "Ciao!": 2 wds.
28. General pardon
29. Accountant's closing time: 2 wds.
30. Hand and shoulder connector
32. Inheritance
36. Hospital staffer: abbr.
38. Moving vehicle
40. Bygone block deliverers
41. It has five sides
42. Gave sustenance
44. French possessive pronoun
47. Observes Yom Kippur
48. Tab key function
52. Commercials
54. It might be headed "To Do"
56. Fake vending machine coin
57. School group: abbr.
58. Big coffee server
59. 18-wheeler
60. "Mayday!"
61. Be in arrears
62. "How was _____ know?": 2 wds.
63. Golfer's standard
64. Timid

MAGIC SQUARE

Place the numbers 1 through 25 in the empty squares so that all rows, columns, and long diagonals add up to the same sum. Each number is used once.

17		1	8	
23				16
	6			22
	12	19	21	
11		25		9

Answers on pages 374–375.

AN ACTOR'S BIO

Cryptograms are messages in substitution code. Break the code to read the trivia question and answer. For example, THE SMART CAT might become FVO QWGDF JGF if **F** is substituted for **T, V** for **H, O** for **E,** and so on.

LA ZRY MDWU-VR-MDWU REWDXE QRX "WDBVDTYE WRIXDFARIE"

DYP "MRCE VRZY." LA DSER EVDXXAP TY "QDVLAX RQ VLA

MXTPA." ZLR TE LA?

EBAYWAX VXDWC

JIGSAW

If you visually rearrange these 4 jigsaw pieces to form a square a capital letter will appear in the middle. What is that letter?

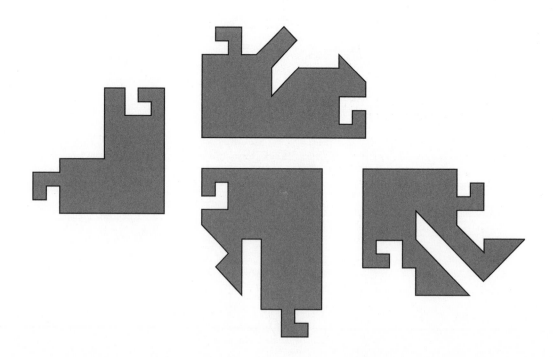

Answers on page 375.

CAPITAL SCRAMBLEGRAM

Four 8-letter words, all of which revolve around the same theme, have been jumbled. Unscramble each word, and write the answer in the accompanying space. Next, transfer the letters in the shaded boxes into the shaded keyword space, and unscramble the 9-letter word that goes with the theme. The theme for this puzzle is world capitals.

Top: N E A R C R A B

Left: I S A T A N G O

Right: R U B S L E S S

Bottom: H U R T A M O K

WORD LADDER

Change just one letter on each line to go from the top word to the bottom word. Do not change the order of the letters. You must have a common English word at each step.

WORK

_____

_____

_____

_____

PLAY

Answers on page 375.

COUNTING UP

What is the next number in this common progression? What do these numbers represent?

1, 5, 10, 25, ___

RHYME TIME

Each clue leads to a 2-word answer that rhymes, such as BIG PIG or STABLE TABLE. The numbers in parentheses after the clue give the number of letters in each word. For example, "cookware taken from the oven (3, 3)" would be "hot pot."

1. Old-fashion watch (4, 4): _____ _____

2. A dive over the line for a touchdown (4, 4): _____ _____

3. Overheated college residence (4, 4): _____ _____

4. Swindle on the tracks (4, 4): _____ _____

5. Swine utensil (4, 4): _____ _____

6. Antique-store purchase (4, 5): _____ _____

7. A most impressive bird of prey (5, 5): _____ _____

8. Sugar cookie (5, 5): _____ _____

9. Clique within the cast (6, 5): _____ _____

10. In-crowd's favorite flick (6, 5): _____ _____

11. Temporary crown (6, 6): _____ _____

12. Mosquito-race timer (7, 5): _____ _____

Answers on page 375.

SUDOKU

Use deductive logic to complete the grid so that each row, each column, and each 3 by 3 box contains the numbers 1 through 9 in some order. The solution is unique.

3	2				6			9
			5					3
						1		
8	3	2			9			
		7				9		
			1			6	3	8
		4						
9					7			
7			3				5	6

RING OF NUMBERS

Arrange the numbers 1 through 11 in the circles below, using each number once, so that any 3 numbers on a straight line add up to 18.

CRISSCROSS PUZZLE

Use each of the words listed here to complete this clue-less crossword grid. The puzzle has only one solution.

3 letters

CAT

DAY

ICE

SAD

TAB

VIA

VAN

4 letters

NOSE

SHOT

5 letters

CATCH

RABID

STEAM

TAKES

6 letters

BORROW

BOUGHT

CLOCKS

GLOBAL

MOTION

NAMING

REPAIR

SQUASH

7 letters

ARRIVED

BARRIER

8 letters

BRIGHTLY

RESTARTS

UPSTAIRS

10 letters

OUTRAGEOUS

ROUNDABOUT

11 letters

TRANSACTION

Answer on page 375.

ISOMETRIC ROGUES

Identify the one figure in each row of designs that is different from the others. Are there any rows that contain identical figures?

Answers on page 375.

Every word listed is contained within the group of letters below. Words can be found horizontally, vertically, or diagonally. They may read either backward or forward. The leftover letters will reveal a hidden message that will tell you "where hurricanes hardly happen."

HADDON HALL

HA-HA

HALFHEARTED

HALF HITCH

HALF HOUR

HAM-HANDED

HAMMERHEAD

HANDHOLDS

HAPHAZARD

HARDHACK

HARDHEAD

HARD-HITTING

HARTSHORN

HARVEST HOME

HAZEL HEN

HEADHUNTER

HEATH HEN

HEAVYHANDED

HEDDA HOPPER

HEDGEHOG

HEE-HAW

HEIGH-HO

HELEN HAYES

HEXAHEDRON

HIGH HOLIDAY

HITCHHIKE

HOBBYHORSE

HOGSHEAD

HO HO

HO-HUM

HOLLYHOCK

HOMO HABILIS

HOP

HOPHEAD

HOREHOUND

HORNBEAM

HORSEHAIR

HORSEHIDE

HOTHOUSE

HOUSEHOLD

HULL HOUSE

HUNTING HORNS

```
Y H G R H S R                                        H E H K H N H
A O N E A D U                                        E S O C I O A
D M I T P L O                                        D U U O T R L
I O T N H O H                                        G O S H C D F
L H T U A H F                                        E H E Y H E H
O A I H Z D L                                        H T H L H H E
H B H D A N A                                        O O O L I A A
H I D A R A H E H H C T I H F L A H G H L O K X R
G L R E D H E R H T H U L L H O U S E F D H E E T
I I A H A M H A N D E D S N R O H G N I T N U H E
H S H A R I A H E S R O H A Z E L H E N O M H E D
A E O R R D H A R D H A C K A H P E N N R U O A A
D Y B V D N U O H E R O H D E F O P R E R H P V E
D A B E D I H E S R O H M A E B N R O H P O H Y H
O H Y S D H E                                        H H W H E H R
N N H T A A I                                        S T A N A A E
H E O H D H G                                        T A H D D N M
A L R O O A H                                        R E E H D D M
L E S M A H H                                        A H E M P E A
L H E E S H O                                        H I H R E D H
```

Hidden message: _____

Answers on page 375.

FIVE-LETTER ANAGRAMS

Fill in the blanks in each sentence below with 5-letter words that are anagrams (rearrangements of the same letters) of one another.

1. We _____ our car to _____, Delaware.

2. The guide took great _____ to point out that the capital of _____ is still Madrid.

3. She spilled ink, which left a permanent _____ on her new _____ dress.

4. The judge took a shortcut on the _____ through the woods to make it to the courtroom in time for the _____.

5. _____ bread should at _____ be cheaper than fresh bread.

6. It is impolite to _____ at someone whose face is covered with _____.

ALL IN THE FAMILY

Three 3-letter family members can be found in this grid. MOM is the first. Additionally, each of their 3-letter first names can be found (one of which starts with the same letter as their position within the family). Every family member and each of their names appears the same number of times in the grid. Can you find them all reading horizontally, vertically, and diagonally?

As a bonus, can you determine the name of their hometown? It's 5 letters long, is a major U.S. city, and appears only once in the grid.

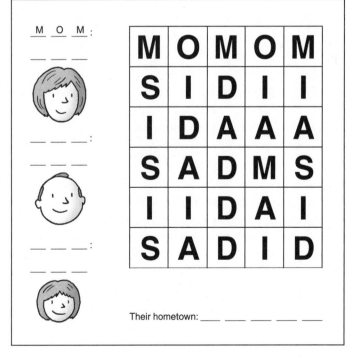

M O M : _ _ _

_ _ _ : _ _ _

_ _ _ : _ _ _

M	O	M	O	M
S	I	D	I	I
I	D	A	A	A
S	A	D	M	S
I	I	D	A	I
S	A	D	I	D

Their hometown: ___ ___ ___ ___ ___

Answers on page 375.

FOUR SISTERS

Upon her return from living abroad, Alberta, the youngest of 4 sisters, announced her shipboard marriage. Her 3 sisters, Carla, Paula, and Roberta were amazed by her husband's name. With the aid of the clues below determine Alberta's husband's first and last name, as well as Carla's, Paula's, and Roberta's husbands' first and last names. The 4 men are Albert, Carl, Paul, and Robert. Their last names are Albertson, Carlson, Paulson, and Robertson.

1. No woman's husband has a first name that consists of her first name without the final "a"; no sister's last name consists of her first name without the final "a" and with "son" on the end; and no man's last name consists of his first name with "son" added at the end.

2. Paul is not married to Roberta, and Robert is not married to Paula.

3. No husband and wife have "bert" in both of their first names, but there is a man who has "bert" in his first and last names.

4. Carl's last name is not Paulson.

	ALBERT	CARL	PAUL	ROBERT	ALBERTSON	CARLSON	PAULSON	ROBERTSON
ALBERTA								
CARLA								
PAULA								
ROBERTA								
ALBERTSON								
CARLSON								
PAULSON								
ROBERTSON								

COIN DILEMMA

I have 10 coins in my pocket (no silver dollars). I can't make change for $1.00, 50¢, 25¢, 10¢, or 5¢. What are the denominations of the 10 coins?

Answers on page 375.

WORD PATHS

Each of these word paths contains a familiar saying. To figure out the saying, read freely from letter to letter, starting with the letter indicated by the arrow. Some letters will be used more than once, and you can move forward and backward along the straight lines. The blanks indicate the number of letters in each word of the saying.

1.

2.

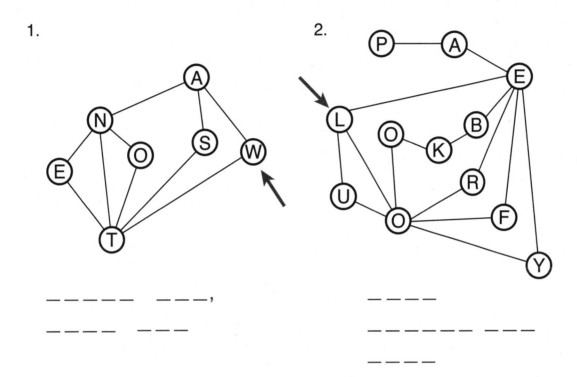

1.

_ _ _ _ _   _ _ _,

_ _ _ _   _ _ _

2.

_ _ _ _

_ _ _ _ _ _   _ _ _

_ _ _ _

3.

4.

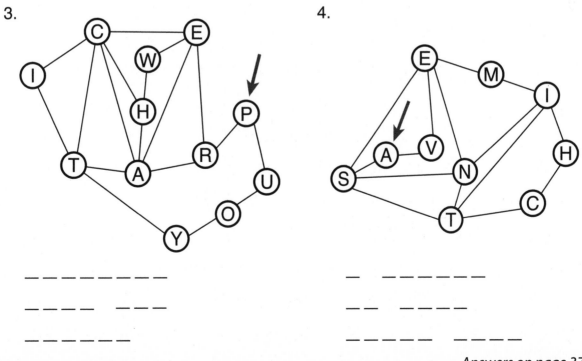

3.

_ _ _ _ _ _ _ _

_ _ _   _ _ _

_ _ _ _ _ _

4.

_   _ _ _ _ _ _

_ _   _ _ _ _

_ _ _ _ _   _ _ _ _

Answers on page 376.

FIFTY-STATE HIGHWAY

Use each of the state names listed here to complete the clue-less crossword grid on the next page and create a superhighway that connects all 50 states. The puzzle has only one solution.

4 letters

IOWA

OHIO

UTAH

5 letters

IDAHO

MAINE

TEXAS

6 letters

ALASKA

HAWAII

KANSAS

NEVADA

OREGON

7 letters

ALABAMA

ARIZONA

FLORIDA

GEORGIA

INDIANA

MONTANA

NEW YORK

VERMONT

WYOMING

8 letters

ARKANSAS

COLORADO

DELAWARE

ILLINOIS

KENTUCKY

MARYLAND

MICHIGAN

MISSOURI

NEBRASKA

OKLAHOMA

VIRGINIA

9 letters

LOUISIANA

MINNESOTA

NEW JERSEY

NEW MEXICO

TENNESSEE

WISCONSIN

10 letters

CALIFORNIA

WASHINGTON

11 letters

CONNECTICUT

MISSISSIPPI

NORTH DAKOTA

RHODE ISLAND

SOUTH DAKOTA

12 letters

NEW HAMPSHIRE

PENNSYLVANIA

WEST VIRGINIA

13 letters

MASSACHUSETTS

NORTH CAROLINA

SOUTH CAROLINA

Answer on page 376.

CRYPTO-QUOTES

Cryptograms are messages in substitution code. Break the code to read the quotes and their sources. For example, THE SMART CAT might become FVO QWGDF JGF if **F** is substituted for **T**, **V** for **H, O** for **E,** and so on. The code is different for each cryptogram.

1. "WRLB, OZ XGRW BX XHFDRAYRD, OD SXB WRLB LHB CS OSYRDBERSB."

—ZFCSPAOS W. FXXDRYRAB

2. "UOB LQ OACOGPYD QY BY URPO BVGB FVOA FO JYWO BY CRO OPOA BVO LACODBGIOD FRUU XO QYDDH."

—WGDI BFGRA

TIMES SQUARE

Fill each square in the grid with a number from 2 through 9. When the numbers in each row are multiplied, you should arrive at the total in the right-hand column. When the numbers in each column are multiplied, you should arrive at the total on the bottom line. Note: This puzzle does not contain the number 1.

Hint: Factor each product into its component prime numbers. For example, 432 is 2×2×2×2×3×3×3.

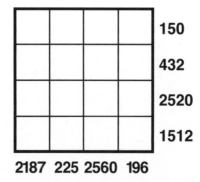

				150
				432
				2520
				1512
2187	225	2560	196	

Answers on page 376.

ABCD

Every cell in this grid contains 1 of 4 letters: A, B, C, or D. No letter can be horizontally or vertically adjacent to itself. The tables above and to the left of the grid indicate how many times each letter appears in that column or row. Can you complete the grid?

	A	1	2	1	3	0	2
	B	2	2	2	0	2	1
	C	3	0	1	2	2	1
A B C	D	0	2	2	1	2	2
3 1 1							
2 0 2 2							D
0 3 1 2							
3 0 2 1							
0 3 1 2							
1 2 2 1						D	

BOOKEND LETTERS

Each word below is missing a pair of identical letters. Add the same letter to the beginning and end of each word to create new words. Do not use any pair of letters twice.

__ANGLE__

__CLIPS__

__RIM__

__TRAIT__

Answers on page 376.

THE INTERNATIONAL SCENE

ACROSS

1. Ooze
5. Excuse
10. Soothing ointment
14. Summon
15. A difficulty or complication
16. Double-reed woodwind
17. They're fiercer than city apes: 2 wds.
20. Member speaking for the whole ball team: hyph.
21. Lacks
22. Enola _____
23. Untidy place
24. Performer
27. This gun for hire
33. Central part
34. Military barracks
35. Quilting party, perhaps
36. Countries just hatched: 2 wds.
39. Turn over the engine
40. National song
41. Quote or mention
42. White-collar bag
44. Cuts from copy
45. "_____ Were King": 2 wds.

46. Defeater of the Luftwaffe: abbr.
47. Nappy leather
50. Mermaids have them
56. Controlled by the military: 3 wds.
58. German river or dam
59. God's fishbowl
60. Peru's capital
61. Boys
62. Squeeze in
63. Observed

DOWN

1. Atlantic porgy
2. English noble
3. Noted island prison
4. Theater lover: hyph.
5. Quite incensed
6. Turn down: var.
7. Fixe or reçue: Fr.
8. Expel air
9. Middle East country: abbr.
10. Henry's first Anne
11. Fit
12. Burden
13. Army meal
18. Close
19. Meaning
23. Beat it!

24. Sharp and biting
25. Person on way to success
26. Famous fountain of Rome
27. Devilfish
28. Baltic natives
29. Opera's Fleming
30. Seething
31. French income
32. Affirmatives
34. Beatrice, "The Beautiful Parricide"
37. Lighting director
38. Chunks dropping off glaciers
43. Downy ducks
44. Computer input or output
46. Class of German wines
47. Takes to court
48. Loosen a knot
49. Happy place
50. Confront
51. Steamed
52. Men only
53. Mr. Nastase
54. Feeble, as an excuse
55. Singer of one last song
57. Shorten the grass

CIRCLES AND NUMBERS

Study the circles and numbers below. Can you replace the question mark with the correct number?

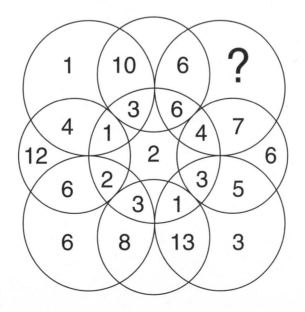

Answers on page 376.

267

A FOUR-MIDABLE MAZE

The object of this maze is to form a path from the 4 diamond on the left to the 4 diamond on the right. You can only move only through diamonds containing a multiple of 4 and only through diamonds connected by a line.

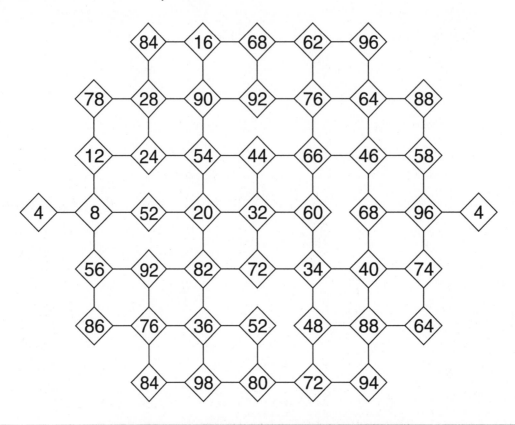

FOUR-LETTER ANAGRAMS

Fill in the blanks in each sentence below with 4-letter words that are anagrams (rearrangements of the same letters) of one another.

1. She put _____ and pepper on her _____ ear of corn.

2. The coach told the _____ to eat a lot of _____ for dinner before the big game.

3. My _____ and uncle offered us _____ fish sandwiches.

4. How can she be so _____ when she's out in the sun every day playing _____ frog?

5. If you don't wear gloves while doing dishes in the _____, the smooth _____ of your hands will pucker.

6. She wrote a _____ to the phone company expressing her displeasure with their dial _____.

Answers on page 376.

SHOE SALE

The shoe sale is over, and now the clerk needs to match up the 21 remaining pairs. Can you help him out? Look closely: There's one shoe with no match.

JIGSTARS

These 12 jigsaw pieces can be put together in pairs to form perfect 6-pointed stars. Can you visually determine the 6 pairs?

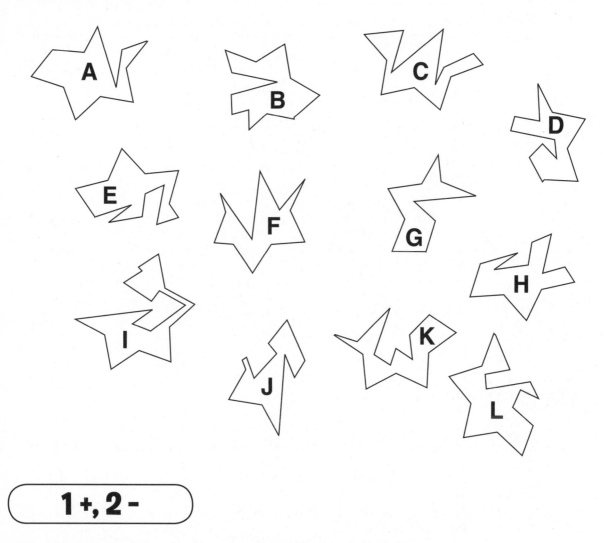

1 +, 2 −

Put one plus sign (+) and two minus signs (−) somewhere between the digits below so the equation is correct.

1 2 3 4 5 6 7 8 9 = 100

Answers on page 376.

SUDOKU

Use deductive logic to complete the grid so that each row, each column, and each 3 by 3 box contains the numbers 1 through 9 in some order. The solution is unique.

1	3				4			
			8					
2	7			3		6		
		1		4	6			
8			6				4	
	9	8		2				
6		5				8	1	
		7						
	2					5	9	

ARROW WEB

Shade in some of the arrows so that each arrow in the grid points to exactly one shaded arrow.

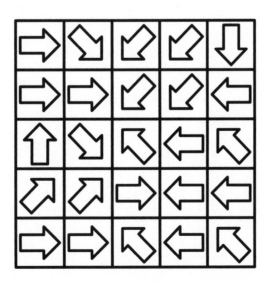

RHYME TIME

Each clue leads to a 2-word answer that rhymes, such as BIG PIG or STABLE TABLE. The numbers in parentheses after the clue give the number of letters in each word. For example, "cookware taken from the oven (3, 3)" would be "hot pot."

1. Underachiever's credo (3, 3): _____ _____

2. They make meals for the masses (4, 4): _____ _____

3. She can afford the best of brooms (4, 5): _____ _____

4. Attorney's excessive billing (4, 5): _____ _____

5. Aid for river crossers (4, 5): _____ _____

6. It has a whistle too (5, 4): _____ _____

7. Time stopper (5, 4): _____ _____

8. They're hooked on omelets (6, 5): _____ _____

9. Revolutionary new pedal (6, 5): _____ _____

10. Require the study of poetry (6, 5): _____ _____

11. How to avoid dog bites (6, 6): _____ _____

12. Where to find roots (7, 5): _____ _____

13. Underachiever's credo (5, 8): _____ _____

14. In search of comic relief (5, 8): _____ _____

15. Monotonous tiles (6, 8): _____ _____

Answers on page 376.

MONDRIANIZE IT!

Inspired by the artwork of Belgian artist Piet Mondrian, these puzzles consist of stars and circles. Using the checkered pattern as a guide, draw in lines so that each star is in its own square, and each circle in its own rectangle.

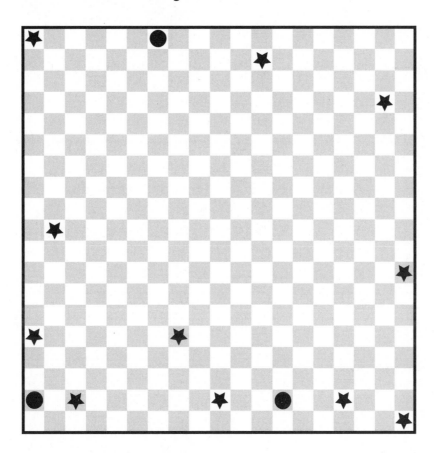

WORD JIGSAW

Fit the pieces into the frame to form common words reading across and down. There's no need to rotate the pieces; they'll fit as shown, with each piece used once.

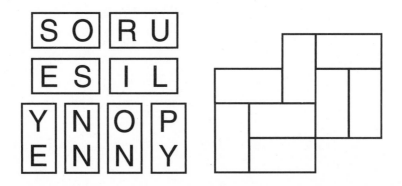

SNOW

Every word listed is contained within the group of letters below. Words can be found horizontally, vertically, or diagonally. They may read either backward or forward. The leftover letters reveal a movie title related to the puzzle's title.

ALASKA

BANK

CAP

CHRISTMAS

CLOUD

COLD

COOL

CRYSTALS

DAMP

DRIFT

FINLAND

FIRN

FLAKE

FORECAST

```
                S               E                   M
                N           C O T                   A
                J         I D H O W                 I
        W H D W A       A L A S K A F       S N P I T
                U E N     W M W E I       T O E
                  O A U     P O R       O R A
        S           L T A     N       R W K             F
        W L K       C H R I S T M A S         A O N
      C H A R Y         E Y D T Y         A K R A P
    N O I T A T I P I C E R P S Y G O L O R O E T E M
    D O T S W I T Z E R L A N D I K S N O W S C A P E
      L E Y H E         N O E A N         S B A N K
      O R E       S E W N W D G A D         V S E
      C         L Z T     E       G L R         T
          U O I       L N V       O N I
        S R R     S N G D E       B I F
      W A H F E   L A P L A N D     O F T R F
          S       F L A K E           T
          K       S N C               E
          I       D                   W
```

FROZEN   NORWAY   SKY   SWITZERLAND

ICE   PARKA   SLED   THAW

JANUARY   PEAKS   SLUSH   TOBOGGAN

LAPLAND   PRECIPITATION   SNOWSCAPE   WEATHER

MAINE   RAW   SNOWSHOE   WET

METEOROLOGY   SKI   SNOW TIRES   WHITE

NEVE   SKID   STORM

NEW ENGLAND

Hidden movie title: _____

Answers on page 377.

NAME THAT NICKNAME

Five male friends are of different ages, drive different vehicles, have different nicknames, have different jobs, and root for different pro football teams. Using the clues below, can you determine the age, vehicle, job, and favorite football team of the man nicknamed Tubba?

• The man who drives a station wagon roots for the Raiders.

• The man who drives a Hummer is 42.

• The man who roots for the Bengals is a flea trainer.

• The man who roots for the Cowboys has a 2-year age difference with the competitive eater.

• The man who drives an SUV is a toothpick tester.

• The man who drives an RV has a 2-year age difference with the 40-year-old.

• The man who roots for the Browns is nicknamed Dubba.

• The oldest man is 4 years older than the apple dewormer.

• The 38-year-old man roots for the Steelers.

• The man whose age is in the middle is an apple dewormer.

• The man nicknamed Rubba has a 2-year age difference with the man who roots for the Steelers.

• The man who drives an RV is the youngest.

• The 44-year-old man is a beer-bottle capper.

• The man who roots for the Cowboys has a 2-year age difference with the man nicknamed Hubba.

• The man who drives a pickup is nicknamed Bubba.

THE UPPER CRUST BY ALPHA SLEUTH™

Move each of the letters below into the grid to form common words. You will use each letter once. The letters in the numbered cells of the grid correspond to the letters in the phrase at the bottom. Completing the grid will help you complete the phrase and vice versa. When finished, the grid and phrase should be filled with valid words, and you will have used all the letters in the letter set.

Hint: The numbered cells in the grid are arranged alphabetically, so the letter in the cell marked 1 will appear in the alphabet before the letter in the cell marked 2, and so on.

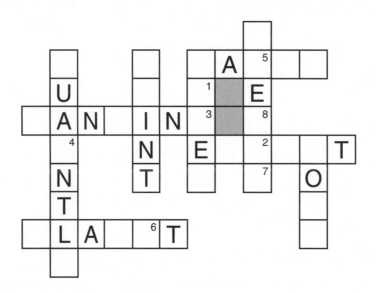

Answers on page 377.

MIND STRETCHER

Reveal the horizontal phrase by completing the merging phrases.

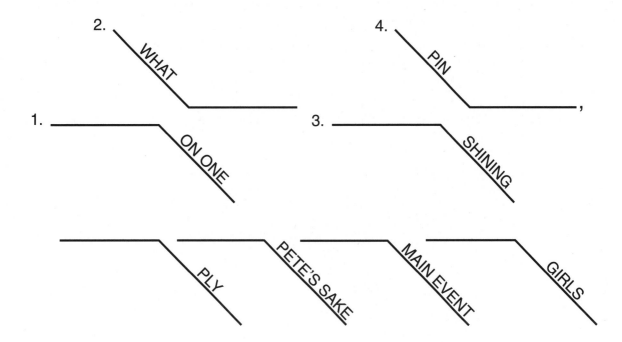

2. WHAT

4. PIN

1. ON ONE

3. SHINING

PLY

PETE'S SAKE

MAIN EVENT

GIRLS

DISSECTION

Separate the figure into 4 identical parts following the grid lines. The parts may be rotated and/or mirrored.

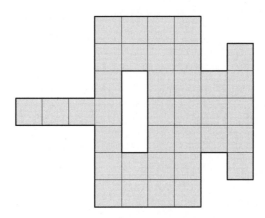

Answers on page 377.

DIAGONAL JUMP

Can you find a single, unbroken path from the circle in the upper-left corner to the circle in the lower right? Your path must move from circle to circle, with one twist—you can jump over any one diamond at a time, provided there is a circle on the other side of it.

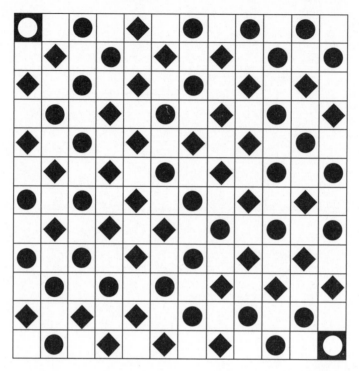

WORD JIGSAW

Fit the pieces into the frame to form common words reading across and down. There's no need to rotate the pieces; they'll fit as shown, with each piece used once.

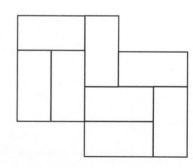

Answers on page 377.

YOU SAID IT!

Cryptograms are messages in substitution code. Break the code to read the humorous observations. For example, THE SMART CAT might become FVO QWGDF JGF if **F** is substituted for **T**, **V** for **H**, **O** for **E**, and so on. The code is different for each cryptogram.

1. XG GXQ AQQIA OG YXGC TGD ARDQ CVJO SQGSKQ CJXO
   OVQAQ PJFA, QEMQSO OVJO OVQF CGX'O JMMQSO J SQXXF
   KQAA.

2. GYQKJ'F GCKTSDSCF XKTS NCYTSL GXKG GXS RYCDQ VF
   OSCGKVLDJ CYWLQ. VG VF GXSVC RKDDSGF GXKG KCS ZDKG.

3. VSXZ LV SGDKWU'V QUGSKD TKDDUW. LD'V EWKSEYJ, MLRV
   OXPU LD, GSR LD EOLSNV DX DYU WXXH XH JXKW YXKVU.

4. RAH QLYUIF ZSA FD ACXZSSZFFYUI ZF HZQWLYUI JDGS XDFF
   MD HLZQ JDG NGFQ FZYM WDGVM UDQ XA MDUA.

TIMES SQUARE

Fill each square in the grid with a number from 1 through 5. When the numbers in each row are multiplied, you should arrive at the total in the right-hand column. When the numbers in each column are multiplied, you should arrive at the total on the bottom line. The numbers in each diagonal must multiply to the totals in the upper- and lower-right corners.

120

3	2		1	2	48
2	2		2	5	80
3	1		1	2	30
	3	1	4		48
2	3	1		2	48
144	36	40	32	40	240

Answers on page 377.

CURVACEOUS CUBE CONSTRUCTION

Which one of the cubes can be formed from the unfolded sample in the middle?

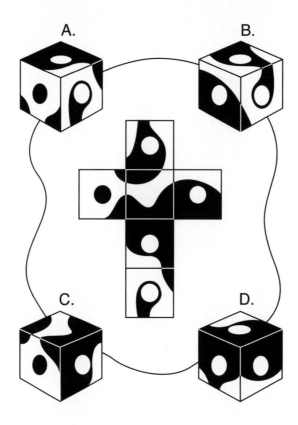

A.

B.

C.

D.

FITTING WORDS

In this miniature crossword, the clues are listed randomly and are numbered for convenience only. It is up to you to figure out the placement of the 9 answers. To help you, we've inserted one letter in the grid, and this is the only occurrence of that letter in the completed puzzle.

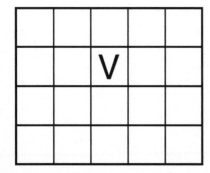

CLUES

1. Academy Award, for example
2. Academy Award winner, perhaps
3. Visionary
4. Band gear
5. Label information
6. Accumulate
7. Hungry
8. Meal with matzoh
9. Seconds

Answers on page 377.

RED, WHITE, AND BLUE

Each row, column, and long diagonal contains 2 reds, 2 whites, and 2 blue. From the clues given, can you complete the grid?

1. The reds are adjacent.

2. One of the blues is bounded by the whites.

3. The blues are somewhere between the whites.

4. One of the reds is bounded by the whites.

5. One blue has a red directly to its left, and the other blue has a red directly to its right.

6. The pattern in cells A, B, and C is repeated in D, E, and F.

A. The reds are somewhere between the blues.

B. The blues are adjacent.

C. One blue is bounded by the reds and the other by the whites.

D. The pattern in cells 1, 2, and 3 is repeated in 4, 5, and 6.

E. The whites are somewhere between the blues.

F. The blues and the reds are bounded by the whites.

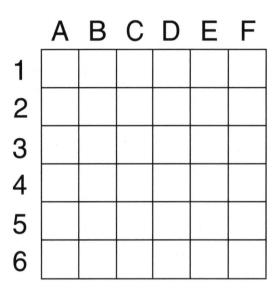

Answer on page 377.

GRAM'S BIRTHDAY

ACROSS

1. Dangerous when it flows
5. He wrote "The Stars and Stripes Forever"
10. Like a senior citizen
14. Milton wrote them
15. Surrounding atmospheres
16. Sideless cart
17. Small units of weight
19. Unusual
20. Chant
21. Law: Fr.
22. Mean little kids
23. Branch of the service: abbr.
25. Northeastern state of India
27. Enroll
32. Comb. of high cards: 2 wds.
35. The Southwest's Bret
36. Actress Debra
38. Reagan, to friends
39. Ages
40. Sprayed defensively
41. If it's "half," it's small
42. Where to get $$: abbr.
43. Welfare allotments
44. Civil War general
45. Oklahoman
47. Kitchen utensil
49. Showers with stones
51. Eternally: poet.
52. Sounds of laughter
54. Once _____ blue moon: 2 wds.
56. Things to eat
61. Smell
62. Heart examination
64. Eat
65. Silkworms
66. Tear down: sp. var.
67. English monetary abbreviation
68. Coarse grass
69. Tennis stadium honoree

DOWN

1. Places
2. Between Yemen and Oman
3. Escape port for air
4. Regarding: 2 wds.
5. Wisest
6. Belonging to us
7. _____ Mountains
8. Where R.L.S. died
9. Helped
10. Name of six popes
11. Parser
12. Wyatt _____
13. Colors
18. Sign on a lab door: 2 wds.
24. Himalayan kingdom
26. Part of a tennis match
27. Flightless S.A. birds
28. "An _____ the ground": 2 wds.
29. Record player
30. Possessive pronoun
31. "The Camptown _____"
33. Spanish earl
34. "Abandon hope, all ye who _____ here" (Dante)
37. "Beau _____"
40. Tenons' companions
41. Charlottetown is its capital: abbr.
43. Singer Shannon
44. Driver Andretti
46. Closer
48. Edit
50. Trap
52. Devices for carrying bricks
53. Mine entrance
55. Sere
57. Taj Mahal city
58. Depression agencies: abbr.
59. Elan
60. Duck
63. Hammarskjöld

HEXAGONAL SHIFT

Make your way from one hexagon to the other in this dizzying maze!

Answers on page 377.

ANAGRAM PRESIDENT

Find a 5-letter anagram for each of the words below. The anagrams will provide answers to the clues. Write the correct anagram on the line by each clue. When completed, the first letter of the answers will spell the name of a U.S. president.

ANAGRAM WORDS

REBUT   LATER   HYDRA   SIREN   PLANE

UNBAR   BLAME   LEMON   LAYER   BURMA   SNAKY

CLUES

1. Strong: _____
2. Stroll: _____
3. Latin dance: _____
4. Washer cycle: _____
5. Jerks: _____
6. Potato, e.g.: _____
7. _____ race
8. Of the city: _____
9. Large fruit: _____
10. Change: _____
11. Katmandu's country: _____

President: _____

FINDING A DIGIT

In the grid, find a stylized digit exactly like that shown next to the grid. The digit can be rotated but not mirrored.

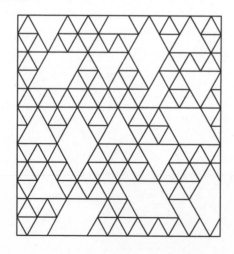

Answers on pages 377–378.

WORD COLUMNS

Find the hidden punny sentence by using the letters directly below each of the blank squares. Each letter is used only once. A black square indicates the end of a word.

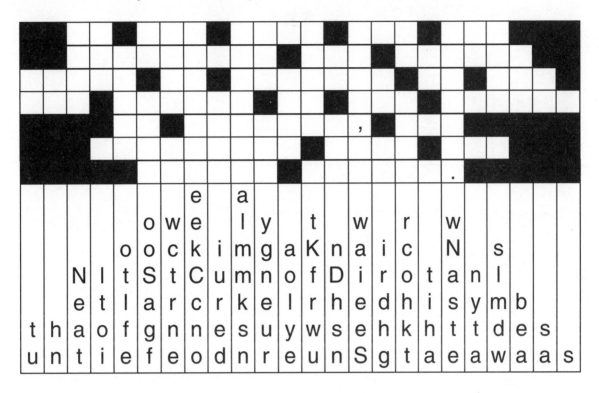

WORD LADDER

Use the clues to change just one letter on each line to go from the top word to the bottom word. Do not change the order of the letters. You must have a common English word at each step.

PLANE

_____

_____ a braid

_____

_____ an inflammation

_____

TRAIN

Answers on page 378.

CRYPTO-ANIMAL FAMILIES

Cryptograms are messages in substitution code. Break the code to discover the animals in each of the categories below. For example, THE SMART CAT might become FVO QWGDF JGF if **F** is substituted for **T, V** for **H, O** for **E,** and so on. The code is different for each cryptogram family.

1. ON THE FARM	2. AT THE ZOO	3. IN THE OCEAN
AMBANHD	EFAAGAGHIDJK	FLEPC
CEFK	LEFMG	ICEP
AEJ	HFPNL	AGBAPC
MEGIH	PFLIBBN	IAHKDBEJ
CEEIH	NONAEIMH	RMPNLHK
OPANRBDC	PGLFOOI	PMSIACB
IMHHS	RNCLI	MJIACB
IJBDH	SIMPILGG	IAEBTHIL
GFTTBK	KMISNK	UCPPJTHIL
MEPDO	OFGM	ILEBV

PSYCHICS FOR HIRE

One hundred people showed up to be interviewed by a brokerage company looking to hire psychics. Stock certificates from 5 different blue-chip companies were placed in a 5-drawer filing cabinet, one in each drawer. The psychics were asked to predict which stock was in which drawer. In order to meet new government hiring regulations, the company would only be hiring psychics who correctly predicted the contents in 4 out of 5 drawers. After the psychics made their predictions and the drawers were opened, the company found that 7 psychics got none of the drawers right, 13 got only one drawer right, 22 got only 2 drawers right, and 39 got only 3 drawers right. How many psychics did the brokerage company hire?

Answers on page 378.

SUDOKU

Use deductive logic to complete the grid so that each row, each column, and each 3 by 3 box contains the numbers 1 through 9 in some order. The solution is unique.

			2			6		
7		8	1					3
	4		5			1		
1	3			4				
				5				
				7			2	1
		7			5		8	
5					4	9		6
	6			8				

DON'S DINER AND PART-TIME ARCADE

We would never recommend that you eat at Don's Diner. Every time we've eaten there, something's gone completely crazy. Look at this illustration of a typical lunch hour at Don's. We count 12 things that are wrong. How many can you find?

Answers on page 378.

STAR POWER

Fill in each of the empty squares in the grid so that each star is surrounded by numbers 1 through 8 with no repeats.

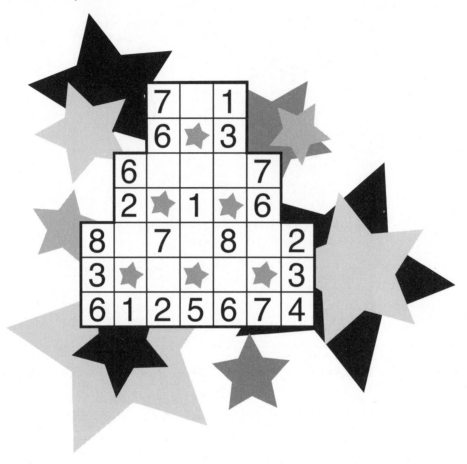

FOUR SQUARES TO THREE

Reposition only 3 lines in order to create 3 squares of equal size.

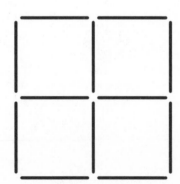

Answers on page 378.

FRAME GAMES™

Can you "read" the phrase below?

WEIRD WORD SEARCH (PART I)

Every word listed is contained within the group of letters below. The words can be found in a straight line horizontally, vertically, or diagonally. They may read either backward or forward. After you've circled all the words, study them for two minutes and try to remember all 14. Then turn the page for a quiz.

ARCANE

BIZARRE

CHILLING

CREEPY

FREAKY

GHOSTLY

HAUNTED

MACABRE

SCARY

SPOOKY

STRANGE

SURREAL

UNCANNY

UNEARTHLY

```
P  A  F  R  E  A  K  Y  G  Y  S
W  U  Q  C  H  R  Y  M  O  L  P
B  Y  C  Y  H  A  B  F  D  H  O
I  L  Q  R  N  I  U  A  E  T  O
Z  T  Y  U  E  N  L  N  C  R  K
A  S  U  R  R  E  A  L  T  A  Y
R  O  D  A  A  C  P  C  I  E  M
R  H  U  F  R  C  I  Y  N  N  D
E  G  N  A  R  T  S  S  D  U  G
```

Answers on page 378.

WEIRD WORD SEARCH (PART II)

Don't read this until you have read the previous page!

Circle the words that appeared in the word search on the previous page.

FANTASTIC	BIZARRE	FREAKY
EERIE	SHADOWY	HALLOWEEN
GHOSTLY	STRANGE	ARCANE
UNCANNY	CHILLY	HUNTED
CHILLING	UNREAL	CREAKY
SCARED	SUPERNATURAL	MACABRE
SÉANCE	PHANTASMAL	SPECTER
	SPIRITUAL	CREEPY

LOGIDOKU

The numbers 1 through 9 appear once in every row, column, long diagonal, irregular shape (indicated by marked borders), and 3 by 3 grid. From the numbers already given, can you complete the puzzle?

Answers on page 378.

BUNGLED BURGLARY

We count 17 things that are wrong in this scene. Can you find them?

JELLY BEAN JAR MAZE

To complete this sweet maze, find a path through the jelly beans to reach the bottom of the candy jar.

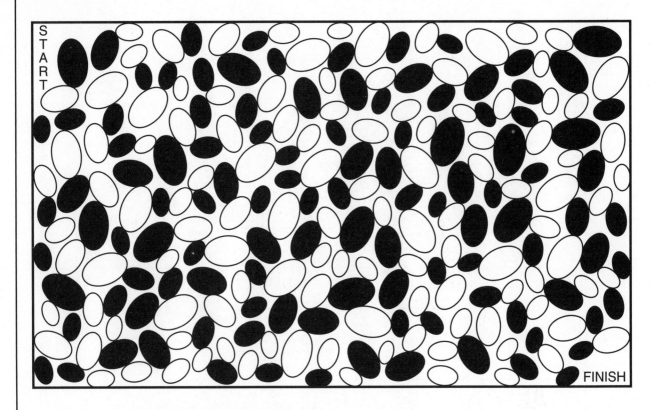

FITTING WORDS

In this miniature crossword, the clues are listed randomly and are numbered for convenience only. It is up to you to figure out the placement of the 9 answers. To help you, we've inserted one letter in the grid, and this is the only occurrence of that letter in the completed puzzle.

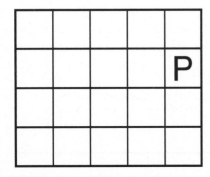

CLUES

1. Boring item
2. Nimble
3. Floor coverings
4. Greenish-blue
5. Foul
6. Try to lose
7. Outfit
8. Poets
9. Hit on the noggin

Answers on page 378.

GO FIGURE

Fill in the missing spaces with numbers 1 through 9. The numbers in each row must add up to the sums in the right-hand column. The numbers in each column must add up to the sums on the bottom line. The numbers in each diagonal must add up to the totals in the upper- and lower-right corners.

								35
1		4	3	1		6	5	29
2	3	1	4			5	8	35
4	2	6		2	7	8		43
2	3		7	6	1		4	31
1	6			5	7	8	5	42
3	5	3	8		4		2	39
		8	7	5	3		3	34
	8	7	5	9		4	1	41
18	34	38	48	38	41	43	34	29

ALPHABET FILL-IN

The first and last letters have been removed from the 5-letter words below. Your task is to reinsert the letters to correctly spell the words. However, you can only use each letter of the alphabet once.

1. ___OLI___

2. ___HAK___

3. ___AYO___

4. ___ENO___

5. ___ELA___

6. ___UNT___

7. ___ILC___

8. ___UER___

9. ___GRE___

10. ___REE___

11. ___LUM___

12. ___HAR___

13. ___ING___

A B C D E F G H I J K L M N O P Q R S T U V W X Y Z

Move each of the letters below into the grid to form common words. You will use each letter only once. The letters in the numbered cells of the grid correspond to the letters in the phrase at the bottom. Completing the grid will help you complete the phrase and vice versa. When finished, the grid and phrase should be filled with valid words, and you will have used all the letters in the letter set.

HINT: The numbered cells in the grid are arranged alphabetically, so the letter in the cell marked 1 will appear in the alphabet before the letter in the cell marked 2, and so on.

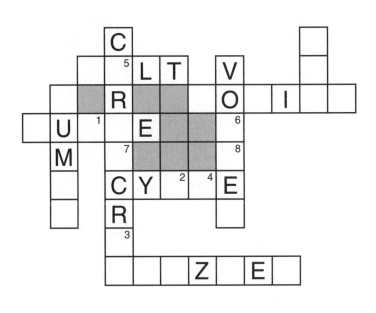

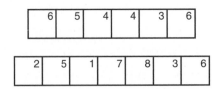

Answers on page 379.

INWARD/OUTWARD BOUND

This puzzle requires an ability to think in circles. Determine the word that answers each clue, and place the letters in the numbered spaces that correspond to the number of letters in your answer. Work in both an outward and inward direction.

OUTWARD

1-4. Pale red
5-13. Ruckus
14-17. Nautical call
18-21. Tropical tree
22-26. Citrus fruit
27-31. Rub out
32-40. Passing
41-46. Disgust
47-52. Diamond or graphite
53-57. Apportion
58-62. Well known
63-68. Although
69-71. Macadamia, e.g.
72-74. And not
75-80. Weasel-like animal

INWARD

80-76. _____ Haute, Indiana
75-71. Facade
70-66. Loosen laces
65-61. Cutting part
60-56. The Lone Ranger's
        sidekick
55-51. Grassy plain
        (Spanish)
50-46. Support (oneself)
45-40. Servant's uniform
39-37. Rodent
36-33. Verne's captain

32-29. High plateau
28-25. Casino city
24-20. Fight
19-16. Knockout, briefly

15-11. Capital of Vietnam
10-8. Male cat
7-4. Ridicule
3-1. _____ it in the bud

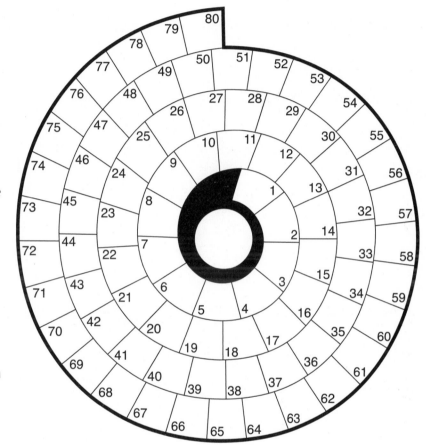

Answers on page 379.

RHYME TIME

Each clue leads to a 2-word answer that rhymes, such as BIG PIG or STABLE TABLE. The numbers in parentheses after the clue give the number of letters in each word. For example, "cookware taken from the oven (3, 3)" would be "hot pot."

1. Subdued startled reaction (4, 3): _____ _____

2. Dull colored crustacean (4, 4): _____ _____

3. Fail to keep up (4, 5): _____ _____

4. Shine sufficiently (4, 6): _____ _____

5. Sophisticated lad (5, 5): _____ _____

6. Dog bark (5, 5): _____ _____

7. Redundant sort of cliff (5, 6): _____ _____

8. Pious pathfinder (6, 5): _____ _____

9. Visitor roster (7, 4): _____ _____

10. He unhappily takes you for a ride (6, 6): _____ _____

11. Overfed pet (6, 5): _____ _____

12. Heist featured on the big screen (7, 5): _____ _____

13. Fountain drink fit for a king (7, 6): _____ _____

14. Appliance deal (7, 7): _____ _____

15. Entertainers at the ballpark (10, 4): _____ _____

16. The road to the Final Four (7, 7): _____ _____

Answers on page 379.

DECORATING DILEMMA

A strange letter arrived recently at the office of Black and Brown Interiors. The letter set the entire staff on its ear until Black and Brown visited the Davis house personally. From the letter below determine each family member's name, how he or she wants the family room decorated, and the bedroom location of each individual. Note: Two individuals share a room.

Dear Sirs:

Everyone in my family wants to redecorate our rec room differently. Lee is dead set on having an entire wall finished with black-and-white carpeting. Like a checkerboard! My son threatens to move out if such a wall is built. He's already told his friends that the room will be Day-Glo orange. Just right for his black light!

Dale and my daughter disagree with Leslie's choice to wallpaper the west wall. Dad wants the whole room rustically paneled—but nobody will listen to him!

There's no phone in the rec room. An occupant in the bedroom next door is sick and tired of having people running up and down the stairs delivering phone messages. Our upstairs occupant refuses to run messages to the converted garage every time her brother's girlfriends call. The woman of the house says, "No messages!"

Help!

Sincerely yours,

Pat Davis

	DAD	DAUGHTER	SON	MOM	B&W CARPET	DAY-GLO PAINT	PANELING	WALLPAPER	CONVERTED GARAGE	ROOM NEXT DOOR	UPSTAIRS ROOM	W/ ONE OF THE ABOVE
DALE												
LEE												
LESLIE												
PAT												
CONVERTED GARAGE												
ROOM NEXT DOOR												
UPSTAIRS ROOM												
W/ ONE OF THE ABOVE												
B&W CARPET												
DAY-GLO PAINT												
PANELING												
WALLPAPER												

Every cell in this grid contains 1 of 4 letters: A, B, C, or D. No letter can be horizontally or vertically adjacent to itself. The tables above and to the left of the grid indicate how many times each letter appears in that column or row. Can you complete the grid?

				A	0	1	3	1	2	2
				B	2	2	0	2	1	2
				C	2	2	0	3	0	2
A	B	C	D	2	1	3	0	3	0
2	1	2	1							
1	3	1	1							
1	1	3	1							
2	2	0	2							
1	2	2	1							
2	0	1	3							

A CAPITAL PUZZLE!

Can you find a state capital hiding in each of the sentences below?

1. "Here's the plan: Sing along with the karaoke and try not to embarrass yourself!"

2. Radioactive isotope? Ka-boom!

3. "Oh yes," said the florist, "I know that garden very well."

4. You can get good deals on the wholesale market.

5. Architect: "Send those gazebos to Newark."

Answers on page 379.

BIG SCREEN LETTERBOX

The letters in MARX can be found in boxes 1, 2, 11, and 20, but not necessarily in that order. Similarly, the letters in all the other names can be found in the boxes indicated. Your task is to insert all the letters of the alphabet into the boxes. If you do this correctly, the shaded cells will reveal 2 more film stars.

1	2	3	4	5	6	7	8	9	10	11	12	13

14	15	16	17	18	19	20	21	22	23	24	25	26

BULLOCK: 6, 7, 15, 19, 21, 26

CLIFT: 7, 8, 13, 16, 19

DE NIRO: 3, 6, 8, 9, 20, 24

GIBSON: 3, 4, 6, 8, 15, 18

JACKSON: 3, 4, 5, 6, 11, 19, 26

KIDMAN: 1, 3, 8, 11, 24, 26

MARX: 1, 2, 11, 20

MCQUEEN: 1, 3, 9, 19, 21, 25

PACINO: 3, 6, 8, 11, 17, 19

SCHWARZENEGGER: 3, 4, 9, 11, 12, 18, 19, 20, 22, 23

SMITH: 1, 4, 8, 16, 23

VALENTINO: 3, 6, 7, 8, 9, 10, 11, 16

WAYNE: 3, 9, 11, 12, 14

Answers on page 379.

GO FIGURE

Fill each square in the grid with a digit from 1 through 9. When the numbers in each row are added, you should arrive at the total in the right-hand column. When the numbers in each column are added, you should arrive at the total on the bottom line. The numbers in each long diagonal must add up to the totals in the upper- and lower-right corners.

									48
1	5	3	6	7	4	9		8	50
4			4	3	5		6	9	46
9	8	3		1	5	4		7	46
	3	4	4		3	5	5	9	43
1	9	3		7		6	7		45
8	2		4	3	9		4	5	49
7		3		3	7	8		4	48
2	4		8	2		3	2		40
	8	3	7		6	8	5		53
49	47	40	51	32	42	58	39	62	39

CODE-DOKU

Solve this puzzle just as you would a sudoku. Use deductive logic to complete the grid so that each row, column, and 3 by 3 box contains the letters from the words PET SALMON. When you have completed the puzzle, read the shaded squares to form a phrase that describes a great feat of exploration.

	L	T					P
		N					
	N				O		
	M				L		
O			L	P	M		
E		A	M				
			O			A	
		N				S	
S	P		A	T			

300

WORD COLUMNS

Find the hidden humorous advice by using the letters directly below each of the blank squares. Each letter is used only once. A black square indicates the end of a word.

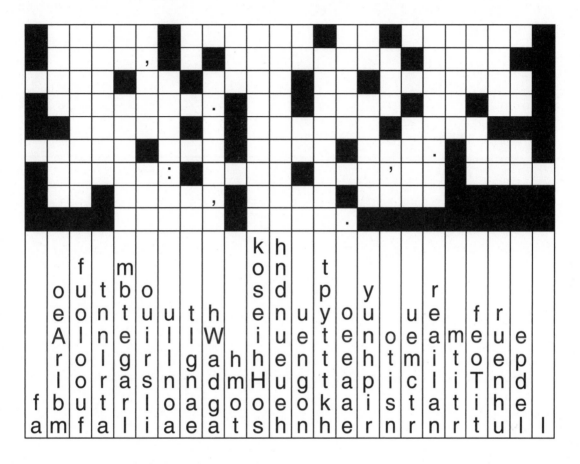

CRYPTO-QUOTE

Cryptograms are messages in substitution code. Break the code to read the following quote and its source. For example, THE SMART CAT might become FVO QWGDF JGF if **F** is substituted for **T, V** for **H, O** for **E,** and so on.

"ALTCT BCT ADK ALEFSJ ALBA BCT IKCT GEMMENOPA ALBF

IBREFS BF BMATC-GEFFTC JUTTNL: NPEIWEFS B DBPP DLENL EJ

PTBFEFS AKDBCG VKO BFG REJJEFS B SECP DLK EJ PTBFEFS

BDBV MCKI VKO."

—DEFJAKF NLOCNLEPP

ACROSTIC ANAGRAM

Unscramble the letters below to form words, then place the letters in their corresponding spots in the grid to reveal a quote from Sir John Vanbrugh. The letter in the upper-right corner of each grid square refers to the clue the letter comes from. A black square indicates the end of a word.

A. P A N I I A T D E C A T C
    ___ ___ ___ ___ ___ ___ ___ ___ ___ ___ ___ ___ ___
    40 60 57 18 28 31 50 68 10 65 4 16 46

B. I E S P R H E D
    ___ ___ ___ ___ ___ ___ ___ ___
    64 25 34 36 70 51 23 20

C. S U E N S E S L F U
    ___ ___ ___ ___ ___ ___ ___ ___ ___ ___
     5 52 35 54 33 72 37 59 8 67

D. R U E V S Y
    ___ ___ ___ ___ ___ ___
    26 53 3 1 71 66

E. D E O A R H F E
    ___ ___ ___ ___ ___ ___ ___ ___
    55 12 24 30 22 6 27 38

F. I G S I N F H
    ___ ___ ___ ___ ___ ___ ___
    73 56 32 48 58 14 42

G. I N I T W T G
    ___ ___ ___ ___ ___ ___ ___
    47 7 21 61 9 41 43

H. I W L W L O
    ___ ___ ___ ___ ___ ___
    17 49 29 62 45 13

I. T R I S Y O R O
    ___ ___ ___ ___ ___ ___ ___ ___
    11 44 19 39 15 2 69 63

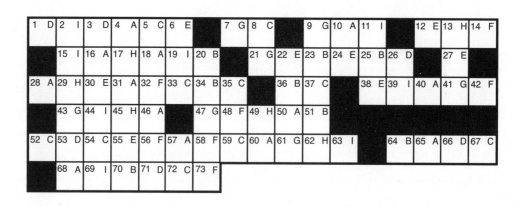

Answers on page 379.

SUDOKU

Use deductive logic to complete the grid so that each row, each column, and each 3 by 3 box contains the numbers 1 through 9 in some order. The solution is unique.

		3				8		
	8			9		2		
5			6					
	1		2					
2	8	9	3	1	7	5		
			8			6		
			7					5
	9		4			8		
		6			2			

A CAN-DO CANDLE ATTITUDE

It's birthday time at the Shady Rest Village for Feisty Grandmas and Grandpas. Mona is turning 100. The other residents gave Dan $100 to buy Mona a variety of cool candles for the cake that Kate is baking. At the store, Dan found cheap candles for 50 cents, nice candles for $5.50, and really hot candles for $9.50. The gang at Shady Rest wanted Mona's 100th birthday party to be special, so they told Dan to spend the entire $100 and that's what he planned to do. How many of each type of candle did he need to buy to end up with exactly 100 candles and spend exactly $100?

TV DOCUMENTARIES

It's time for the annual TV documentary awards, but the cue-card writer has mixed up the 2-word titles of the nominated documentaries as well as the last names of their directors. Although each word and name is in the correct column, only one entry in each column is correctly positioned. Using the clues below, can you correctly match each first title word, second title word, and director?

1. Cloth is 2 places below Alhen but only one below Painting.

2. Ripping is 2 places below Newspapers, which is one place above Torrentino.

3. Capri is somewhere below Bread, which is somewhere below Stealing.

4. Making is somewhere below Cloth, which is somewhere above Jockson.

5. Rodrigo is 2 places above Wallpaper but only one below Cutting.

	First word	Second word	Director
1	Making	Money	Torrentino
2	Stealing	Newspapers	Spoolbag
3	Cutting	Cloth	Rodrigo
4	Eating	Bread	Alhen
5	Painting	Pizza	Capri
6	Ripping	Wallpaper	Jockson

DIGITAL SUDOKU

Fill in the grid so that each row, column, and 2 by 3 block contains a number from 1 to 6 exactly once. Numbers are in digital form and some segments have already been filled in.

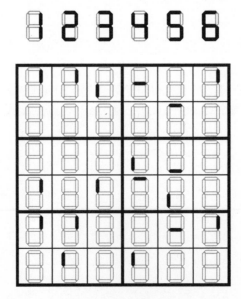

Answers on page 380.

WORD LADDER

Use the clues to change just one letter on each line to go from the top word to the bottom word. Do not change the order of the letters. You must have a common English word at each step.

CLUSTER

_____

_____ a worker employed to use explosives

_____

_____ serving dish

PLANTER

ODDBALL OF THE GROUP

Which figure is the odd one out?

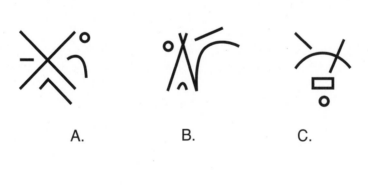

A.   B.   C.

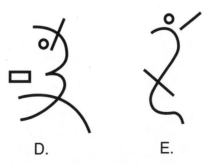

D.   E.

MORE THAN A WORD

Every phrase listed is contained within the group of letters below. The words can be found in a straight line diagonally. The words can be read backward or forward.

BASE RUNNER

BLUE MONDAY

COARSE CLOTH

COMMON ERA

CRUDE OIL

DIRTY RICE

FOUL SHOT

GROSS WEIGHT

LOW PROFILE

MEAN INCOME

OFFENSIVE LINE

POOR RICHARD

RANK AND FILE

RAW RECRUIT

ROUGH IT

SALTY SNACKS

SORRY ABOUT THAT

VULGAR LATIN

```
            A S Y G C T B N O N T
            Y M F R R A O D O A R
              I S U R S O R H H N E
        L E G B D K E A A S T S V A C N T
        T H M E A R C H W T S U L O A E T
        M R O E U D C A U R L W A U N E A
        E I A N A I N O N G E R E I O N S
        L L N N R N B E A S S C L I Y F S
        D E I R K A I R W E Y E R A G A O
        R I O F Y A L N C B V T D U R H M
        R O R R O A N L C I E N L E I E T
        P O R T T R O D S O O A N A T T H
        I O U I Y T P N F M M O R N S G E
        S L N G H R E W E I M E S S E B E
            G H F I U O M L I N S
            E F I L C O L A E C H
            O P B T C E H R A S E
```

Answers on page 380.

RHYME TIME

Each clue leads to a 2-word answer that rhymes, such as BIG PIG or STABLE TABLE. The numbers in parentheses after the clue give the number of letters in each word. For example, "cookware taken from the oven (3, 3)" would be "hot pot."

1. Special occasion at the aquarium (3, 3): _____ _____

2. Record of online journal entries (4, 3): _____ _____

3. A midnight snack, for example (5, 4): _____ _____

4. Backward kicker's aid (5, 4): _____ _____

5. Part of a pol's preparation (5, 5): _____ _____

6. Mark of the biggest Texas ranch (5, 5): _____ _____

7. Brit's unexpected discovery (5, 5): _____ _____

8. Auto museum (6, 4): _____ _____

9. Bobsledder's favorite spot (6, 4): _____ _____

10. Retaliate (6, 4): _____ _____

11. Fit to be tying (5, 6): _____ _____

12. Mass extra (5, 6): _____ _____

13. Thanksgiving meet, cut and dried (6, 5): _____ _____

14. She hoards certain appliances (7, 6): _____ _____

15. Suggest the plan (7, 9): _____ _____

Answers on page 380.

STARBOARD COURSE MAZE

Don't be a landlubber! Find your way from start to finish in this maritime maze.

TINY'S SOCK DRAWER

Tiny Tom can barely reach into the top drawer of his highboy where he keeps his socks. He knows he has 11 pairs of black socks and 6 pairs of brown socks scattered in the drawer with no pairs knotted together.

How many socks would he have to pull out of the drawer in order to ensure that he gets a matching pair?

Answers on page 380.

WORD WEB

Use each of the state capitals listed here to complete this clue-less crossword grid. The puzzle has only one solution.

ATLANTA

AUGUSTA

AUSTIN

BOISE

BOSTON

CONCORD

HELENA

JACKSON

JUNEAU

LANSING

LINCOLN

MADISON

PIERRE

RALEIGH

SALEM

TOPEKA

TRENTON

WACKY WORDY

Can you "read" the phrase below?

TOM OOOOOOO

GO FIGURE

Fill each square in the grid with a digit from 1 through 9. When the numbers in each row are added, you should arrive at the total in the right-hand column. When the numbers in each column are added, you should arrive at the total on the bottom line. The numbers in each diagonal must add up to the totals in the upper- and lower-right corners.

								35
1		4	3	1		6	5	29
2	3	1	4			5	8	35
4	2	6		2	7	8		43
2	3		7	6	1		4	31
1	6			5	7	8	5	42
3	5	3	8		4		2	39
		8	7	5	3		3	34
	8	7	5	9		4	1	41
18	34	38	48	38	41	43	34	29

THE PERFECT SQUARE

Make 2 identical straight line cuts, 1 in each of the irregular figures below, so that the resulting 4 pieces can be arranged to form a perfect square.

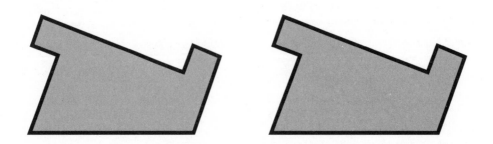

Answers on page 380.

MASYU

Masyu has a simple goal: to draw a single, nonintersecting loop through all of the pearls on the grid.

There are 2 rules according to the color of the pearl:

Black pearls: A line must enter and exit at right angles from the pearl. It must also extend straight for 2 squares in the chosen direction.

White pearls: A line goes straight through each pearl and must turn immediately before or after. It is optional for the line to turn both before and after.

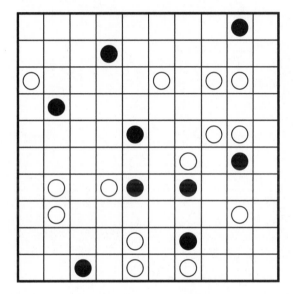

SOMEONE WILL GET THIS RIGHT!

Study these 5 sets of numbers carefully.

25: 7 9 4 5   19: 1 3 8 7   20: 4 6 9 1   22: 2 8 8 4   15: 1 3 9 2

Based on your observations, which 4 numbers should be included in this set?

31: _____?

A. 7 9 9 1   B. 8 7 9 7   C. 3 3 3 3   D. 9 2 6 8

Answers on page 380.

STAR POWER

Fill in each of the empty squares in the grid so that every star is surrounded by the numbers 1 through 8 with no repeats.

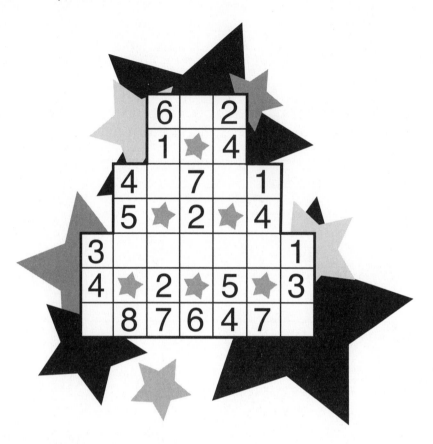

FRAME GAMES™

Can you "read" the phrase below?

feeligns

feleings

feelsgni

Answers on page 380.

CROSS-MATH

Place the digits 1 through 9 in the empty white squares so that the 3 horizontal and 3 vertical equations are true. Each digit will be used exactly once. Calculations are done from left to right and from top to bottom.

	+		−		=	6
+		−		+		
	×		−		=	2
+		+		÷		
	÷		+		=	10
=		=		=		
10		6		2		

PRIME SUSPECT

The police have drawn up a list of suspect descriptions for a recent bank robbery. However, due to a clerical error, only one entry in each column is correctly positioned, although each item is in the correct column. The following facts are true about the correct order:

1. Yellow is one row below medium and somewhere above mauve.
2. Thin is two rows above Spanish.
3. Hunched is three places below English.
4. White is somewhere above dark and two places above fat.
5. Italian is two places above purple.
6. Brown is one row below both yellow and African.
7. Cream is immediately below purple but three places below none.

Can you find the correct nationality, hair color, coat color, and build for each suspect?

	Nationality	Hair	Coat	Build
1	English	none	green	slim
2	Italian	white	yellow	thin
3	Spanish	red	mauve	fat
4	Mexican	gray	blue	round
5	African	brown	purple	medium
6	Chinese	dark	cream	hunched

Answers on page 381.

ANIMAL HOUSE

ACROSS

1. Concordes: abbr.
5. Bass and treble
10. Teases
14. Lotion additive
15. Aged: Lat.
16. Concerning: Lat., 2 wds.
17. Biggest portion: 2 wds.
19. Amateur sports group: abbr.
20. Editor's equipment
21. Owl hours
23. Paul, the guitar guy
24. Ready supply
26. Greek physician
29. Exclude
30. _____ plea (pleads guilty): sl., 2 wds.
34. Military address: abbr.
35. Greek flier
38. Pinches
39. Ivy League team: 2 wds.
42. Ireland
43. Fuel vessel
44. Regret
45. Lots and lots: var.
47. Kleindienst, Kennedy, Civiletti, etc.: abbr.
48. Beginning
50. O'Casey and Connery
52. One: Fr.
53. Former CBS newsman Dan
56. Mournful
60. Surrounding atmosphere
61. String game: 2 wds.
64. Put away
65. Wipe out
66. Young adult
67. Make like a goose
68. Put off
69. Orient

DOWN

1. Mineo and Maglie
2. Sales receipt
3. Implement
4. Mentally deteriorated
5. Examples
6. Annealing oven
7. Timetable heading: abbr.
8. Distant
9. Office skill, for short
10. Giant simian: 2 wds.
11. Traverse little by little
12. Mild oath
13. Oceans
18. Like some views
22. Transport watchdogs: abbr.
24. East Indian dresses
25. Ring apparel
26. Stares open mouthed
27. March follower
28. French river
29. WWII battle site
31. Breakwaters
32. Mold opening
33. Plus quality
36. That: Fr.
37. Sault _____ Marie
40. Reporter: 2 wds.
41. Presser
46. Match the bet
49. Nullify
51. Curved
52. Worrier's worry
53. Allergic evidence
54. Manual's companion, for short
55. 1982 animated Disney feature
56. Being: Lat.
57. Concept
58. Pub drinks
59. Penny
62. 100 square meters
63. Make lace

FITTING WORDS

In this miniature crossword, the clues are listed randomly and are numbered only for convenience. It is up to you to figure out the placement of the 9 answers. To help you, we've inserted one letter in the grid, and this is the only occurrence of that letter in the puzzle.

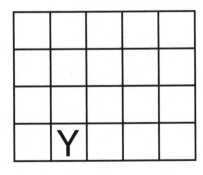

CLUES

1. Spin doctor's concern
2. Bishoprics
3. Lose ground?
4. Team from West Point
5. Bride's headgear
6. Flower holders
7. Boundary
8. Ancient stringed instruments
9. Fly like an eagle

Answers on page 381.

PRETZEL LOGIC

Arrange each of the numbers 1 through 9 in the shaded circles below so that any 5 numbers around a big circle add up to 22. Use each number only once. Can you come up with more than one solution?

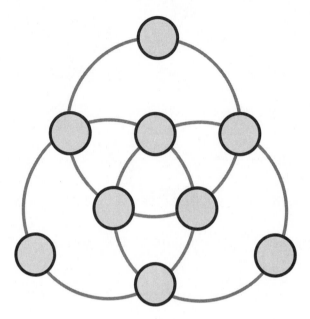

NAME CALLING

Decipher the encoded words in the proverb below using the numbers and letters on the phone pad. Remember that each number can stand for 3 or 4 possible letters.

Man should 5–4–8–3 if only to 7–2–8–4–7–3–9 his 2–8–7–4–6–7–4–8–9.

Answers on page 381.

STATELY LETTERBOX

The letters in UTAH can be found in boxes 4, 5, 15, and 26, but not necessarily in that order. Similarly, the letters in all the other state names can be found in the boxes indicated. Your task is to Insert all the letters of the alphabet into the boxes. If you do this correctly, the shaded cells will reveal another state.

Hint: Look for words that share a single letter. For example, OREGON shares an **O** with WASHINGTON and an **R** with NEBRASKA. By comparing the number lists, you can then deduce the values of these letters.

1	2	3	4	5	6	7	8	9	10	11	12	13
Q												

14	15	16	17	18	19	20	21	22	23	24	25	26

ARIZONA: 3, 4, 13, 19, 21, 22

CALIFORNIA: 3, 4, 7, 8, 19, 21, 22, 24

MAINE: 4, 11, 20, 21, 22

MICHIGAN: 4, 7, 15, 20, 21, 22, 23

NEBRASKA: 3, 4, 11, 12, 16, 22, 25

NEVADA: 4, 6, 9, 11, 22

NEW JERSEY: 2, 3, 11, 12, 17, 18, 22

NEW YORK: 3, 11, 17, 18, 19, 22, 25

OREGON: 3, 11, 19, 22, 23

PENNSYLVANIA: 4, 6, 8, 11, 12, 14, 18, 21, 22

TEXAS: 4, 10, 11, 12, 26

UTAH: 4, 5, 15, 26

WASHINGTON: 4, 12, 15, 17, 19, 21, 22, 23, 26

Answers on page 381.

ACROSTIC ANAGRAM

Unscramble the letters below to form words, then place the letters in their corresponding spots in the grid to reveal a quote from Simone Weil. The letter in the upper right corner of each grid square refers to the clue the letter comes from. A black square indicates the end of a word.

A. R E E O U C B N N C L T A A

‾‾ ‾‾ ‾‾ ‾‾ ‾‾ ‾‾ ‾‾ ‾‾ ‾‾ ‾‾ ‾‾ ‾‾ ‾‾ ‾‾
56 66 3 52 14 59 35 60 19 71 9 26 27 41

B. R O E D S I S

‾‾ ‾‾ ‾‾ ‾‾ ‾‾ ‾‾ ‾‾
47 30 74 69 12 34 68

C. D I H F G O L S

‾‾ ‾‾ ‾‾ ‾‾ ‾‾ ‾‾ ‾‾ ‾‾
44 51 8 42 38 55 13 57

D. R E R O N T H I

‾‾ ‾‾ ‾‾ ‾‾ ‾‾ ‾‾ ‾‾ ‾‾
32 2 37 4 20 64 28 24

E. A R C A E H S E H T

‾‾ ‾‾ ‾‾ ‾‾ ‾‾ ‾‾ ‾‾ ‾‾ ‾‾ ‾‾
54 23 48 45 17 1 10 40 25 36

F. A E E H F R R E T T

‾‾ ‾‾ ‾‾ ‾‾ ‾‾ ‾‾ ‾‾ ‾‾ ‾‾ ‾‾
5 33 73 18 61 62 6 11 70 63

G. F A T W S

‾‾ ‾‾ ‾‾ ‾‾ ‾‾
58 46 22 29 21

H. U E N E V

‾‾ ‾‾ ‾‾ ‾‾ ‾‾
72 16 65 7 43

I. T I T H W O U

‾‾ ‾‾ ‾‾ ‾‾ ‾‾ ‾‾ ‾‾
53 50 39 15 31 67 49

1 E		2 D	3 A	4 D	5 F	6 F	7 H	8 C		9 A	10 E	11 F		12 B	13 C		14 A	15 I	16 H
	17 E	18 F	19 A	20 D	21 G	22 G	23 E	24 D	25 E	26 A	27 A	28 D		29 G	30 B		31 I	32 D	33 F
34 B	35 A	36 E		37 D	38 C		39 I	40 E	41 A		42 C	43 H	44 C	45 E	46 G	47 B	48 E	49 I	50 I
51 C	52 A		53 I	54 E	55 C	56 A	57 C		58 G	59 A		60 A	61 F	62 F	63 F		64 D	65 H	
66 A	67 I	68 B	69 B	70 F	71 A	72 H	73 F	74 B									

Answers on page 381.

SUDOKU

Use deductive logic to complete the grid so that each row, each column, and each 3 by 3 box contains the numbers 1 through 9 in some order. The solution is unique.

			4	7				
			3			5	8	
	6					3		7
7			1			8		
5				3				6
		4			7			2
2		8					4	
	1	3			8			
				2	1			

MONEY FOR A BUNNY

"Step right up, and try your luck!" yelled the carnival barker to anyone who looked like he had money to lose and a girlfriend to impress. That fit the description of Mel, who had just cashed his paycheck and wanted to win a 7-foot-tall stuffed purple rabbit for his girlfriend, LouAnn. The game was called "Spinning Wheel Gotta Go Round," and it was played by spinning a ball in a wheel with 50 evenly spaced holes. The chances were 1 in 50 that the ball would fall into any one particular hole and win the player who picked it a coupon for a free fried candy bar on a stick. But LouAnn had her eye on the 7-foot purple rabbit. The barker offered Mel a special challenge: He could have the huge hare for his honey if he could tell the barker the odds that 2 balls circling the wheel at the same time would fall into the same hole. What odds did Mel tell the barker to win LouAnn the bunny of her dreams?

JAPANESE CULTURE

This free-form crossword has spaces for 20 words that relate to the culture of Japan.

ACROSS

2. Zen planting of rugged charm: 2 wds.
4. Old-time Japanese governor
9. Sash for Miss Japan?
10. Japanese wrestling
11. 17-syllable verse
12. Japanese board game
15. Japanese warrior
17. Paper-folding art
18. Ancient Japanese drinking ritual?: 2 wds.

DOWN

1. Japan's unofficial national flower: 2 wds.
3. Japanese writing
4. It may come with seaweed
5. Japanese robe
6. Graceful writing form
7. Onsen (baths popular in Japan): 2 wds.
8. Sliding panel covered with rice paper: 2 wds.
12. Female entertainer
13. Chopping skill?
14. Japanese cartoons
16. Flower arranging art

ALIEN REVOLUTION

Can you form something recognizable out of these strange shapes?

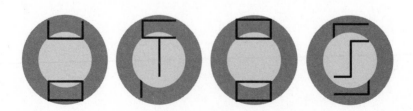

Answers on page 381.

MONDRIANIZE IT!

Inspired by the artwork of Belgian artist Piet Mondrian, these puzzles consist of stars and circles. Using the checkered pattern as a guide, draw in lines so that each star is in its own square, and each circle in its own rectangle.

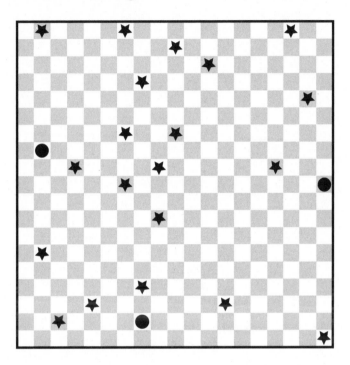

FITTING WORDS

In this miniature crossword, the clues are listed randomly and are numbered only for convenience. It is up to you to figure out the placement of the 9 answers. To help you, we've inserted one letter in the grid, and this is the only occurrence of that letter in the puzzle.

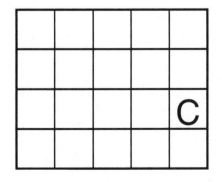

CLUES
1. More than plump
2. Ancient Greek garment
3. China setting
4. Violin part
5. Touch on
6. Infidel
7. Cookware
8. T-bone
9. Trait carrier

Answers on page 381.

COLE PORTER SONGS

American composer Cole Porter wrote some of the most memorable tunes of the early 20th century. The titles of many of his hits and not-as-well-known songs are listed on the opposite page and can be found in the group of letters below. Words can be found diagonally. They may read either backward or forward.

```
N N B Y T O F R I E E W H N I G E Y W L B R U S H U P Y
H O T O H I O L E T T N D G A Y I O E L E T S D O S O R
Y U I U B F O V A N Y P M N I W G U O O I C B E G U N B
O N E H B R O D R S O D Y I E H E D P D T H L A R N R I
U L E T S O U C S T T T O O E F N B E O S E N E T U I I
D E I M G A S O E T H O P W T R M I N N I P S N S E B E
B H V I G E F H Y I E E C A N I R U D T E E G H E U R C
E F Y O E O T Y N E N L T E E I O A S I N D U I O D U E
S R B F L E N G M I B F R O S Y N D E S R P I Y L O S S
O I E I R O G V N N T O U Y F T E T A B Y M N F W N H T
Y E G U N O T V T G I H T O A L M T H O S O Y R T T U M
I B O G E S E Y A E I U T T O O I A U E S N O O N F P A
F Y B S D N I E S T N U O V H O I R G E D S U M I E I E
R I L O I O D O W A O O E Y N G S D Y N I E R I G N N W
I C O C L B N S H K E L T A O H U E T Y I G P S H I Y E
E H E I T S D T C A Y O L N A T Y O S F E F N T U E W O
N E B R U S I I F G V U S K E M E D S T N I I G H H D L
D P D O N S K L O E S E E E T M O U O E G O E Q Y S O W
S L I E R A R G O O N S U O B W O U R H I B L S U E N E
H E G H T C D O N V P C G O U D T M T T E P H L O E T L
A T I E S I T S D E E E E Y O U A S H S O Y V W S F L
N H G N L D G I A E V P P M F D N O T I U Y E R E U E D
Y I C E S T N R Y I L H A T E D I N Y L H I A R R H N I
T U R I O T E E N D E D O R D I I D D S L T N W D E I D
H N Y O U D B B I H T W N A I G N N L I L O M A L E H Y
I Y O U D B E T Y R N L Y I E S T S I L C H E O S A T C
N N I G W E O P E N F D H B P I M L E T E D O N R O M V
Y O U B R U S H U P Y W F R I E N D S L E W T T S F A I
```

Answers on page 381.

ABCD

Every cell in this grid contains 1 of 4 letters: A, B, C, or D. No letter can be horizontally or vertically adjacent to itself. The tables above and to the left of the grid indicate how many times each letter appears in that column or row. Can you complete the grid?

Column totals (top table):

A	3	0	0	2	2	2
B	0	3	2	1	2	1
C	1	3	2	1	1	1
D	2	0	2	2	1	2

Row totals (left table) and grid:

A	B	C	D						
2	2	1	1						
1	1	2	2						
3	2	0	1						
1	1	1	3						
0	3	3	0						
2	0	2	2				C		

Answer on page 381.

GET IT STRAIGHT

Don't get too caught up in the twists and turns as you negotiate your way to the center of this intricate labyrinth.

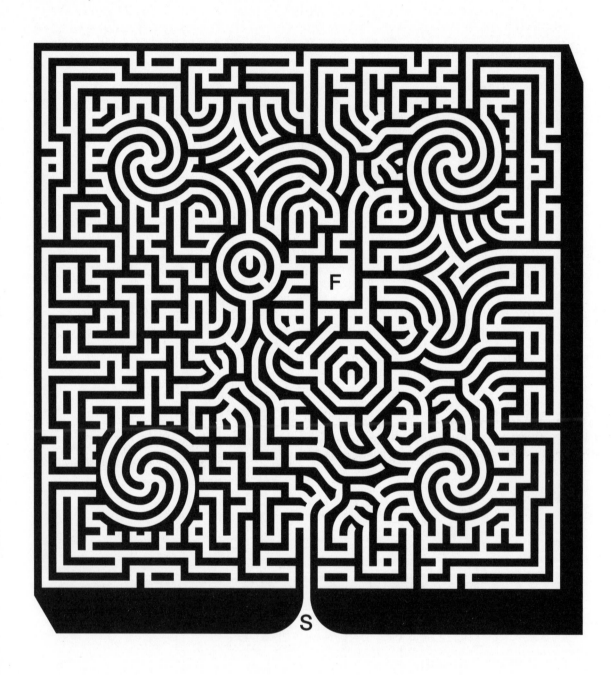

Answer on page 381.

THE FRIENDLY SKIES BY ALPHA SLEUTH™

Move each of the letters below into the grid to form common words. You will use each letter once. The letters in the numbered cells of the grid correspond to the letters in the phrase at the bottom. Completing the grid will help you complete the phrase and vice versa. When finished, the grid and phrase should be filled with valid words, and you will have used all the letters in the letter set.

Hint: The numbered cells in the grid are arranged alphabetically, so the letter in the cell marked 1 will appear in the alphabet before the letter in the cell marked 2, and so on.

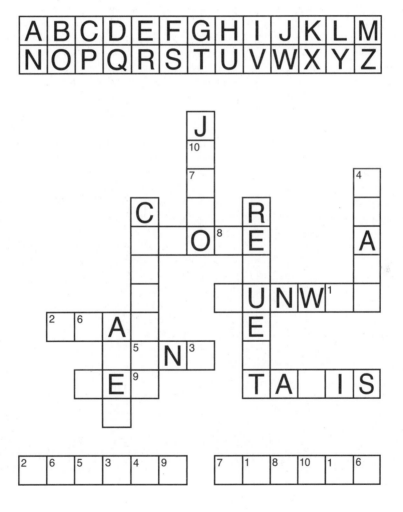

Answers on page 382.

RED, WHITE, AND BLUE

Each row, column, and long diagonal contains 2 reds, 2 whites, and 2 blues. From the clues given, can you complete the grid?

1. The blues are adjacent.

2. Each white is immediately to the left of each red.

3. The whites are somewhere between the reds.

5. The reds are somewhere between the whites

6. The whites are somewhere between the blues.

A. The whites are adjacent.

C. The whites are somewhere between the blues.

E. One white is bounded by the reds, the other by the blues.

Answer on page 382.

ODD-EVEN LOGIDOKU

The numbers 1 through 9 appear once in every row, column, long diagonal, irregular shape, and 3 by 3 grid. Cells marked with the letter **E** contain even numbers. From the numbers already given, can you complete the puzzle?

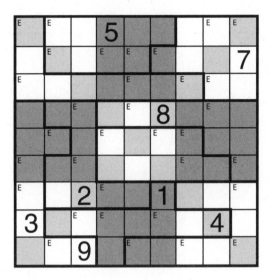

WORD COLUMNS

Find the hidden quote from Mark Twain by using the letters directly below each of the blank squares. Each letter is used only once. A black square indicates the end of a word.

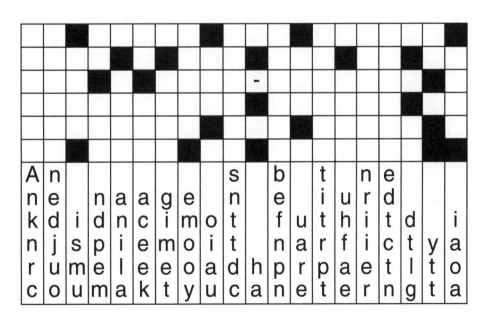

Answers on page 382.

MIRROR IMAGES

Study the drawing on the left for 2 minutes, then turn the page upside down and find the 22 things in the companion picture that differ from the original. No fair turning the picture right-side up until you've found them all (or given up)!

Answers on page 382.

HITORI

The object of this puzzle is to have a number appear only once in each row and column. By shading a number cell, you are effectively removing that number from its row and column. There's a catch though: Shaded number cells are never adjacent to one another in a row or column.

4	4	1	8	5	2	7	5
7	5	3	2	6	3	1	4
8	4	3	7	5	5	6	1
4	6	3	5	4	8	4	2
5	3	8	8	7	1	2	4
8	1	5	3	5	7	2	6
3	5	7	4	1	6	8	5
6	8	4	8	2	2	5	1

FRAME GAMES™

Can you "read" the phrase below?

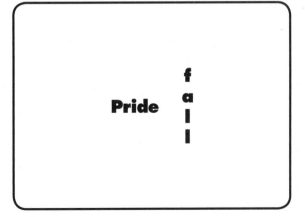

MENAGERIE NURSERY

ACROSS

1. Skating event
6. Rick's "Casablanca" love
10. Door feature
14. Comedian Murphy
15. Former Georgia senator
16. College in New Rochelle
17. It's below the knee: 2 wds.
19. Lara Croft raids it
20. Short joke: hyph.
21. Knockout drink
23. Hot under the collar
24. City on the Po River
26. Was in session
27. Thankless one
31. The Pips, to Gladys Knight
35. Hits the roof: 2 wds.
36. Utah's Hatch
37. Little boy
38. Youth with a lamp
41. Suitability
43. Iceberg alternative
44. Swedish flier
45. Palindromic vehicle
47. Melville captain
51. Seaport of Italia
54. Phone call opener: 2 wds.
56. Citizens' rights group: abbr.
57. Revolver maker: 2 wds.
59. It smooths things over
60. German auto
61. March honoree, familiarly: abbr., 2 wds.
62. Off-color
63. Part in a play
64. Actor Davis

DOWN

1. River to the Rio Grande
2. Hersey's "A Bell for _____"
3. Time waster
4. Biathlon weapon
5. Prefix with "sweet"
6. Newspaper pullouts
7. Monetary gain
8. Weekend TV fare: abbr.
9. Flower or swimmer
10. Scout of the Old West: 2 wds.
11. Secluded spot
12. Round-buyer's words: 2 wds.
13. Diaper wearer
18. Take the lid off
22. Swallows
25. Prefix with -place or -print
26. Old timer
28. Composer Thomas
29. Cash register section
30. Ice cream brand
31. Sow's mate
32. Alice's Restaurant patron
33. Overcrowd
34. Engage in horseplay: 2 wds.
39. Tooth for gnawing
40. Name divider
41. In general: 3 wds.
42. French capital, in song
46. Water-conserving critter
47. Bank units: abbr.
48. Gym game
49. Ike's opponent
50. Actress Davis
51. Execute perfectly, slangily
52. Approx. 4,047 square meters
53. Clear snow-covered roads
55. Furthermore
58. GI mail drop

WORD LADDER

Use the clues to change just one letter on each line to go from the top word to the bottom word. Do not change the order of the letters. You must have a common English word at each step.

HILL

_______ the handle of a sword

_______ stop

_______ a mark of purity

_______ large room for assembly

_______ one of the bladders

_______ a very forceful wind

PALE

Answers on page 382.

STAR POWER

Fill in each of the empty squares in the grid so that each star is surrounded by numbers 1 through 8 with no repeats.

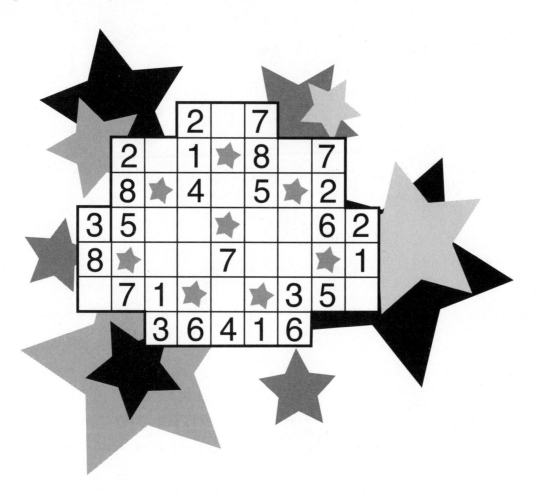

SIX-LETTER ANAGRAMS

Fill in the blanks in the sentence below with 6-letter words that are anagrams (rearrangements of the same letters) of one another.

Several hours can _____ quickly if you're _____, so _____ try to stay awake.

Answers on page 382.

PAINTERLY LOGIC

Painter Pat has been hired to paint the walls, doors, and roofs (yes, roofs!) of the brand-new trailers in Prefabulous, the world's tackiest trailer park, where it seems that each owner wants their walls, doors, and roofs to be painted with three different colors. Being individualists, the owners also want their doors, walls, and roofs to be painted different color combinations from their neighbors, with every trailer using three colors. Painter Pat arrived at the park and saw that the trailers are addressed 101 through 105 as they line up consecutively on Paisley Way. The colors the owners asked him to use to paint the walls, doors, and roofs of their trailers are red, orange, yellow, green, blue, indigo, and violet. None of the owners were home, but they left the following instructions for Pat.

The owner who wants orange doors and indigo walls does not live in Trailer Number 103.

The owner of Trailer 103 wants a green roof.

The owner of Trailer 102 wants yellow walls and a red roof.

The owner of Trailer 105 wants red doors.

The owner who wants the walls of his trailer painted orange and the roof blue lives directly next door to the owner who wants his trailer painted with green doors and violet walls.

What colors did Painter Pat paint the walls, doors, and roofs of each trailer?

ODD-EVEN LOGIDOKU

The numbers 1 through 9 appear once in every row, column, long diagonal, irregular shape (indicated by marked borders), and 3 by 3 grid. Cells marked with the letter **E** contain even numbers. From the numbers already given, can you complete the puzzle?

DIGITAL SUDOKU

Fill in the grid so that each row, column, and 2 by 3 block contains the numbers 1 through 6 exactly once. Numbers are in digital form and some segments have already been filled in.

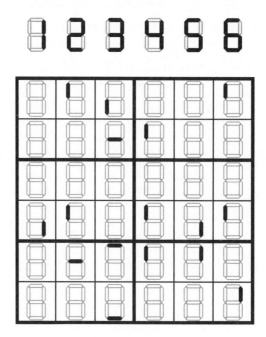

SIX-LETTER ANAGRAMS

What 2 words, formed from different arrangements of the same 6 letters, can be used to complete the sentences below?

1. The group of hikers retraced the river's _____ back to its _____.

2. The couple enjoyed their _____ trip to the city _____.

3. The park _____ advised us not to _____ from the well-marked trails.

4. A piano student's _____ may be _____ until brought out by a good instructor.

5. Life _____ a cruise ship is relaxing when you travel _____.

Answers on page 382.

TH@'S WACKY

In the words listed below, the @ symbol stands in for the letters **A** and **T**. Every word on the list is contained within the group of letters, and the words appear exactly as they are on the word list (with "@" substituting for "at"). Words can be found in a straight line horizontally, vertically, or diagonally. They may read either backward or forward.

ANTE@ER

ASSASSIN@ION

@LANTIS

@LAS

@MOSPHERE

C@ERWAULS

CH@TERBOX

CR@ER

FR@ERNITY

INFL@E

L@ERAL

N@ION

PAGIN@ION

P@ERNITY

P@TERN

PR@FALL

R@@OUILLE

R@S

REVEL@ION

S@ELLITE

S@URDAY

SC@TERBRAIN

SH@TER

SPL@

TRE@

ZIGGUR@

```
S A L @ P N O I @ L E V E R
C @ N I A R B R E T @ C S S
@ Z I G G U R @ I N M N C F
L E Y T I N R E @ P O @ H @
E C R S N S @ R T I S I @ Y
L @ Y T @ A N A @ @ P O T T
L E A D I B E N @ S H N E I
I R D I O N I T H E E S R N
U W R @ N S S E I @ R @ B R
O A U L S P L @ O L E H O E
@ U @ A C R @ E R F L I X @
@ L S P @ T E R N N V E E R
R S L L A F @ R P I P S @ F
A @ S L A R E @ L A N T I S
```

QUILT QUEST

The small, tricolored shape at right appears twice in the quilt below. Find both instances. The shape can be rotated, but not mirrored.

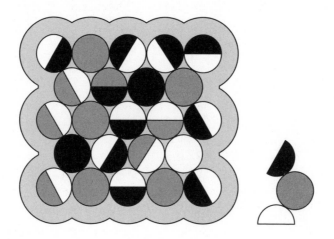

STAR POWER

Fill in each of the empty squares in the grid so that each star is surrounded by numbers 1 through 8 with no repeats.

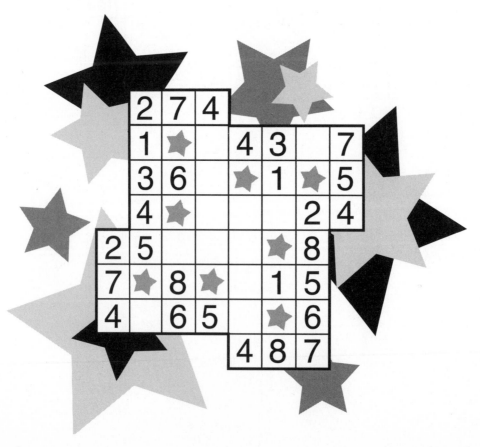

Answers on pages 382–383.

CODEWORD

The letters of the alphabet are hidden in code: They are represented by a random number from 1 to 26. With the letters already given, complete the crossword puzzle with English words and break the code.

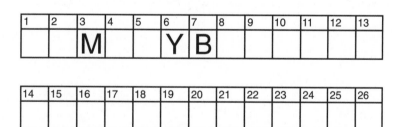

Answer on page 383.

Use deductive logic to complete the grid so that each row, each column, and each 3 by 3 box contains the numbers 1 through 9 in some order. The solution is unique.

						7		
	9					8	4	
3			7					5
		3		9			2	
	2		6		1		9	
	8			4		3		
1					5			6
	4	6					7	
		8						

A PUZZLING PERSPECTIVE

Mentally arrange the lettered balls from large to small in the correct order to spell an 11-letter word.

Clue: Ponderously clumsy

Answers on page 383.

ABCD

Every cell in this grid contains 1 of 4 letters: A, B, C, or D. No letter can be horizontally or vertically adjacent to itself. The tables above and to the left of the grid indicate how many times each letter appears in that column or row. Can you complete the grid?

	A	2	2	1	1	1	2
	B	2	0	2	3	1	1
	C	1	1	2	0	3	2
A B C D	D	1	3	1	2	1	1
2 0 1 3							
1 1 3 1							
1 3 1 1							
3 1 1 1							
1 2 1 2							
1 2 2 1							

FOR YOUR EYES ONLY

Look carefully at the 4 arrows below. Which one is the shortest? Which one is the longest? Are they all the same length? No need to use a ruler—just use your eyes.

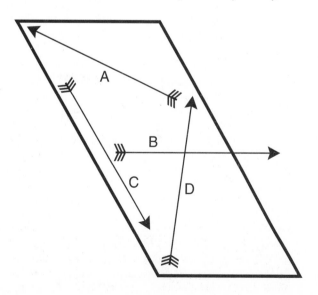

Answers on page 383.

HASHI

Each circle represents an island, with the number inside indicating the number of bridges connected to it. Draw bridges between islands using the number given. There can be no more than 2 bridges going in the same direction, and there must be a continuous path connecting all islands. Bridges can only be vertical or horizontal and may not cross islands or other bridges. We've drawn some bridges to get you started.

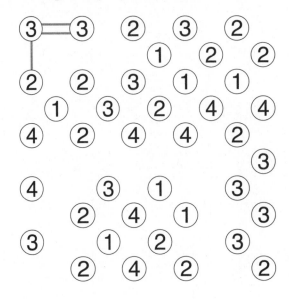

ODD-EVEN LOGIDOKU

The numbers 1 to 9 are to appear once in every row, column, long diagonal, irregular shape (indicated by marked borders), and 3 by 3 grid. Cells marked with the letter **E** contain even numbers. From the numbers already given, can you complete the puzzle?

Answers on page 383.

CODEWORD

The letters of the alphabet are hidden in code: They are represented by a random number from 1 to 26. With the letters already given, complete the crossword puzzle and break the code.

10	8	6	18	8	5	4	26		14	8	11	12
	6		14		3		18		13		17	
6	20	1	6	23	14		14	19	2	5	18	14
	1		2		20	21	6		5		25	
12	14	4	10		6		8	17	18	3	14	22
	6				4				14			
14	17	18	14	3	6		19	5	9	24	6	22
			7				6				1	
10	14	25	14	18	10		7		1	6	10	8
	15		11		5	11	14		17		21	
15	17	21	8	14	9		10	14	11	17	18	14
	6		14		14		8		18		6	
16	1	14	9		10	21	22	20	14	6	4	10

A B C D E F G H I J K L M N O P Q R S T U V W X Y Z

1	2	3	4	5	6	7	8	9	10	11	12	13
								D				

14	15	16	17	18	19	20	21	22	23	24	25	26
	Q									W		

MAKE SENSE OF THE SYMBOLS

Which figure comes next?

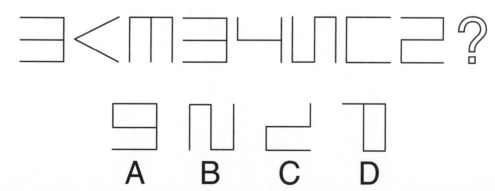

A   B   C   D

RED, WHITE, BLUE, AND GREEN

Each row, column, and long diagonal contains 2 reds, 2 whites, 2 blues, and 2 greens. Using the clues below, can you complete the grid?

1. Each blue is immediately right of each green; each white is immediately left of each red.
2. The greens are directly enclosed by a red and a blue.
4. The pattern of colors takes the form abcdacbd.
6. The whites, a red, and a blue are directly enclosed by the greens.
7. Each white is immediately left of each green.
8. The blues are adjacent.

A. The blues, the whites, and a green are directly enclosed by the reds.
B. The whites and a green are directly enclosed by the blues.
C. There are no greens in cells 1, 2, 3, or 4.
D. The reds are adjacent.
E. The whites are separated by 6 cells.
F. The blues are adjacent.
G. The blues are adjacent; the reds are separated by 2 cells.
H. The whites are separated by 5 cells.

Answer on page 383.

NAME CALLING

Decipher the encoded words in the proverb below using the numbers and letters on the phone pad. Remember that each number can stand for 3 or 4 possible letters.

Don't 7–3–5–6–4–2–3 at your enemy's 3–2–5–5, but don't 7–8–7–4 to pick him up 3–4–8–4–3–7.

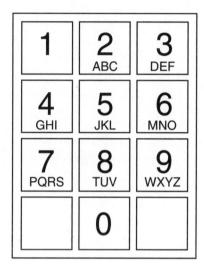

WORD LADDERS

Using the clues, change just one letter on each line to go from the top word to the bottom word. Do not change the order of the letters. You must have a common word at each step.

1. RIVET

_____

_____ a classic dog's name

_____

_____ a structure used to support growing plants

_____

TOWEL

2. BADGER

_____

_____ Macbeth thought he saw one

_____

_____ where baby Jesus slept

_____

BANNER

Answers on page 383.

MONDRIANIZE IT!

Inspired by the work of Dutch artist Piet Mondrian, this puzzle consists of stars and circles. Using the checkered pattern as a guide, draw in lines so that each star is in its own square, and each circle in its own rectangle.

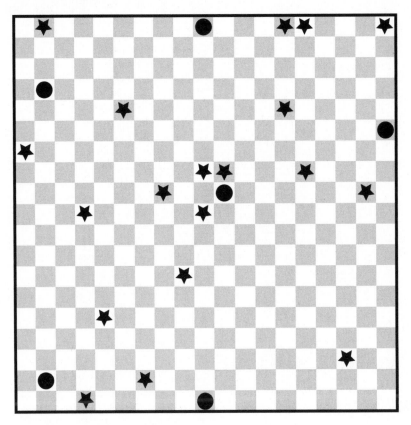

DISSECTION

Separate the figure into 2 identical parts following the grid lines. The parts may be rotated and/or mirrored.

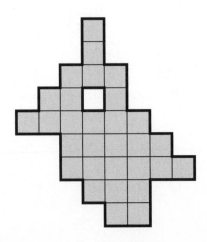

Answers on page 383.

ACROSTIC CLUES

Solve the clues below and then place the letters in their corresponding spots in the grid to reveal a quote by a famous person. The letter in the upper-right corner of each grid square refers to the clue the letter comes from. A black square indicates the end of a word.

A. Source of quote: 2 wds.

___ ___ ___ ___ ___ ___ ___ ___ ___ ___ ___ ___ ___
62 37 4   78 45 30 32 11 12 42 19 21 53

B. Flora

___ ___ ___ ___ ___ ___ ___ ___ ___ ___
75 40 14 3   55 9   5   76 83 84

C. Abstain from drinking

___ ___ ___ ___ ___ ___ ___ ___
25 47 51 81 31 43 52 29

D. Lounging around

___ ___ ___ ___ ___ ___ ___
8   18 23 58 15 16 10

E. "The Fall of the _____": 3 wds.

___ ___ ___ ___ ___ ___ ___ ___ ___ ___ ___ ___
56 66 69 17 63 49 27 60 26 34 35 41

F. More slothful

___ ___ ___ ___ ___ ___
7   71 79 74 57 50

G. Asserts

___ ___ ___ ___ ___ ___ ___
80 48 67 82 38 70 65

H. Brass instrument: 2 wds.

___ ___ ___ ___ ___ ___ ___ ___ ___ ___
36 64 13 72 73 2   68 28 46 61

I. _____ Teresa

___ ___ ___ ___ ___ ___
39 59 33 20 54 24

J. Twirl

___ ___ ___ ___ ___
1   44 6   22 77

1 J	2 H	3 B	4 A	■	5 B	6 J	7 F	8 D	9 B	10 D	11 A	■	12 A	13 H	14 B	15 D	16 D	17 E
18 D	19 A	20 I	21 A	22 J	■	23 D	24 I	25 C	26 E	■	27 E	28 H	29 C	30 A	31 C	32 A	■	33 I	34 E
35 E	■	36 H	37 A	38 G	39 I	40 B	41 E	42 A	■	43 C	44 J	45 A	46 H	47 C	48 G	49 E	50 F	51 C
52 C	53 A	54 I	■	55 B	56 E	57 F	■	58 D	59 I	60 E	61 H	62 A	63 E	64 H	65 G	■	66 E	67 G
68 H	69 E	70 G	71 F	72 H	■	73 H	74 F	75 B	76 B	77 J	78 A	79 F	80 G	81 C	82 G	83 B	84 B

Answers on page 383.

BUY BUY BUY

ACROSS

1. Busy people in April: abbr.
5. Heat broadcasts: abbr.
9. Protrude
12. Bindle carrier
13. National park in Utah
14. She's often blamed for a famous breakup
15. Where Napoleon went in 1814
16. Church volunteer: 2 wds.
18. Math class subject, maybe
20. Tool for a cold mountain climber
21. "Hunny" seeker
24. Money for the golden years: abbr.
27. Hammer's locale
28. Souped-up
29. First name of Oscar nominee for "Hoosiers"
31. Last name of Oscar nominee for "Hoosiers"
32. Weird Al parody of a Michael Jackson song
33. How long a wait might seem to last
34. Thesaurus item: abbr.
35. His game show is often seen with Pat's
36. Treat the turkey
38. Stops moving
43. Glade: 2 wds.
45. It may break in the game The Oregon Trail
46. Amorphous lump
47. Math class subject, for short
48. Burn in the kitchen
49. Bad thing to be poked
50. With all one's marbles
51. SportsCenter network

DOWN

1. "Hell's Kitchen" competitor
2. Sport with chukkers
3. It's shortened, for short
4. "Me too!": 3 wds.
5. Flowery shrubs
6. One of Islam's five
7. Popular injection
8. Wrench in the gears
9. Department of Labor training program: 2 wds.
10. Pizzeria chain
11. A child often leaves it out
17. Destroy, in a way: 2 wds.
19. Nail the test: 2 wds.
22. Tyrant's command
23. It may be leaned on in anger
24. Brainstorming session output
25. "Keep it _____"
26. Come before
28. TV character whose name is Spanish for "stupid"
30. Frost interviewee
31. Bank heist victim, maybe
33. Enter carefully: 2 wds.
36. Quotable baseball catcher
37. Rub out
39. They often have dirt wiped on them
40. Alimony recipients, perhaps
41. Reaction to a bad pick-up line
42. Sea bird
43. Must 44-Down
44. Fork over

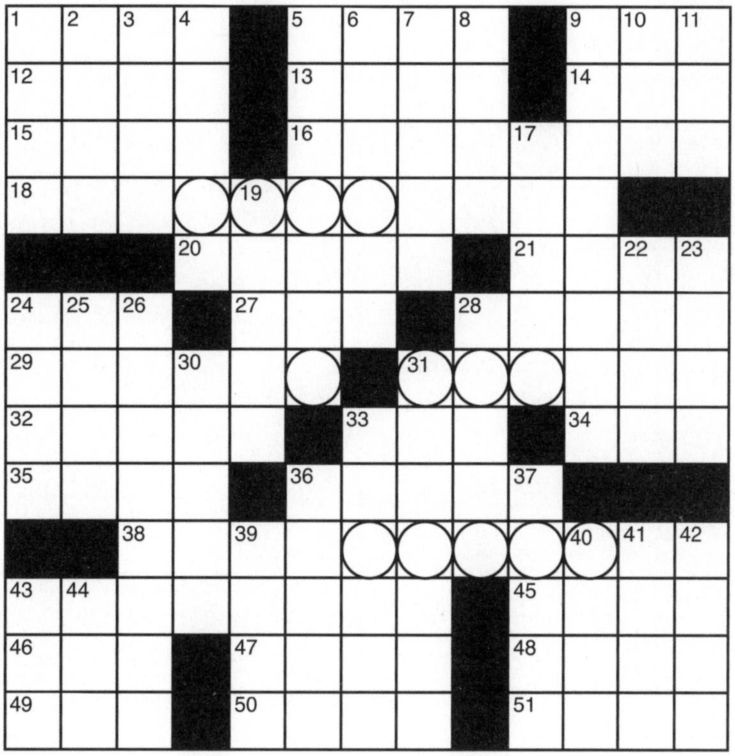

STAR POWER

Fill in each of the empty squares in the grid so that each star is surrounded by numbers 1 through 8 with no repeats.

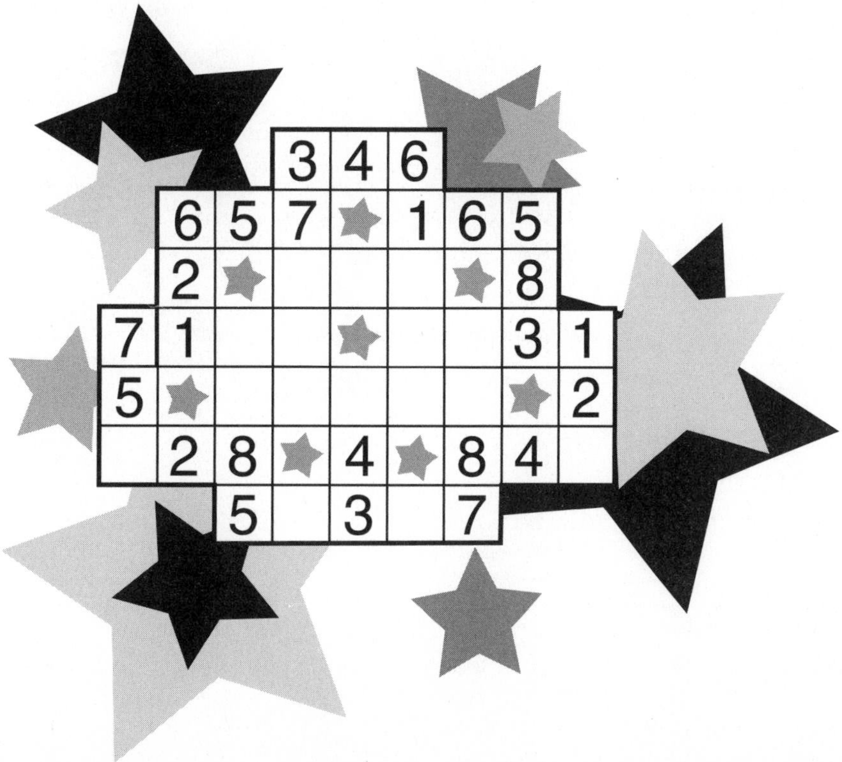

Answers on page 384.

MASYU

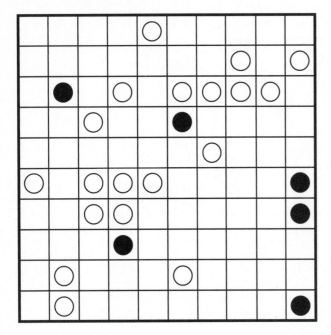

Masyu has a simple goal: to draw a single, nonintersecting loop through all of the pearls on the grid.

There are 2 rules according to the color of the pearl:

Black pearls: A line must enter and exit at right angles from the pearl. It must also extend straight for 2 squares in the chosen direction.

White pearls: A line goes straight through each pearl and must turn immediately before or after. It is optional for the line to turn both before and after.

NUMBER CROSSWORD

Fill in this crossword with numbers instead of letters. Use the clues to determine which number between 1 and 9 belongs in each square. No zeros are used.

ACROSS

1. The 2 outside digits add up to the middle digit
4. A number in the form of aabcc
6. A square
7. A multiple of 19
8. The sum of its first 2 digits is equal to the sum of its last 3 digits
10. A square

DOWN

1. Consecutive digits, ascending
2. A multiple of 13
3. Consecutive digits, descending
4. A cube
5. A square palindrome
9. A multiple of 17

Answers on page 384.

RHYME TIME

Each clue leads to a 2-word answer that rhymes, such as BIG PIG or STABLE TABLE. The numbers in parentheses after the clue give the number of letters in each word. For example, "cookware taken from the oven (3, 3)" would be "hot pot."

1. Farmer's pride (3, 4): _____ _____

2. Chicken server's suggestion (3, 5): _____ _____

3. Corncob, e.g. (4, 4): _____ _____

4. It makes swimmers shiver (4, 4): _____ _____

5. Temporary sales outlet (4, 5): _____ _____

6. Golfer's need, descriptively (5, 4): _____ _____

7. Dead letter office contents (5, 4): _____ _____

8. Hoard money (5, 4): _____ _____

9. Slight blemish (5, 5): _____ _____

10. Timepiece inventory (5, 5): _____ _____

11. It's not a real jail (5, 5): _____ _____

12. Military man in his first battle (5, 6): _____ _____

13. Traveling without baggage (5, 6): _____ _____

14. Race track (5, 6): _____ _____

15. He finds game faster (6, 6): _____ _____

Answers on page 384.

CROSS-MATH

Place the digits 1 through 9 in the empty white squares so that the 3 horizontal and 3 vertical equations are true. Each digit will be used exactly once. Calculations are done from left to right and from top to bottom.

	+		×		=	24
×		+		+		
	+		-		=	6
+		-		×		
	-		×		=	24
=		=		=		
24		5		24		

PATTERN PLACEMENT

When meshed together, which 3 patterns from the 6 labeled below can form the grid shown in the center? Patterns cannot be rotated or flipped.

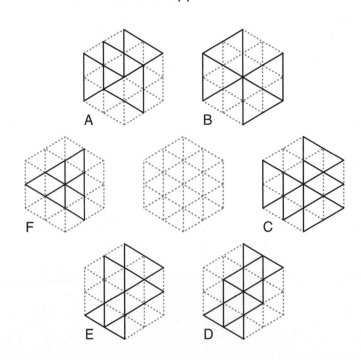

A   B

F

C

E   D

Answers on page 384.

FITTING WORDS

In this miniature crossword, the clues are listed randomly and are numbered for convenience only. It is up to you to figure out the placement of the 9 answers. To help you, we've inserted one letter in the grid, and this is the only occurrence of that letter in the completed puzzle.

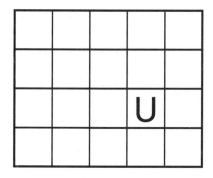

CLUES

1. Refer to
2. Burn treatment
3. Excuse
4. Fountain order
5. Fountain request?
6. Yoga position
7. Colorful parrot
8. Choppers
9. Neighbor

PYTHAGORIZE IT!

Blacken one white dot within the board so that, from this dot, exactly 4 symmetrical squares can be drawn. Squares must be drawn along the black dots. See the example illustration for clarification.

EXAMPLE

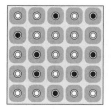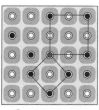

● extra blackened dot

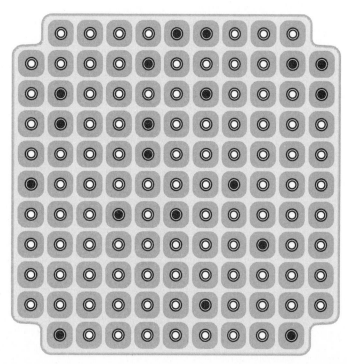

Answers on page 384.

THINK ABCD

Each row and column contains the letters A, B, C, D, and 2 blank squares in random order. Each letter and number indicator refers to the first or second of the 4 letters encountered when traveling inward. Can you complete the grid?

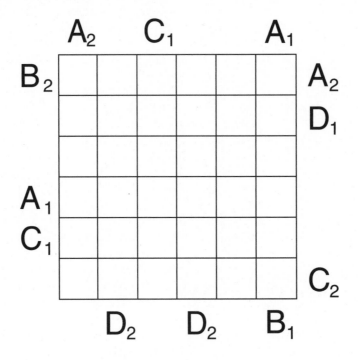

FRAME GAMES™

Can you "read" the phrase below?

Answers on page 384.

ANSWERS

Shrouded Summary
(page 4)
Orphan hides out with thieves before finding real family, but gang leader has other plans for him. "Oliver Twist" by Charles Dickens

True or False? *(page 5)*
1. 3 + 11 = 14 is true; 2. 22 − 19 = 2 is false; 3. 15 + 16 = 31 is true; 4. 90 − 12 = 88 is false; 5. 45 − 40 = 46 is false; 6. 7 + 11 = 18 is true; 7. 80 − 20 = 70 is false; 8. 70 + 13 = 83 is true; 9. 32 − 21 = 12 is false.

Name Calling *(page 5)*
It is difficult to make predictions, especially about the future.

Word Square *(page 6)*

S	A	L	T	S
A	W	A	I	T
L	A	R	G	E
T	I	G	E	R
S	T	E	R	N

Rhyme Time *(page 6)*
1. split pit; 2. neat street; 3. built stilt; 4. tight fight; 5. eight straight
Theme: All 10 answer words end in "t."

Criminals *(page 7)*
bandit, burglar, crook, gangster, mugger, outlaw, robber, thief

Aptagrams *(page 7)*
1. doughnut; 2. clothespins; 3. the Hilton; 4. Barbie doll

Lip Service *(pages 8–9)*

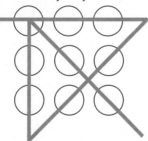

Rhyme Time *(page 9)*
1. bleaker speaker; 2. sad grad; 3. pink drink; 4. frail whale; 5. delay decay; 6. minute fruit; 7. cheery theory; 8. saloon tune

Continuous Line Bet
(page 10)
Answers may vary

Name Calling *(page 10)*
A. Alabama; B. Florida; C. Georgia; D. Indiana; E. Montana; F. New York; G. Vermont; H. Wyoming

Where Are the Animals?
(page 11)
1. dog, cat; 2. skunk, elk; 3. deer, owl; 4. fox, snake; 5. wolf, horse; 6. rabbit, elephant; 7. tiger, lion; 8. monkey, eagle; 9. seal, whale; 10. parrot, eel

Fitting Words *(page 11)*

A	M	B	L	E
K	O	R	E	A
I	R	O	N	S
N	E	W	S	Y

Sudoku *(page 12)*

4	9	5	1	2	6	3	8	7
2	1	7	3	8	5	6	4	9
8	6	3	9	4	7	2	5	1
9	4	2	7	5	3	1	6	8
7	5	6	8	1	9	4	3	2
3	8	1	2	6	4	9	7	5
1	3	8	6	7	2	5	9	4
6	7	4	5	9	1	8	2	3
5	2	9	4	3	8	7	1	6

Theme Park *(page 12)*

Baseball Teams Letterbox *(page 13)*

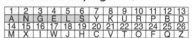

1	2	3	4	5	6	7	8	9	10	11	12	13
A	N	G	E	L	S	Y	K	U	R	P	B	D

14	15	16	17	18	19	20	21	22	23	24	25	26
M	X	I	W	J	H	C	V	T	O	F	Q	Z

Jigshape *(page 14)*

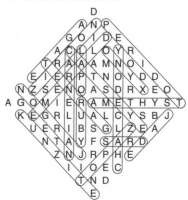

Contain Yourself *(page 14)*
ex(pen)sive, vau(devil)le, c(Handel)ier

Gems *(page 15)*
Leftover letters spell: "Diamonds Are a Girl's Best Friend"

ANSWERS

Acrostic Anagram
(page 16)
A. cabin; B. symphonic; C. level;
D. typing; E. warhead; F. pecan;
G. finalize; H. chore; I. aviator;
J. wearily; K. booze; L. output
"People who cannot recognize a palpable absurdity are very much in the way of civilization."

Dream Man *(page 17)*
P + RING – G + ACE – A + CHAIR – I + M + WING – W = PRINCE CHARMING

Wacky Wordy *(page 17)*
"Sleepy Hollow"

Cities and States *(page 18)*
Fargo, Indiana, Maine, Salem, Seattle, Texas

Word Ladders *(page 18)*
Answers may vary.
1. PEACH, beach, beech, LEECH
2. SHOW, slow, plow, prow, prop, DROP

It's Elementary *(page 19)*
1. c) plutonium; 2. b) lawrencium;
3. a) californium; 4. c) palladium;
5. d) francium; 6. b) germanium;
7. b) gold; 8. b) fluorine

Pardon My French
(page 19)
"What's the French for 'fiddle-de-dee'?"

—Lewis Carroll

Find the Word *(page 20)*
1. She couldn't beliEVE that she won the lottery.; 2. "In sumMARY, we've had a very profitable year," Larry said.; 3. "MacBETH is a classic treat for any connoisseur," Tom loftily replied. ; 4. "What time is it?" PAUL Asked.; 5. To tELL ENds a friendship, to not tell would make me very uncomfortable," she said.; 6. "Wal-MART HAs stuff like that," Hank observed.; 7. "A MAN DAred to refuse you? What is the world coming to these days?" she asked,

astonished.; 8. "Yes! ThaT HELM! And keep her steady!" he growled, ducking another wave and dancing across the wildly pitching deck.; 9. "She isn't too bright, is SHE? I LAid my clothes out the night before," she said, sniffing in obvious disdain.; 10. "He'S A MAN THAt thinks before he speaks," she said, gazing at him with loving eyes.

Tasty Scramblegram
(page 20)

CAIROAMN
MACARONI

Red, Red, Red *(page 21)*
Leftover letters spell: A bottle of catsup

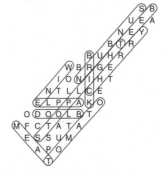

Wacky Wordy *(page 21)*
Change in the weather

Sudoku *(page 22)*

5	6	7	2	8	1	9	4	3
4	8	2	3	9	7	6	1	5
9	1	3	5	6	4	7	2	8
2	4	5	6	7	8	1	3	9
8	7	1	9	5	3	4	6	2
6	3	9	1	4	2	8	5	7
3	9	4	7	2	6	5	8	1
7	2	6	8	1	5	3	9	4
1	5	8	4	3	9	2	7	6

Who's There? *(page 22)*
"Well, if I called the wrong number, why did you answer the phone?"

—James Thurber

It Has a Ring *(page 23)*

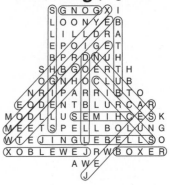

Versatile Verbiage
(page 23)
BAND

Take a Vacation
(pages 24–25)

Word Jigsaw *(page 25)*

	Y	E	W	
S	H	A	V	E
T	O	W	E	D
Y	E	N		

Space Hop *(page 26)*

Crossword Snack
(page 26)

D	R	I	B	S
Y	A	H	O	O
I	V	A	N	A
N	E	V	E	R
G	L	E	S	S

Alphabetics *(page 27)*

1. F; 2. G; 3. D; 4. B; 5. P; 6. C; 7. R; 8. Z; 9. E; 10. X; 11. M; 12. Q; 13. T; 14. Y; 15. A; 16. H; 17. I; 18. J; 19. K; 20. L; 21. S; 22. W; 23. U; 24. V; 25. N; 26. O

Soupy Sailfish *(page 28)*

Flower Girls Letterbox
(page 29)

1	2	3	4	5	6	7	8	9	10	11	12	13
P	E	T	U	N	I	A	C	M	S	V	Y	R
14	15	16	17	18	19	20	21	22	23	24	25	26
L	G	H	J	D	O	B	F	K	Q	W	X	Z

E Pyramid *(page 30)*

E / H E / S H E / S H E D / S H I E D / S H I E L D

Find the Word *(page 30)*

22. Fre**d, og**re of the land of Pra**do G**amma, declared that the **dog**ma of en**dog**amy, requiring him to we**d og**res only, was unfair. Fred **dog**gedly courted En**dog**ia, a lover of avoca**do g**um, but not a weir**do** girl. He wrote her **dog**gerel, sent her hot**dog**s, and took her to a black tie dinner, but his tuxe**do g**ot caught on a nail, and everyone saw his Spee**do g**arment underneath. Fred moped in his con**do g**arage

until En**dog**ia's parents, after much a**do, g**ave their permission to we**d**. **Og**res from Pra**do G**amma thought the wedding was a boon**dog**gle, and they were proven right when Fre**d og**led the maid of honor and En**dog**ia said, "No can **do**—**g**oodbye!"

Initially Yours *(page 31)*

1. big man on campus; 2. Book of the Month Club; 3. cash on delivery; 4. extra-sensory perception; 5. high-definition television; 6. machine-groomed snow; 7. patrol torpedo; 8. standing room only; 9. unidentified flying object; 10. water displacement

Code-doku *(page 31)*

ALL'S WELL THAT ENDS WELL

T	D	N	H	W	S	A	L	E
L	E	H	T	N	A	S	D	W
S	A	W	E	L	D	T	N	H
N	L	S	W	D	T	E	H	A
A	T	D	S	E	H	L	W	N
H	W	E	N	A	L	D	T	S
D	N	L	A	S	W	H	E	T
W	S	T	D	H	E	N	A	L
E	H	A	L	T	N	W	S	D

Donut Maze *(page 32)*

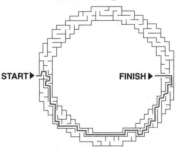

START ▶   FINISH ▶

Wacky Wordy *(page 32)*

Sudden death overtime

Play Ball *(page 33)*

1. catch; 2. bunt; 3. base; 4. single; 5. pitch; 6. umpire; 7. triple; 8. shortstop; 9. manager; 10. diamond

Number Crossword
(page 33)

2	4	6	
3	4	5	6
1	2	4	8
	2	3	6

Doggone Logic *(page 34)*

OWNER	BREED	DOG
LISA	BEAGLE	MAGGIE
JEREMY	DALMATIAN	SAM
ALYSSA	GERMAN SHEPHERD	SHASTA
MIKE	CHIHUAHUA	MR. BIG

Word Ladder *(page 34)*

ALDA, alma, alms, aims, ails, mils, miss, mass, MASH

Crossed Words *(page 35)*

You Auto Like This *(page 36)*

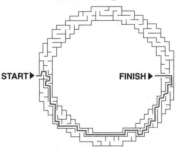

Word Ladder *(page 37)*

There are two possible answers.
1. HATE, date, dote, dove, LOVE;
2. HATE, have, hive, live, LOVE

Word Jigsaw *(page 37)*

		L	A	W
N	E	I	G	H
I	G	L	O	O
B	O	Y		

Acrostic Anagram
(page 38)

A. iodine; B. flowery; C. furious; D. wispy; E. country; F. school; G. nominee; H. snore; I. tornado; J. siege; K. reunion; L. shiny
"Writing is the only profession where no one considers you ridiculous if you earn no money."

ANSWERS

The But-Not Game
(page 39)

Carol likes words with "her" in them.

Class Logic *(page 39)*

Student	Subject	Teacher
Bethany	Computers	Mrs. Simpson
Jordan	History	Mr. Jackson
Kateline	Art	Mrs. Jennings
Mary	Science	Mr. Smith

Rock Around the Record Maze *(page 40)*

Where ARE They? *(page 41)*

17. On a d**are**, **Care**y called Marie, **a re**gular at his favorite b**ar, e**xpecting to get her cell phone. Marie sc**are**s easily so she comp**are**d his number to her speed-dial list and didn't answer. **Care**y ate a pear and decided to visit B**ar, e**x-wife number two, but c**ar e**ngine trouble forced him to take a cab and sh**are fare** with a fair-haired lass named Claire, who told him he didn't have a prayer with her. Bar doesn't c**are** for **Care**y, so she had current boyfriend Gary bl**are a re**d horn to sc**are Care**y away.

Number Crossword
(page 41)

3	6	
1	2	3	4
3	4	5	6
	8	8

Backyard Barbecue
(page 42)

WET SIGNS = SWING SET; HOSS HEROES = HORSESHOES; THICK TRIO = TIKI TORCH; TOAST PIE = PATIO SET; EAGLE CUSHION = CHAISE LOUNGE; CLONE HELP = CELL PHONE; RUM LABEL = UMBRELLA; NO HBO CONCERT = CORN ON THE COB; PRESCRIBE MAD HUB = BARBECUED SHRIMP; TO CHOKE SKIS = KISS THE COOK

Evens/Odds *(page 42)*

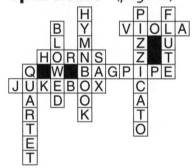

Perfect Harmony by Alpha Sleuth™ *(page 43)*

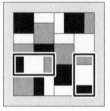

MUSIC MAKERS

Sudoku *(page 44)*

8	7	4	6	9	5	1	2	3
2	3	9	1	7	8	5	6	4
6	5	1	2	3	4	7	9	8
1	9	3	5	8	2	6	4	7
7	8	6	9	4	1	3	5	2
4	2	5	3	6	7	9	8	1
9	1	7	8	2	6	4	3	5
5	6	8	4	1	3	2	7	9
3	4	2	7	5	9	8	1	6

Don't Forget to Count the Donuts *(page 44)*

The answer is 19.

30 − 10 (who ate less than 6) − 1 (who ate more than 9) = 19.

Rhyme Time *(page 45)*

1. cellar dweller; 2. gory story; 3. lazy daisy; 4. muddy buddy; 5. funny bunny; 6. little fiddle; 7. legal eagle; 8. jelly belly; 9. soggy doggy; 10. better letter

Times Square *(page 45)*

			75	
6	4	5	120
4	5	6	120
3	1	2	6

72 20 60 60

Spin the Dials *(page 46)*

Quilt Quest *(page 46)*

Flying High *(page 47)*

COANFL	FALCON
RIOBN	ROBIN
CAALINRD	CARDINAL
NAARYC	CANARY
BIRDULEB	BLUEBIRD
WOCR	CROW
EGLAE	EAGLE
WSROPRA	SPARROW
GASLIRNT	STARLING

FREE AS A BIRD

Word Ladder *(page 47)*

LEAP, heap, hemp, hump, JUMP

Shenanigans *(page 48)*

MOON − O + KEY + BUS + LINES − L + S = MONKEY BUSINESS

Cross-Math (page 48)

5	–	2	÷	3	=	1
+		+		×		
9	×	8	–	6	=	66
÷		×		–		
7	–	1	–	4	=	2
=		=		=		
2		10		14		

Let's Play Some Music (page 49)

Leftover letters spell: Electric or acoustic guitar.

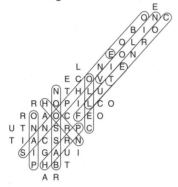

Word Ladder (page 49)

COLD, cord, word, worm, WARM

Many Mice (page 50)

5. Ta**mi ce**ntered the cera**mic e**gg that Mick eventually gave her so she wouldn't miss him while he worked for the Ato**mic E**nergy commission. Tami smoothed the egg with a pu**mice** stone, the only one in her domicile. Tami enjoyed the egg, but Mike's gift of an imported sala**mi ce**mented their relationship and helped her to miss him less.

Name Calling (page 50)

The hardest thing when learning to skate is probably the ice.

Trees in Words (page 51)

1. teak; 2. yew; 3. elm; 4. elder; 5. pine; 6. ash; 7. fir

Oddball of the Group (page 51)

The oddball figure is D. It's the only one where the intersection of the two parts does not reproduce the same shape as each of its figures.

Birthday Party (page 52)

SAW – A + EYE – Y + T + SIX + TEE + N = SWEET SIXTEEN

Colors Letterbox (page 52)

1	2	3	4	5	6	7	8	9	10	11	12	13
N	U	O	B	L	A	C	K	Q	F	X	J	S

14	15	16	17	18	19	20	21	22	23	24	25	26
Z	G	P	W	H	I	T	E	R	M	V	D	Y

Answer in the Round (page 53)

dining room table

Solve This ASAP! (page 54)

1. Baltimore & Ohio; 2. Cooperative for American Relief Everywhere; 3. electrocardiogram (or -graph); 4. Greenwich Mean Time; 5. International Standard Book Number; 6. light-emitting diode; 7. National Aeronautics and Space Administration; 8. répondez, s'il vous plaît; 9. surface-to-air missile; 10. sealed with a kiss

Hashi (page 54)

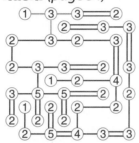

Edible Anagrams (page 55)

1. diary, dairy; 2. sauce, cause; 3. west, stew; 4. last, salt; 5. team, meat

Go Figure (page 55)

			19
2	1	7	10
3	4	9	16
8	5	6	19
13	10	22	12

Crossword for Dummies (pages 56–57)

D	I	V	A	■	D	D	T	■	F	O	P	S
O	V	E	R	T	O	O	K	■	O	D	I	E
V	E	N	T	R	I	L	O	Q	U	I	S	T
E	S	T	■	I	N	T	■	U	L	N	A	S
■	■	■	J	O	G	■	D	E	S	■	■	■
W	H	E	E	■	C	U	E	■	F	E	Z	■
A	U	C	T	I	O	N	B	R	I	D	G	E
G	T	O	■	S	A	N	■	I	R	O	N	■
■	G	A	R	■	T	A	I	■	■	■	■	■
G	H	A	N	A	■	P	A	C	■	D	I	S
A	U	T	O	C	R	A	S	H	T	E	S	T
S	L	I	M	■	B	A	K	E	S	A	L	E
H	A	T	E	■	I	R	S	■	P	R	E	P

Name Calling (page 57)

1. moral; 2. Virtue; 3. giraffe; 4. travel; 5. stronger

A-MAZE-ing Race (page 58)

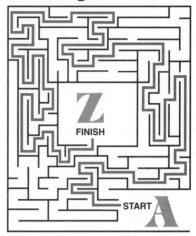

Ho-Hum Advice (page 58)

"When in doubt, sing loud."
—Robert Merrill

Honeycomb (page 59)

Word Columns (page 59)

"Logic takes care of itself; all we have to do is look and see how it does it."

Inherit the Win (page 60)

Misers aren't much fun to live with but they make great ancestors!

A Whale of a Challenge (page 60)

ANSWERS

Ten-Five, Good Buddy
(page 61)
1. Hitchhiker in tree; 2. deer head in tree trunk; 3. branch growing out of truck; 4. company name runs off end of truck; 5. missing back wheels; 6. driver on wrong side; 7. missing headlight; 8. tree is growing in the middle of the road; 9. pie in the sky

Word Columns *(page 61)*
As soon as you sit down to a cup of hot coffee, your boss will ask you to do something which will last until the coffee is cold.

Strike a Pose *(page 62)*
Leftover letters spell: "Better to live one year as a tiger than a hundred as sheep."

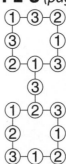

A Tuneful Love Story
(page 63)
A. the trolley; B. bamboo; C. Yourself; D. magnifying; E. Esther; F. whooped; G. Truett; H. entertaining; I. "You and I"; J. mayhem

"My dear, when you get to be my age, you'll find out there are more important things in life than boys."

Animal House *(page 64)*

	Name	Animal	Location
1	Brenda	elephant	cave
2	Clive	goat	wood
3	Andy	horse	field
4	Dolly	flamingo	shed

Word Ladder *(page 64)*
SOFT, sort, sore, core, cord, card, HARD

Rhyme Time *(page 65)*
1. got hot; 2. snub Cub; 3. slow flow; 4. dorm form; 5. finer liner; 6. rift shift; 7. muddy study; 8. reach beach; 9. stock shock; 10. regal eagle

Sudoku *(page 65)*

2	5	9	6	7	1	4	3	8
7	3	8	2	5	4	9	1	6
1	4	6	8	3	9	2	5	7
4	9	7	5	1	8	3	6	2
8	6	1	7	2	3	5	9	4
5	2	3	9	4	6	8	7	1
6	8	2	1	9	5	7	4	3
9	7	4	3	6	2	1	8	5
3	1	5	4	8	7	6	2	9

Life's Little Mysteries
(page 66)
1. Why do they call it a TV set when you only get one?; 2. Why is it that when you transport something by car, it's a shipment, but when you send it by ship, it's called cargo?; 3. How does the guy who drives the snowplow get to work in the morning?; 4. Can an ambidextrous person make an offhand remark?; 5. Why don't they just make food stamps edible?

Playing the Market
(page 67)
When he bought the stock, Steve was a billionaire.

Word Jigsaw *(page 67)*

		A	R	E
	T	I	B	I	A
	I	N	E	P	T
	E	N	D		

Gone Fishin' *(page 68)*
1. River running uphill; 2. fishing line behind bridge; 3. perspective on tiles is wrong; 4. top and bottom of barrel showing; 5. man on hill couldn't touch man in window; 6. giant bird on tree

Grid Fill *(page 68)*

Anagrammed to Homonyms *(page 69)*
Real/reel; leek/leak; lane/lain; meat/meet; soar/sore

All 26 *(page 69)*

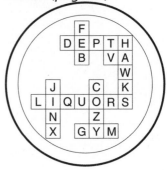

1-2-3 *(page 70)*

Six-Letter Anagrams
(page 70)
meteor/remote

Star Power
(page 71)

Vex-a-Gon (page 71)

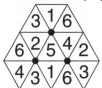

Sailing Smarts (pages 72–73)

Wacky Wordy (page 73)

Get in shape

Word Math (page 74)

Three-Letter Anagrams (page 74)

1. Now/own; 2. ten/net;
3. Who/how; 4. gum/mug

The Dark Side (page 75)

A. unique; B. Corpse; C. guava;
D. "Planet of the Apes"; E. bratty;
F. Juice; G. virtuosity; H. "Big Fish";
I. mammogram; J. theater;
K. meatballs
"There's just something visceral about moving a puppet frame by frame. There's a magical quality about it."

Sudoku (page 76)

2	3	7	1	4	5	9	8	6
5	4	8	9	6	7	2	1	3
6	1	9	3	8	2	7	5	4
3	2	1	5	9	4	6	7	8
9	7	4	6	2	8	5	3	1
8	6	5	7	3	1	4	2	9
1	9	2	8	7	6	3	4	5
4	5	6	2	1	3	8	9	7
7	8	3	4	5	9	1	6	2

Frame Games™ (page 76)

Neither here nor there

Girls' Names Letterbox (page 77)

Crossed Words (page 78)

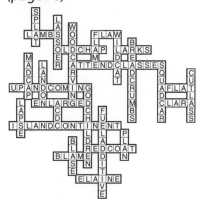

Can You Be Picture-Perfect? (page 79)

1. Boy in bottom picture has longer hair; 2. coffee gone from cup; 3. cup handle rotated right; 4. fluting on neck of vase is different

No Touching! (page 80)

Football Fever by Alpha Sleuth™ (page 81)

Quic-Kross (page 82)

REGIME

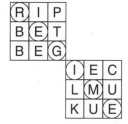

Wacky Wordy (page 82)

Wait and see

Codeword (page 83)

Bee-Bop Jive (page 84)

Word-a-Maze: On the Go (page 85)

ANSWERS

Cross-Math (page 85)

3	+	6	÷	1	= 9
+		÷		+	
9	×	2	+	8	= 26
-		+		-	
4	+	7	+	5	= 16
=		=		=	
8		10		4	

Flock of F's (page 86)
Other answers are possible.
1. fan; 2. fedora; 3. feet; 4. finger bowl; 5. fingers; 6. flying saucer; 7. football field; 8. frankfurter; 9. frog

Wacky Wordy (page 87)
Play above the rim (a basketball term)

Cool Café (page 87)

	Surname	Drink	Sugars
1	Dribble	latte	1
2	Aviary	coffee	2
3	Crumple	mocha	0
4	Bloggs	tea	3

Acrostic Clues (page 88)
A. Thomas Paine; B. blitz; C. dwelt; D. Hoover; E. forthright; F. Kong; G. inequities; H. Delhi; I. nephew; J. fleshy; K. unity
"When men yield up the privilege of thinking, the last shadow of liberty quits the horizon."

What's Wrong with This Picture? (page 89)
1. One of the essays is posted sideways; 2. there are no hands on the clock; 3. the carnival poster uses the wrong spelling of "week"; 4. the world map is labeled as a map of the United States; 5. the first math problem is wrong; 6. the teacher is a woman, so her name isn't Mr. Grimm; 7. the cabinet has a big envelope for a drawer; 8. there is a hand floating in the air; 9. desk in the front row is actually a big book; 10. the bookcase is upside down; 11. child has a balloon for a head; 12. the boy in the striped shirt is sitting without a chair; 13. whispering girl's chair is missing legs; 14. boy the whispering girl is talking to has a big button for a desk; 15. boy's shirt is on backward; 16. boy throwing paper has two different shirt sleeves

Star Power (page 90)

	5	2	4	8	7	
8	6	1	★	6	★	1
4	★	7	8	3	5	2
8	5	2	3	■	6	★ 8
6	★	3	■	2	1	7 4
1	4	7	5	4	★	5
3	★	6	★	8	3	6
5	8	2	1	3		

Snack Time (page 91)
Hubert H. Humphrey Jr., vice president under Lyndon Johnson, on what constituted his favorite sandwich: "Peanut butter, bologna, cheddar cheese, lettuce and mayonnaise on toasted bread with lots of catsup on the side."

Crypto-Logic (page 91)
The word is NEAT. If S is 5, I is 10. If I is 10, T is 1. Therefore N is 4. 4 − A = 1, so A is 3. Therefore, E is 9.

Passport Letterbox (page 92)

1	2	3	4	5	6	7	8	9	10	11	12	13
G	S	W	I	T	Z	E	R	L	A	N	D	H

14	15	16	17	18	19	20	21	22	23	24	25	26
P	Y	Q	K	U	J	X	C	V	B	M	O	F

Frame Games™ (page 93)
Jekyll & Hyde

Word Ladder (page 93)
Answers may vary.
FORD, fore, sore, sole, SOLO

Can't See the Trees for the Forest? (page 94)
1. pine; 2. yew; 3. cedar; 4. elm; 5. ash; 6. teak; 7. fir; 8. larch

Elevator Words (page 94)
1. KNOW how; 2. how come; 3. come clean; 4. clean hands; 5. hands off; 6. off base; 7. base HIT

Auto Showcase by Alpha Sleuth™ (page 95)

STOCKCAR RACING

Acrostic Anagram (page 96)
A. catamaran; B. thereabout; C. leaflet; D. succumb; E. bench; F. facade; G. haggle; H. convergence; I. telephone; J. hyphen
"Change the changeable, accept the unchangeable, and remove yourself from the unacceptable."

No Shoes, No Shirt, No Service (page 97)
12 people were allowed in. Of the people turned away, 3 wore only socks, 1 wore only shoes, and 4 wore both.

Quic-Kross (page 97)
BRAGGART

B	O	A	T
G	R	A	M
H	E	A	T
H	A	N	G

G	S	M	T
R	A	A	A
I	N	R	R
T	D	T	T

Shooting Star (page 98)

SLING

The But-Not Game (page 98)
Carol likes words with alternating consonants and vowels.

ABCD *(page 99)*

	A	B	C	D	
A	3	0	2	0	2 2
B	1	2	0	2	2 2
C	1	2	2	2	1 1

A	B	C	D
1	2	2	2	1 1

0	2	2	2	B D C D B C
3	0	2	1	A C A C A D
0	3	0	3	D B D B D B
2	0	2	2	A D C D C A
1	3	1	1	C B D B A B
3	1	2	0	A C A C B A

Vex-a-Gon *(page 99)*

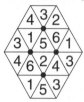

Summertime Fun
(pages 100–101)

C	E	D	E		A	Y	E		L	A	S	S
B	A	I	L		L	A	P		E	L	I	A
S	U	N	S	H	I	N	E		M	E	N	U
		G	E	E		K	E	R	O	U	A	C
T	A	B		R	U	E		U	N	T	I	E
S	L	A	V		S	E	P	I	A			
P	E	T	A	L	S		E	N	D	E	A	R
		C	O	R	E	R		E	X	P	O	
A	M	M	A	N		A	U	G		P	E	T
B	O	O	T	E	E	S		A	O	L		
A	C	T	I		S	E	A	S	H	O	R	E
S	H	O	O		A	L	B		O	R	A	L
E	A	R	N		U	S	E		H	E	N	S

Grid Fill *(page 101)*

S	P	I	C	E	S
N	I	C	K	E	L
A	P	P	E	N	D
B	O	S	T	O	N
L	I	P	T	O	N
S	H	I	V	E	R
C	A	N	A	R	Y

Odd-Even Logidoku
(page 102)

4	2	7	9	1	6	8	3	5
3	1	9	8	5	4	2	6	7
5	8	6	3	7	2	4	9	1
9	5	4	7	3	1	6	2	8
2	6	1	4	9	8	5	7	3
8	7	3	2	6	5	9	1	4
6	4	8	1	2	7	3	5	9
1	3	2	5	4	9	7	8	6
7	9	5	6	8	3	1	4	2

Wacky Wordy *(page 102)*
"Bad Moon Rising"

Rhyme Time *(page 103)*
1. big pig; 2. buy pie; 3. seek peak; 4. shrill drill; 5. scare bear; 6. mail trail; 7. mean queen; 8. chilly filly; 9. cheese please; 10. bigger rigger

How'd He Do It? *(page 103)*
The other end of the chain wasn't attached to anything.

Picnic Puzzle *(page 104)*
No: It's impossible to cover the remaining tablecloth squares with the hoagies. Draw an 8×8 checkerboard with alternating red-and-white squares. When you draw a pitcher of lemonade covering the diagonal corners, you will be covering either 2 red or 2 white squares (let's say red). When you put a hoagie on the table, it must cover a red and a white square. But there are now 32 white squares and only 30 red ones. Sally won't be able to do it.

Fitting Words *(page 104)*

A	L	O	H	A
R	I	V	A	L
A	M	A	Z	E
B	A	L	E	S

Flowers Letterbox
(page 105)

1	2	3	4	5	6	7	8	9	10	11	12	13
X	J	C	V	I	O	L	E	T	F	Q	G	U
14	15	16	17	18	19	20	21	22	23	24	25	26
Z	W	R	M	K	D	P	A	N	S	Y	B	H

Circus Time *(page 106)*

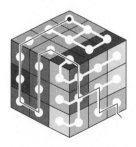

Totally Cubular! *(page 107)*

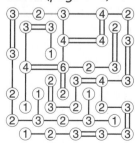

Word Ladder *(page 107)*
DINNER, winner, winter, hinter, hunter, HUNTED

Sudoku *(page 108)*

6	4	1	5	3	8	9	2	7
7	8	3	2	9	4	5	6	1
2	9	5	1	7	6	4	8	3
5	6	7	9	4	3	8	1	2
3	1	4	8	2	7	6	9	5
9	2	8	6	5	1	7	3	4
1	5	2	4	8	9	3	7	6
4	7	9	3	6	2	1	5	8
8	3	6	7	1	5	2	4	9

Three-Letter Anagrams
(page 108)
1. won/now; 2. tap/pat; 3. tea/ate; 4. car/arc; 5. ewe/wee

Grid Fill *(page 109)*

		F	L	Y		
	P	I	T	C	H	
B	A	T	T	E	R	S
P	E	A	N	U	T	S
I	N	F	I	E	L	D
	G	L	O	V	E	
		B	A	T		

Sign Here, Please
(page 109)
99

Word Ladders *(page 110)*
Answers may vary.
1. DAWN, darn, dark, dank, dunk, DUSK; 2. JUMP, lump, lamp, lame, lane, LAND; 3. BOOT, book, took, tock, tick, KICK; 4. BOAT, moat, most, mist, fist, FISH; 5. WAVE, wove, wore, sore, sure, SURF; 6. KISS, miss, moss, loss, lose, LOVE

Hashi *(page 110)*

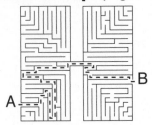

H Is for Help! *(page 111)*

A ··· B

Cube Quandary *(page 111)*

The length is 6 times the height and 3 times the width.

Codeword *(page 112)*

S	U	P	P	O	R	T	E	R		E	A	R	T	H
H		I		E		X				A				A
O		H	A	N	D	I	C	A	P		C			C
U				Y		O		L			K			K
T	I	M	I	N	G		I	G	N	O	R	E	D	
I					N		R		V					
N	O	V	E	L	T	Y		I	M	A	G	E	S	
G					T		T		R					Q
	A	M	P		E	X	H	I	B	I	T			U
	O		F			O		O					B	O
B	R		O		F		O		N		B	E	T	
E	E		U		J		A							
B		T	R	E	E		M	E	N	T	I	O	N	
O			T		A		S			Z				G
W	L	A	D	H	E	R	E			T		E		

| P | O | Q | W | R | J | Y | I | M | X | K | H | A |

14	15	16	17	18	19	20	21	22	23	24	25	26
N	T	S	D	L	C	Z	V	G	U	F	E	B

Rhyme Time *(page 113)*

1. ode code; 2. old cold; 3. hot yacht; 4. bass mass; 5. dark park; 6. nail sale; 7. sword cord; 8. small haul; 9. lack black; 10. great bait or sure lure; 11. beam team; 12. quick stick; 13. terse verse; 14. fair éclair; 15. school pool

Prvrbs *(page 113)*

1. A stitch in time saves nine.
2. Better late than never.
3. All's well that ends well.

Animal Farm *(page 114)*

NE'ER RIDE = REINDEER
BALD GUY = LADYBUG
GLARING BEET = BENGAL TIGER
THE PLANE = ELEPHANT
AMHERST = HAMSTER
LEG RIB = GERBIL
GOLF DISH = GOLDFISH
EGO NIP = PIGEON
PALE NOTE = ANTELOPE

Cross-Math *(page 114)*

3	+	5	÷	4	=	2
×		+		+		
7	+	8	+	6	=	21
×		-		×		
1	+	9	+	2	=	12
=		=		=		
21		4		20		

Hitori *(page 115)*

6	4	4	4	7	6	2	1
5	8	7	6	4	1	2	2
6	4	2	5	8	7	3	
3	1	3	8	8	4	5	7
7	7	1	2	3	5	6	8
8	2	6	4	1	3	2	5
8	7	5	8	6	2	1	1
8	3	2	1	2	7	8	4

The First Lady of Cinema
(page 115)

"Why slap them on the wrist with feathers when you can belt them over the head with a sledgehammer?"

Bad Weather
(pages 116–117)

U	S	E		N	Y	P	D		V	I	N	E
P	U	G		O	A	H	U		I	R	O	N
L	I	G	H	T	N	I	N	G	B	O	L	T
A	T	T	A	C	K			E	R	N	I	E
T	O	O	T	H		A	S	S	A	Y	E	R
E	R	S			A	M	U	S	T			
		S	T	O	R	M	D	O	O	R		
	I	O	T	A	S			E	S	P		
S	A	G	E	H	E	N		F	A	C	T	O
O	S	S	I	E		T	A	I	L	O	R	
T	H	U	N	D	E	R	S	T	R	U	C	K
T	O	I	T		M	E	A	T		S	K	Y
O	T	T	O		S	P	R	Y		E	S	S

Calcu-doku *(page 117)*

2	4	3	1
4	1	2	3
3	2	1	4
1	3	4	2

Go Figure *(page 118)*

Answers may vary.

					20
8	4	4	3	1	20
3	2	6	7	7	25
9	8	1	1	6	25
8	9	9	2	5	33
2	3	1	3	8	17
30	26	21	16	27	21

Rhyme Time *(page 118)*

1. see me; 2. top cop; 3. fat bat; 4. chow now; 5. last cast or past cast; 6. Mars czars; 7. wrong thong; 8. pony's cronies

Star Power *(page 119)*

	8	1	3	2	4	
5	3	4	★	6	★	5
1	★	2	5	7	8	1
5	8	7	6		4	3
3	★	2		3	5	6	2
6	4	1	8	4	★	8
5	★	3	★	2	1	7
8	2	7	5	6	

Desert Island Quiz
(page 119)

Dean tore out pages 7 and 8. There were 14 pages in the book.

Chick Flick by Alpha Sleuth™ *(page 120)*

	G		T			F	
S	Q	U	E	E	Z	A	B	L	E
N		S	A			O		F	
I		H	U	R	R	Y		W	A
F			J			E		E	I
F				E	X	C	E	R	P	T
L	O	V	E	R		S		H	
E				K					
D	A	M	S	E	L				
				R					

| M | O | V | I | E | | D | R | A | M | A |

Fitting Words *(page 121)*

R	A	T	T	Y
I	N	U	R	E
D	E	B	I	T
S	W	A	M	I

Unmistakable Aroma
(page 121)

You can't act like a skunk without someone getting wind of it.

How Will You Conduct Yourself? *(page 122)*

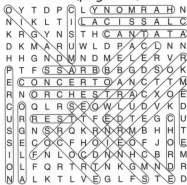

Smart Scramblegram
(page 123)

	I	N	W	A	R	D	
	D	A	R	W	I	N	
N	J				P	A	
J	E				A	C	
E	N				S	L	
N	N				C	A	
R	E				A	S	
E	R				L	P	
	L	I	S	T	E	R	
	L	I	T	R	E	S	

I	N	E	N	E	S	I	T
E	I	N	S	T	E	I	N

Quic-Kross *(page 123)*
RESERVED

(R)	E	S	T
B	E	A	R
L	A	(S)	T
L	A	T	(E)

		(R)	O	S	D
		A	(V)	E	I
		T	E	(E)	E
		E	R	P	(D)

Sudoku *(page 124)*

5	3	9	7	2	1	8	6	4
1	4	8	6	5	3	2	9	7
7	2	6	8	4	9	3	1	5
2	9	5	1	6	4	7	8	3
8	6	7	9	3	2	5	4	1
3	1	4	5	7	8	6	2	9
4	7	2	3	1	6	9	5	8
9	5	1	2	8	7	4	3	6
6	8	3	4	9	5	1	7	2

Wise Words *(page 124)*
The next letter is "E." The sequence is A, P, S, I, A, P, E, as in: "A penny saved is a penny earned."

Circular Reasoning
(page 125)

Rhyme Time *(page 125)*
1. Gates skates; 2. Blass class;
3. worry Murray; 4. Haley's dailies;
5. Clinton hintin'
Theme: Famous people named Bill.

Star Power *(page 126)*

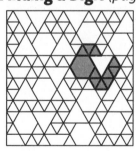

Boys' Names Letterbox
(page 127)

1	2	3	4	5	6	7	8	9	10	11	12	13
P	I	J	C	H	A	R	L	E	S	U	F	W

14	15	16	17	18	19	20	21	22	23	24	25	26
M	X	D	Q	B	K	Z	T	O	N	Y	G	V

Degrees of Confusion
(page 127)
The letter "e" is at the end of time.

Acrostic Clues *(page 128)*
A. Julian; B. "Yesterday"; C. curfew;
D. Yellow; E. "Hey Jude"; F. Happy;
G. Harrison; H. stats; I. full house;
J. Fool on the; K. Stuart; L. toured;
M. Coyote
"Would those of you in the cheaper seats clap your hands? And the rest of you, if you'll just rattle your jewelry."

Finding a Digit *(page 129)*

Wacky Wordy *(page 129)*
Seventh-inning stretch

Presidential Puzzle
(pages 130–131)

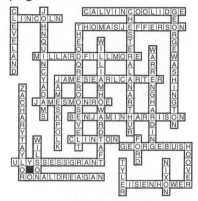

Odd-Even Logidoku
(page 132)

3	6	7	5	4	9	8	1	2
2	1	9	3	6	8	4	7	5
4	5	8	7	2	1	9	3	6
7	8	5	9	1	6	2	4	3
9	3	1	4	5	2	7	6	8
6	2	4	8	3	7	1	5	9
5	7	3	2	8	4	6	9	1
8	4	6	1	9	5	3	2	7
1	9	2	6	7	3	5	8	4

Go Figure *(page 132)*
Answers may vary.

							25
2	4	6	8	2	4	26
1	3	5	7	9	1	26
4	6	8	2	4	6	30
9	7	5	3	1	9	34
2	4	6	8	1	3	24
1	3	5	7	9	1	26

19 27 35 35 26 24 18

Vowel Play *(page 133)*

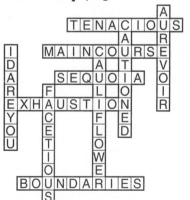

ANSWERS

Honeycomb (page 133)

```
  B O E D E D
 M 1 D 2 F 3 G
  E Y L O O O
 K 4 L 5 W 6 I
  C A A W G N
 S 7 L 8 E 9 U
  D E C D M T
```

Gesundheit! by Alpha Sleuth™ (page 134)

```
      B L O W I N G
    P     H       L
    H A N D K E R C H I E F
    J     E       L     Q
    E X A M     Z O     U
    M     Y     T H     I
    A           H       D
    S H I V E R
```

COLD   AND   FLU

Wacky Wordy (page 134)

Underhand serve

Downtown (page 135)

Leftover letters spell: "The bright array of city lights, as far as I can see."

It's All Relative (page 136)

"When a man sits with a pretty girl for an hour, it seems like a minute. But let him sit on a hot stove for a minute—and it's longer than an hour. That's relativity."

—Albert Einstein

Word Ladder (page 136)

RANGER, ringer, linger, longer, lodger, Dodger, dodder, fodder, folder, solder, solver, SILVER

Sudoku (page 137)

```
2 3 7 4 5 1 6 9 8
4 5 8 9 3 6 7 1 2
1 9 6 8 2 7 3 4 5
6 2 5 1 8 3 9 7 4
8 1 9 2 7 4 5 6 3
7 4 3 6 9 5 8 2 1
5 8 4 7 1 9 2 3 6
3 7 1 5 6 2 4 8 9
9 6 2 3 4 8 1 5 7
```

Bottom of the Dice (page 137)

There are 9 dots in all. On standard dice the numbers on opposite sides of a die always add up to 7.

Grid Fill (page 138)

```
W O R K E R
G O L D E N
A L M O N D
A R R E S T
S M A C K S
C H A I N S
F I R S T S
```

Maxims to Ponder (page 138)

1. Eagles may soar but weasels don't get sucked into jet engines.
2. Never argue with a spouse who is packing your parachute.
3. Never moon a werewolf.

Hats Off (page 139)

1. Feather is different on top left hat; 2. zebra fabric on same hat; 3. buckle different on top right hat; 4. flower instead of feather pouf; 5. no rings on top of cap; 6. shelf longer; 7. brim different on hat with bow; 8. feather is white; 9. stand missing; 10. top of hat different; 11. no apostrophe in HATS; 12. triangle feathers going in opposite direction on bottom hat.

Training Exercise (page 140)

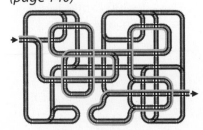

Calcu-doku (page 140)

```
4 2 3 1
1 4 2 3
2 3 1 4
3 1 4 2
```

Can You Conjugate a Beatle? (page 141)

John

Superfluity (page 141)

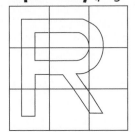

Acrostic Anagram (page 142)

"You can't say that civilization don't advance . . . for in every war they kill you a new way."
A. anyway; B. arctic; C. watery; D. tower; E. chain; F. annoys; G. ozone; H. utility; I. heaved; J. flank; K. layout; L. vivid

Code-doku (page 143)

T	O	H	U	M
H	U	M	T	O
M	T	O	H	U
O	H	U	M	T
U	M	T	O	H

Name Search (page 143)

ROB wins. His name appears 13 times. BOB, even though it can be spelled forward and backward, appears only 12 times. The word ORB is hidden twice.

Helloo (page 144)

Calcu-doku (page 144)

3	4	1	2
1	3	2	4
2	1	4	3
4	2	3	1

December the What?
(page 145)

The Festival of Games is Sunday, December 13: Clue 1 eliminates December 5, 10, 15, 20, 25, and 30. Clue 2 eliminates December 24 and 31. Clue 3 eliminates December 1, 2, 3, 4, 6, 7, 8, 9, 11, 12, 22, and 23. Clue 4 eliminates December 16, 17, 18, 19, 26, 27, 28, and 29. Clue 5 eliminates December 14 and 21.

What's Flipped in Vegas, Stays in Vegas (page 146)

The coin came up heads 12 times.

Totally Cubular!
(page 146)

A and B

Go for the Gourd
(page 147)

24. **Go**mer **go**t the urge to dra**g** **o**ut an orange **go**urd even though it wasn't Halloween. He carved his own face (which shows that his **e**go was a bi**g o**ne!). **Go**mer **go**t more **go**urds and carved a **go**ose with **go**ut, an eg**g o**n a wall, and a gan**g** of **go**rillas **go**ing ape. He showed them to his gal Gloria, a former **go**-**go** dancer who was now a bi**g o**ld **go**urd grower from Georgia. She gave **Go**mer a ba**g of** seeds to grow more **go**urds and **go** whole-ho**g** **o**ut on his porch carving them.

Don't Miss the Boat on This One (page 147)

The number 1. The sum of each row is 20.

"Easy" Does It
(pages 148–149)

Word Jigsaw (page 149)

Let It Shine by Alpha Sleuth™ (page 150)

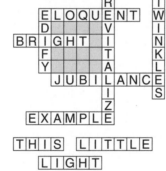

THIS LITTLE LIGHT

Wacky Wordy (page 151)

Download songs

Name Calling (page 151)

1. So easy to use a child can do it. Child sold separately.
2. Common sense ain't.
3. A king's castle is his home.
4. Length, width, height, and cost are the four dimensions.

At the Movies (page 152)

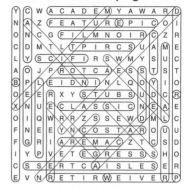

Barbershop Duet
(page 153)

1. Three men in the mirror; 2. customer still has hair in mirror image; 3. person hanging on coat rack; 4. magazine is upside down; 5. sandwich on price list; 6. everyone is bald; 7. shampoo costs more than a haircut

Quic-Kross (page 153)

BEVERAGE

Triple-Jointed (page 154)

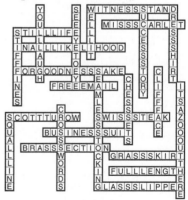

Sudoku (page 155)

4	2	1	7	5	3	6	8	9
6	3	8	9	4	2	1	7	5
9	5	7	1	8	6	2	3	4
2	9	3	8	7	1	4	5	6
7	1	4	6	2	5	8	9	3
5	8	6	4	3	9	7	2	1
1	6	2	3	9	7	5	4	8
8	7	9	5	6	4	3	1	2
3	4	5	2	1	8	9	6	7

ANSWERS

Number Crossword
(page 155)

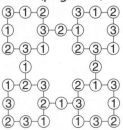

2	3	4	
5	2	5	2
	3	6	6	3
		7	8	9

Word Ladders *(page 156)*
Answers may vary.
1. GRAY, bray, brat, boat, goat, goad, GOLD
2. BLUE, flue, flux, flax, flay, fray, GRAY
3. BLACK, blank, bland, blend, bleed, breed, greed, GREEN
4. ROSE, rode, mode, made, JADE
5. TEAL, tell, till, tile, time, LIME

1-2-3 *(page 156)*

Match-Up Twins *(page 157)*
The matching pairs are: 1 and 8, 2 and 9, 3 and 6, 4 and 7, 5 and 10.

Wacky Wordy *(page 157)*
Made in China

Talk Show *(page 158)*

	Name	Surname	Topic
1	Jackie	Bore	book
2	Bruce	Ponds	baseball
3	Hal	Rawlings	movie
4	Gary	Wells	politics

Code-doku *(page 158)*
CAMBRIDGE

M	B	C	D	E	R	G	A	I
D	A	I	C	G	M	E	B	R
G	R	E	I	A	B	D	C	M
I	C	D	A	R	G	B	M	E
R	M	B	E	I	D	A	G	C
A	E	G	B	M	C	I	R	D
E	D	R	G	C	A	M	I	B
B	G	M	R	D	I	C	E	A
C	I	A	M	B	E	R	D	G

Star Power *(page 159)*

Wacky Wordy *(page 159)*
Piece of cake

Color-Coded
(pages 160–161)

D	I	R	T	S		S	L	O	E		O	H	M	S
A	R	I	E	L		E	A	R	N		R	I	O	T
I	M	G	R	E	E	N	W	I	T	H	E	N	V	Y
S	A	S	S	E	D		N	E	R	O		D	I	E
			E	P	I	C		L	E	A	G	U	E	S
E	L	K		S	T	A	B		E	R	R			
L	O	I	S		O	N	U	S		S	E	A	M	Y
B	O	L	T	F	R	O	M	T	H	E	B	L	U	E
A	P	N	E	A		E	P	E	E		E	M	I	T
			N	E	B		Y	E	A	R		S	R	I
F	E	D	O	R	A	S		D	R	A	T			
O	R	R		I	N	C	A		T	R	U	S	T	S
Y	O	U	R	E	J	U	S	T	Y	E	L	L	O	W
E	D	G	E		O	L	E	O		L	L	A	M	A
R	E	S	T		S	L	A	P		Y	E	M	E	N

Hashi *(page 161)*

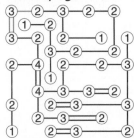

Sudoku *(page 162)*

4	7	3	2	6	9	1	8	5
2	5	8	1	4	7	6	9	3
9	6	1	8	5	3	7	2	4
3	4	2	6	7	8	5	1	9
5	8	9	3	1	4	2	6	7
7	1	6	9	2	5	4	3	8
8	2	7	5	9	1	3	4	6
1	9	4	7	3	6	8	5	2
6	3	5	4	8	2	9	7	1

To the Letter *(page 162)*

A	B	C	D	E	F
3	5	1	2	4	7

Acrostic Anagram
(page 163)
A. breathless; B. thermometer; C. forgoes; D. fortify; E. euthanasia; F. faction; G. eunuch; H chunky; I. widowed
"More firm and sure the hand of courage strikes, when it obeys the watchful eye of caution."

What's for Dinner?
(page 164)
In the bottom picture: 1. Rounded chair back; 2. girl has toy soldier; 3. girl wearing black skirt; 4. bowl on plate in front of girl; 5. sailboat flag points right; 6. dad wearing bowtie; 7. dad holding screwdriver; 8. ham on platter; 9. corn on table; 10. pitcher half full; 11. cake on windowsill; 12. window has 2 panes; 13. square pattern on curtain; 14. boy is eating yams; 15. boy is wearing sweater; 16. mom not wearing oven mitts; 17. Square tray cover; 18. mom's apron shorter.

Anagrammatically Correct *(page 165)*
1. this/hits; 2. toms/most; 3. left/felt; 4. tale/late; 5. acre/race; 6. sore/rose; 7. cats/cast/acts; 8. snap/pans/naps

Times Square *(page 165)*

3	1	3	3	27
1	5	5	9	225
7	5	5	1	175
7	2	1	2	28

147 50 75 54

Spiral: Classic Movies
(page 166)

G	A	R	B	O	G	A
N	E	A	L	D	A	R
N	O	N	T	A	V	T
A	M	A	R	N	I	I
I	M	Z	I	D	D	S
D	E	A	N	Y	A	T
N	L	N	G	A	N	A
I	L	A	O	N	N	N
A	E	L	E	G	E	G
T	T	S	E	N	R	E
R	E	T	N	E	L	L

Cruising Along (page 167)

A word search grid with circled answers including: CLASSES, ACTIVITIES, PROMENADE, MASSAGE, BINGO, MEALS, ROLES, CRUISE, STORE, SALON, LECTURES, VIDEOS, LOUNGE, SOLARIUM, HEATER, TOURS, etc.

Have a Taste, Bud
(page 168)
56 students have tasted both Cola A and Cola B.

Animal Safari (page 168)
bat; bear; cat; dingo; doe; dog; goat; goose; hare; horse; lion; mole; moose; mouse; mule; pig; rat; tiger

Star Power (page 169)

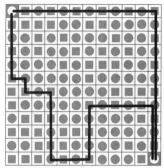

			1	6	3		
6	1	7	☆	2	8	6
4	☆	8	4	5	☆	3
3	5	2	☆	1	4	7
6	☆	7	3	6	☆	5
4	8	1	☆	8	2	3
3	☆	2	4	5	☆	1
7	5	6	☆	4	6	7

Word Jigsaw (page 169)

E	A	R		
W	R	I	T	E
E	M	B	E	R
		S	E	A

Awfully Nice
(pages 170-171)

A	S	I	A		E	L	B	A		L	I	M	O	S
L	A	C	S		C	O	O	L		I	L	O	V	E
G	U	E	S	T	H	O	S	T		F	L	U	E	S
E	N	R	O	B	E		S	A	M	E	H	E	R	E
R	A	S	C	A	L		A	R	O	S	E			
			R	O	T		S	T	P	A	U	L	S
P	E	S	O		N	A	P		H	A	L	V	E	S
E	P	O	X	Y		P	E	T		N	T	E	S	T
R	E	D	Y	E	D		Z	A	P		H	A	T	S
T	E	A	M	S	U	P		G	A	G				
		O	S	O	L	E		P	O	S	S	E	S
R	E	P	R	I	S	A	L		A	N	E	M	I	A
E	R	R	O	R		G	O	O	D	G	R	I	E	F
A	L	I	N	E		U	P	T	O		A	L	I	E
R	E	E	S	E		E	E	O	C		C	E	O	S

Word Ladder (page 171)
Answers may vary.
READ, road, rood, rook, BOOK

Girlfriends (page 172)
NAN appears 24 times. ANN appears 18 times. ANNA appears 6 times, and NANA appears 3 times.

Four-Letter Anagrams
(page 172)
1. odor/door; 2. lids/slid; 3. runt/turn; 4. part/rapt; 5. ring/grin; 6. lamp/palm; 7. form/from; 8. pace/cape

Word Ladders (page 173)
Answers may vary.
1. CALF, call, ball, BULL; 2. WORK, pork, port, pert, pest, REST; 3. MOON, moan, mean, bean, BEAM; 4. TRAIN, trait, tract, track, wrack, WRECK; 5. HARD, card, care, core, sore, sort, SOFT; 6. FOOL, foot, loot, lost, list, lisp, wisp, WISE

Say What? (page 173)
"All happy families resemble one another, each unhappy family is unhappy in its own way."

Pyramid (page 174)
```
        E
       D E
      D E N
     R E N D
    U N D E R
   E N D U R E
  D E N T U R E
 V E N T U R E D
A D V E N T U R E
U N T R A V E L E D
```

Go Figure (page 174)

						29
6	5	4	9	1	2	27
3	4	3	2	5	6	23
2	2	7	1	6	4	22
1	6	5	7	5	3	27
8	9	4	3	3	1	28
7	4	3	4	4	5	27
27	30	26	26	24	21	32

Square the Circle
(page 175)

A grid puzzle with a looping line path.

It's a Wrap! (page 176)
The answer is B.

Word Ladder (page 176)
Answers may vary.
SLEEP, bleep, bleed, breed, bread, dread, DREAM

Quic-Kross (page 177)
TUMULTUOUS

T	R	A	I	N
B	U	L	L	Y
H	U	M	A	N
B	E	G	U	N
T	O	T	A	L

T	L	A	A	T
R	U	L	B	A
I	C	O	O	X
C	K	N	U	E
E	Y	E	T	S

Initially Yours (page 177)
1. also known as; 2. Bay Area Rapid Transit; 3. frequently asked question; 4. International Business Machines; 5. Mobile Army Surgical Hospital; 6. monosodium glutamate; 7. President of the United States; 8. polyvinyl chloride; 9. supersonic transport; 10. videocassette recorder

Sudoku (page 178)

7	3	8	5	1	4	6	9	2
5	2	9	3	7	6	8	4	1
4	6	1	8	9	2	5	3	7
6	8	5	7	2	9	4	1	3
2	4	7	1	6	3	9	5	8
9	1	3	4	5	8	7	2	6
3	9	4	6	8	1	2	7	5
1	5	6	2	4	7	3	8	9
8	7	2	9	3	5	1	6	4

ANSWERS

Break This Color's Cover
(page 178)

The next color is black, the color of the eight ball in pool.

Crypto-quote *(page 179)*

"Put all your eggs in one basket—and watch that basket."
—Mark Twain

Famous Address
(page 179)

"Four score and seven years ago…"

Acrostic Anagram
(page 180)

A. acerbic; B. repetitive; C. gushes; D. entity; E. overjoys; F. navigational; G. enviable; H. belonged; I. follower

"If your job is to leaven ordinary lives with elevating spectacle, be elevating or be gone."

20-Sided Triangle *(page 181)*

Two possible solutions are:

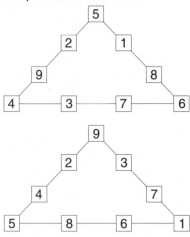

B Nice *(page 181)*

before, benign, and behalf

Word Columns *(page 182)*

I believe for every drop of rain that falls, a flower grows, a foundation leaks, a ballgame gets rained out, a car rusts and…

Sage Advice *(page 182)*

The missing letter is "P." The sequence is: A fool and his money are soon parted.

All the Colors of the Rainbow *(page 183)*

Leftover letters spell: red, orange, yellow, green, blue, indigo, violet

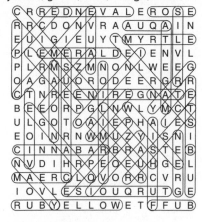

Motel Hideout *(page 184)*

The thief is in room 25.

Numbers Game *(page 184)*

The number is 8694

Triangle Cut *(page 185)*

Find the Booty! *(page 185)*

1. ENTERTAIN; 2. THOUSANDS;
3. SUPERSTAR; ERT+USA+ERS= TREASURES

Things Are Heating Up
(pages 186-187)

Math Grid *(page 187)*

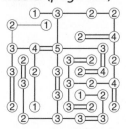

Two Rules *(page 188)*

There are two rules for ultimate success in life. Never tell everything you know.

Hashi *(page 188)*

Car Chase *(page 189)*

Fit It *(pages 190-191)*

Star Power (page 192)

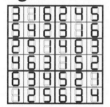

	4	2	1			
4	1	7	★	6	3	1
3	★	8	3	5	★	2
5	6	2	★	4	7	8
8	★	7	1	6	★	5
1	4	3	★	2	1	3
		4	5	8		

Wacky Wordy (page 192)
C: Catch as catch can

Rhyme Time (page 193)
1. soft loft; 2. mock block; 3. lack black; 4. base place; 5. exalt salt; 6. paste waste; 7. raven haven; 8. swell smell; 9. broth cloth; 10. create great; 11. change range; 12. center renter; 13. locket pocket; 14. leather tether; 15. boomer consumer

Digital Sudoku (page 194)

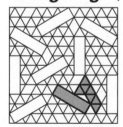

Season's Greetings (page 194)

The missing letter is C, as in "Cupid." The sequence: Dasher, Dancer, Prancer, Vixen, Comet, Cupid, Donder, Blitzen

Finding a Digit (page 195)

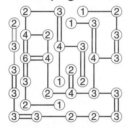

Pork Puzzler (page 195)
First place: Gomer's Berkshire
Second place: Homer's Hampshire
Third place: Romer's Duroc
Fourth place: Domer's Chester White

Cube Fold (page 196)
Figure 8 would not form a cube.

Next Letter? (page 196)
E as in "eight." The other letters are the first letters of the numbers 1 through 7.

Math Scramblegram (page 197)

	A	D	R	I	A	N	
	R	A	D	I	A	N	
F	F					O	T
O	A					B	O
R	C					E	U
C	T					U	B
A	O					S	U
T	R					E	S
	S	E	C	A	N	T	
	E	N	A	C	T	S	

KEYWORD

N	A	T	O	T	S	C	N
C	O	N	S	T	A	N	T

Hashi (page 197)

Logidoku (page 198)

3	7	6	4	2	8	1	5
2	8	7	3	5	1	6	4
5	6	1	8	3	4	2	7
1	4	2	5	7	6	8	3
6	3	8	2	4	7	5	1
7	5	3	1	6	2	4	8
4	1	5	6	8	3	7	2
8	2	4	7	1	5	3	6

Land of the Free (page 198)
The next letter is S. The sequence is O, S C Y S, as in "Oh, say can you see?"—the first line of "The Star-Spangled Banner."

Horsing Around (page 199)

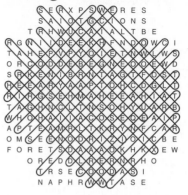

The theme is: If you add the first word of each phrase to the word "horse," you create a common idiom, such as CLOTHES HORSE or GIFT HORSE

Day at the Zoo (page 200)
Changes in the right-hand picture:
1. County changed to Country; 2. pennants are white; 3. extra post supporting zoo sign; 4. extra bush below sign; 5. child with balloons holding man's right hand; 6. tiger cage narrower; 7. only 1 tiger; 8. person in front of cage has back turned to tiger; 9. person in front of cage is now a woman; 10. child walking has no cotton candy; 11. adult giraffe has no mane; 12. same giraffe has gained an ear; 13. baby giraffe's spots are different; 14. more hay around baby giraffe; 15. bars missing from giraffe pen; 16. boy at giraffe pen wearing extra shirt; 17. girl taking giraffe photo has stripes on her shirt; 18. woman pushing stroller is wearing a hat; 19. same woman wearing skirt instead of pants; 20. child in stroller has 3 balloons; 21. only 1 boy watching elephant; 22. no branch in elephant's trunk; 23. elephant's tusk is shorter; 24. elephant's trunk outside of fence.

Go Figure (page 201)

								26
2	3	6	8	7	3	5	34
3	4	3	9	1	4	7	31
8	2	7	5	3	6	8	39
9	6	2	6	7	3	9	42
1	3	1	9	5	2	1	22
3	5	4	7	1	8	6	34
2	4	9	5	8	2	4	34

28 27 32 49 32 28 40 36

ANSWERS

Costarring *(page 201)*
A and E are the correct pieces.

High Times *(pages 202-203)*

B	E	T	A	■	P	O	W	E	R	■	S	T	A	G
I	C	O	N	■	A	B	A	C	I	■	P	I	M	A
T	H	E	T	O	W	E	R	O	F	B	A	B	E	L
S	O	R	E	N	E	S	S	■	L	A	R	I	N	E
■	■	D	A	R	E	■	R	E	R	E	A	D	S	■
S	C	R	A	G	S	■	D	U	M	B	■	■	■	■
E	L	A	T	E	■	G	I	N	A	■	■	W	A	N
T	O	W	E	R	I	N	G	I	N	F	E	R	N	O
S	T	S	■	C	A	I	N	■	■	A	M	A	T	I
■	V	E	S	T	■	S	U	P	P	E	R	■	■	■
W	A	S	P	I	S	H	■	R	I	C	E	■	■	■
A	C	K	A	C	K	■	G	E	N	E	R	A	T	E
T	H	E	L	E	A	N	I	N	G	T	O	W	E	R
T	O	I	L	■	T	A	S	T	E	■	R	A	N	I
S	O	N	S	■	E	N	T	E	R	■	S	Y	N	E

Rhyme Time *(page 203)*
1. aisle pile; 2. choppy copy;
3. snail tale; 4. usher's gushers;
5. vandals' sandals

The Logic of Crayons *(pages 204-205)*
Sabrina likes fruits and vegetables, so her lip gloss is either Strawberry Lip Smackers or Plum Wicked. Her crayon color is either Neon Carrot or Vivid Tangerine. Kelly borrowed the Vivid Tangerine crayon, so that's not her crayon color. The Bubble Gum lip gloss isn't hers, either. The item that could remind Jill of her doll Elmo is Tickle Me Pink (a la Tickle Me Elmo), so that's a given for her crayon. The only lip gloss with a "seductive" and "devilish" sound is Plum Wicked, and it's also a "fruity flavor," so that must be Kris's lip gloss. The crayon color Mauvelous is the only one that's a shade of violet/ purple, and the punny "Mauvelous" sounds like the breezy "wunnerful," so that's a lock for Kelly's crayon. Kris doesn't have pink, and she doesn't like vegetables, so she doesn't like Neon Carrot. If so, then Sabrina must have it, so you can plug that in for Sabrina's crayon. If Kelly likes violet shades and also "all-day" suckers, she must have the Hard Candy Lollipop lip gloss. The strawberry is the only fruit with its seeds on the outside, so Sabrina's lip gloss must be the Strawberry Smackers. By now we know 3 of the lip glosses, so the fourth one, by elimination, must be Bubble Gum for Jill.

Girl	Crayon Color	Lip Gloss
Sabrina	Neon Carrot	Strawberry Smackers
Jill	Tickle Me Pink	Bubble Gum
Kelly	Mauvelous	Hard Candy Lollipop
Kris	Vivid Tangerine	Plum Wicked

Fitting Words *(page 205)*

F	I	L	T	H
A	D	I	E	U
T	O	M	E	S
S	L	O	S	H

Take 30 *(page 206)*
Alf turned the candle on its side and balanced it on the candleholder. Then he lit the wick at both ends. The flames met in the middle exactly 30 minutes later.

Hidden Critters *(page 206)*
1. **She ep**itomizes elegance.;
2. Soap is an**ti-ger**m.; 3. He ma**de er**rors.; 4. Urban rene**wal rus**hes on.; 5. He did the ta**sk unk**nowingly.; 6. Her **badge r**evealed her mission.; 7. I went **to a d**andy party.; 8. Smell ne**w olf**actory sensations.; 9. Would you re**buff a lo**cal swain?; 10. Yes, i**f Rog**er will.

Say It Again, Sam *(page 207)*
1. ate eight; 2. add ad; 3. pale pail; 4. peace piece; 5. pear pair; 6. pier peer; 7. plain plane; 8. whole hole; 9. wholly holy; 10. Whig wig; 11. one won; 12. whale wail; 13. vain vein; 14. toe tow; 15. write right; 16. wry rye; 17. sole soul; 18. packed pact; 19. prophet profit; 20. colonel kernel

Acrostic Clues *(page 208)*
A. Leonardo da Vinci; B. daydreams; C. dived; D. vested; E. desktop; F. fungus; G. disbands; H. windiest; I. offensively; J. immensely. "As every divided kingdom falls, so every mind divided between many studies confounds and saps itself."

Logidoku *(page 209)*

7	4	6	1	5	2	8	3
1	6	4	3	7	8	2	5
5	3	8	2	6	1	4	7
8	2	7	5	4	3	1	6
2	5	3	8	1	6	7	4
3	1	5	7	2	4	6	8
4	7	2	6	8	5	3	1
6	8	1	4	3	7	5	2

Quilt Quest *(page 209)*

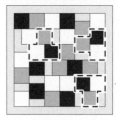

Sudoku *(page 210)*

2	5	7	1	9	3	4	6	8
8	4	3	5	2	6	7	9	1
9	6	1	4	7	8	3	2	5
3	7	5	2	8	9	6	1	4
6	9	4	3	1	5	8	7	2
1	8	2	7	6	4	9	5	3
4	3	6	9	5	1	2	8	7
7	1	9	8	4	2	5	3	6
5	2	8	6	3	7	1	4	9

Wacky Wordy *(page 210)*
The long and the short of it.

Red, White, and Blue *(page 211)*

	A	B	C	D	E	F
1	R	W	R	B	B	W
2	B	W	B	R	W	R
3	W	R	W	R	B	B
4	R	B	R	B	W	W
5	W	B	B	W	R	R
6	B	R	W	W	R	B

Quic-Kross (page 211)

BACKSEAT

```
B L E D
S A I D
L A C E
R A C K
      S B P N
      L E E E
      E A A A
      D D T T
```

For the Fellas (page 212)

```
      N I N E J A M B
      B E N J A M I N
D R                 L N
O A                 A E
N N                 W W
R D                 R C
A O                 E L
L L                 N A
P P                 C R
H H                 E E
      J O N A T H A N
      T H A N J O A N
```

KEYWORD

```
E A I N L A N T H
N A T H A N I E L
```

Number Crossword (page 212)

```
3 4 3
4 7 7
    7 3 6
    4 7 3
```

Wacky Wordy (page 213)

Forty acres and a mule

What a Whistle (Part II) (page 214)

1. Connecticut; 2. b) American kestrel; 3. 14; 4. False; 5. c) raw meat; 6. a) a bad wing; 7. b) falcon; 8. b) retrained it to fly; 9. a) a certain whistle; 10. b) a screech owl

Logical Hats (page 214)

The numbers on A and C are 10 and 5. B sees these and realizes he either has 15 or 5 on his hat. He then realizes that if he had 5 on his hat, A would have seen 5 and 5 and would have known his own hat had a 10. Since A didn't know his number, B eliminates this possibility.

Word Columns (page 215)

A husband said to his wife, "No, I don't hate your relatives. In fact, I like your mother-in-law better than I like mine."

Hashi (page 215)

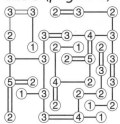

Color Scheme Word Search (pages 216-217)

1. BLACK MARKET
2. BLUE JEANS
3. BROWNIE
4. EBONY AND IVORY
5. GOLDFINGER
6. GRAPE-NUTS
7. GREEN CARD
8. JADED
9. OLIVE OYL
10. ORANGE JUICE
11. PEACHY
12. PINKIE
13. PLUMBER
14. RED SEA
15. ROSEBUD
16. SCARLETT O'HARA
17. SILVER SPOON
18. SNOW WHITE
19. TANNING
20. YELLOW SUBMARINE

Leftover words spell: Aquaman and the Navy Seal enjoyed "Grey's Anatomy."

```
E B O N Y A N D I V O R Y
N O O P S R E V L I S B A
I Q U A M L Y O E V I L O
R E G N I F D L O G A A N
A R A H O T T E L R A C S
M P E A C H Y B D A N K D
B R S T H E L N A A M S
U E D V T Y S U E A J A N
S B E C I U J E G N A R O
W M R L E N N J O Y K W
O U E O R O S E B U D E W
L L D G W R E A P Y S T H
L P A N G N I N N A T A I
E I K N I P I S T O R M T
Y D R A C N E E R G Y G E
```

Panagram (pages 218-219)

```
S E E M S   A S I F   G A R B
A R T I N   T E L L   A L O E
T I T L E   S E L A   L A B S
S Q U E E Z E D   P H A S E S
    A R E A   A J A X
S I N G E D   P L A T Y P U S
C H E E R   B R I C E   I N A
R A G S   Q U A C K   F L I T
A D E   D U N N E   B O O T Y
M A V E R I C K   W E L T E R
    P U Z O   K I D D
A D L I B S   H I N T E D A T
C R O C   H A U L   I D A H O
N A L A   O R E L   M U M M Y
E T A L   W A D S   E P E E S
```

Times Square (page 219)

```
         768
2 3 4 5 6   720
1 5 3 4 2   120
2 3 4 5 1   120
3 2 4 3 2   144
4 5 2 1 3   120
```

48 450 384 300 72 360

Fitting Words (page 220)

```
C O N G A
O K A Y S
P R I M E
S A L S A
```

More Times the Fun (page 220)

```
5 4 3 2 6 1
4 3 2 5 1 6
6 2 4 1 3 5
2 6 1 4 5 3
3 1 5 6 2 4
1 5 6 3 4 2
```

ANSWERS

Times Square *(page 221)*

3	3	2	4	72
4	5	2	1	40
3	5	4	3	180
1	1	5	5	25

40 (top)

36 75 80 60 300

Rhyme Time *(page 221)*
1. more ore; 2. mean dean; 3. tall mall; 4. seek leak; 5. core chore; 6. gray beret; 7. mummy rummy; 8. deeper sleeper; 9. cheaper keeper; 10. last broadcast

Fold-O-Rama
(page 222)

ABCD *(page 223)*

	A	B	C	D				
A	0	1	3	1	2	2		
B	2	1	1	2	2	1		
C	2	3	1	1	0	2		
D	2	1	1	2	2	1		

				A	B	C	D
1	2	2	1	B	C	A	B	D	C
1	2	2	1	C	B	D	C	A	B
2	1	1	2	D	C	A	D	B	A
1	1	2	2	C	D	C	B	A	D
1	1	2	2	D	C	A	D	B	C
3	2	0	1	B	A	B	A	D	A

Cast-a-Word *(page 223)*
Die 1: A, D, I, K, N, V
Die 2: B, E, M, P, S, T
Die 3: C, F, J, Q, R, Y
Die 4: G, H, L, O, U, W

Star Power *(page 224)*

4	7	8					
3	★	5	8	1			
7	2	1	6	★	7	1	6
6	★	3	2	4	3	★	2
8	4	5	★	6	4	8	5
	8	1	7	★	3		
		5	1	2			

Work It! *(page 224)*
designer/resigned/redesign

Fitting Words *(page 225)*

F	A	B	L	E
A	L	L	A	Y
R	O	U	S	E
M	E	E	T	S

Code-Doku *(page 225)*
TALL VANILLA NONFAT LATTE

I	T	A	O	L	N	F	E	V
L	E	V	A	I	F	T	N	O
O	N	F	E	T	V	A	I	L
E	A	L	V	N	I	O	T	F
F	I	T	L	E	O	V	A	N
V	O	N	F	A	T	I	L	E
A	V	E	I	O	L	N	F	T
T	L	O	N	F	A	E	V	I
N	F	I	T	V	E	L	O	A

Sudoku *(page 226)*

2	5	1	7	6	4	8	3	9
9	4	6	3	8	1	2	7	5
8	3	7	2	5	9	4	6	1
7	2	3	4	9	8	1	5	6
1	8	5	6	7	2	3	9	4
6	9	4	5	1	3	7	2	8
3	7	9	1	4	5	6	8	2
4	6	8	9	2	7	5	1	3
5	1	2	8	3	6	9	4	7

Wacky Wordy *(page 226)*
Police lineup

Fourth Assembling
(page 227)

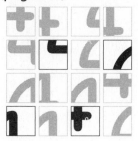

Red, White, and Blue
(page 227)

	A	B	C	D	E	F
1	R	R	B	B	W	W
2	W	B	R	W	B	R
3	B	W	W	R	R	B
4	B	W	R	R	W	B
5	R	B	W	W	B	R
6	W	R	B	B	R	W

Cat Logic *(page 228)*
Mr. Stripes owns Rusty; Mr. Rusty owns Puddles; Mr. Tommy owns Stripes; Mr. Puddles owns Tommy.

Aphorism Code-doku
(page 228)
HERE NOW, GONE TOMORROW

G	H	N	W	M	T	O	R	E
R	M	O	G	E	N	H	W	T
E	W	T	H	O	R	G	N	M
H	T	W	O	G	E	N	M	R
O	N	G	M	R	W	T	E	H
M	R	E	T	N	H	W	G	O
T	E	H	N	W	M	R	O	G
W	O	M	R	H	G	E	T	N
N	G	R	E	T	O	M	H	W

Start Your Day by Alpha Sleuth™ *(page 229)*

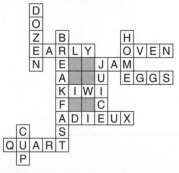

RISE AND SHINE

Get It Straight (page 230)

Hashi (page 231)

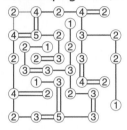

Things That Smell Good (Part II) (page 232)

GARLIC, JASMINE, ONIONS, CHOW MEIN, LICORICE, CARAMEL CORN, DOUGHNUTS, CHOCOLATE

Star Power (page 232)

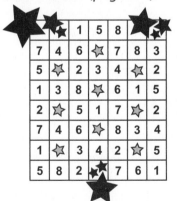

Last Laugh Department (page 233)

1. Agatha Christie's first book, "The Mysterious Affair at Styles," which introduced her Belgian detective Hercule Poirot, was rejected by the first six publishers she submitted it to.

2. John Grisham's first novel, "A Time to Kill," was rejected by twenty-eight publishers.

3. Robert W. Pirsig's "Zen and the Art of Motorcycle Maintenance" was rejected—ouch!—one hundred and twenty-one times before it became a bestseller for Morrow in nineteen seventy-four.

4. Ayn Rand's "The Fountainhead" was rejected by the first twelve publishers she approached.

5. J. K. Rowling's first book, "Harry Potter and the Philosopher's Stone,"* was turned down by nine publishers, including HarperCollins and Penguin, before Bloomsbury signed it up.

6. Dr. Seuss's first children's book, "And to Think That I Saw It on Mulberry Street," was rejected by twenty-six publishers before it was published in nineteen thirty-seven.

*The title of the book is the original, British title. The American edition is called "Harry Potter and the Sorcerer's Stone."

Spring Has Sprung! (pages 234-235)

Greedy Scramblegram (page 235)

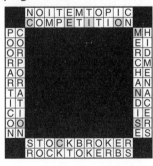

Word Jigsaw (page 236)

Amazing Bout with a Trout (page 236)

Rhyme Time (page 237)

1. slow flow; 2. fish dish; 3. play away; 4. sole goal; 5. full bull; 6. pail tale; 7. worn horn; 8. wide slide; 9. ghost host; 10. third word; 11. horse force; 12. border order; 13. madder adder; 14. better letter; 15. colder shoulder

Number Web (page 238)

(grid of numbers)

Ageless Logic (page 239)

Grandma is 61.

Codeword (page 239)

(codeword grid)

1	2	3	4	5	6	7	8	9	10	11	12	13
F	I	C	A	R	V	U	B	J	L	P	M	N

14	15	16	17	18	19	20	21	22	23	24	25	26
X	S	G	O	Y	K	W	T	D	E	Z	Q	H

ANSWERS

Word Circle (page 240)
cellar, arouse, sequel, eleven, entice

Number Crossword
(page 240)

		5	1	2
	8	7	6	5
7	8		6	6
9	8	4	1	
2	8	9		

Zoo Letterbox (page 241)

1	2	3	4	5	6	7	8	9	10	11	12	13
H	S	W	B	A	D	G	E	R	I	K	P	Z

14	15	16	17	18	19	20	21	22	23	24	25	26
U	M	Y	V	F	O	X	N	Q	C	J	T	L

Mrs. Smith's Daughters
(page 242)
The youngest child is not Sarah, Jane, or Anna, so it is Kate. The oldest child is not Jane or Anna, so it is Sarah. Two girls are older than Anna, so Anna is 2 and Jane is 3. Jane is the blond, so her eyes are brown and Anna's hair is brown. Sarah does not have black hair, so Kate does, and Sarah is the redhead whose eyes are green. Kate does not have hazel eyes, so her eyes are blue and 2-year-old, brown-haired Anna has hazel eyes. In summary:

Age	Name	Hair	Eyes
4	Sarah	red	green
3	Jane	blond	brown
2	Anna	brown	hazel
1	Kate	black	blue

The Perfect Cube
(page 243)

		2	8	7
	1	1	9	2
1	3	5	7	9
2	3	1	6	
5	1	2		

Party Dress (page 243)
We know that no one was wearing a dress to match her name. Since Magenta agreed with the woman in the teal dress, that means the woman in the teal dress was Hazel. It then follows that Magenta was wearing the hazel dress, and Teal was in the magenta dress.

Star Power (page 244)

Find the Word (page 245)
15. Rufus was a kanga**roo f**anatic, and the p**roof** was the kanga**roo** frescoes he painted on his **roof.** Rufus owned a bist**ro, of**ten bringing home food for his pet kanga**roo, F**ido. Fido, a boxing kangaroo, was a semi**pro, of**ten fighting large wallabies. His win total was ze**ro of**ficially, although he once defeated a koala in an unofficial match when the smaller koala pulled a switche**roo, f**alling to throw the fight. Rufus kept Fido in a leak**proof** hut with shatter**proof** windows and read him stories of the jacka**roo, f**antastic creatures that were part rabbit and part kanga**roo. F**ido didn't believe the stories but played along because he had no p**roof** and wanted Rufus to keep bringing foods from the bist**ro, of** which the rooster fondue was his favorite.

A Puzzling Perspective
(page 245)
Nearsighted

All Together Now
(page 246)
The next letter is "R." The sequence is J, P, G, R, as in John, Paul, George, and Ringo—the members of The Beatles.

Math Grid (page 246)

							51	
6	3	2	9	2	6	5		33
5	2	8	4	4	9	6		38
4	7	3	7	5	7	4		37
2	8	4	8	1	3	5		31
7	6	7	2	9	4	8		43
9	8	5	1	3	2	2		30
9	5	6	7	4	6	3		40

42 39 35 38 28 37 33 33

Tessellated Floor
(page 247)

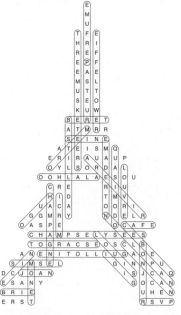

French Connection
(pages 248-249)
Bon Jour; Eiffel Tower; Seine; Champs-Élysées; "Gigi"; café; champagne; escargot; brie; Napoleon; Louis; Guillotine; Bastille Day; Joan; Three Musketeers; Pasteur; Hugo; Quasimodo; Notre Dame; Les Mis; Metro; Louvre; Monet; Ooh-la-la; Cancan; beret; perfume; RSVP; Nice; Riviera; Quebec; Merci

Leftover letters spell: Raise up your glass and say "Cheers!"

Carrying On
(pages 250–251)

P	E	A	L		G	R	A	S		C	A	R	V	E
U	R	S	A		O	U	S	E		A	L	I	E	N
B	A	S	K	E	T	B	A	L	L	G	A	M	E	S
		E	N	C	L		F	I	E					
G	S	A		T	H	E	W	H	O		S	A	Y	A
Y	E	L	L		A	S	H	E	N		E	M	E	R
M	A	B	E	L		E	L	E	V	E	N	A	M	
	B	A	G	P	I	P	E	P	L	A	Y	E	R	
F	I	N	A	N	C	E	D		N	O	S	E	S	
E	R	I	C		E	N	L	A	I		U	T	N	E
D	D	A	Y		M	T	E	T	N	A		Y	D	S
		L	E	A		O	D	D	S					
P	U	R	S	I	N	G	O	N	E	S	L	I	P	S
T	R	I	O	S		O	W	E	N		U	T	A	H
A	N	G	S	T		N	E	S	T		G	O	R	Y

Magic Square *(page 251)*

17	24	1	8	15
23	5	7	14	16
4	6	13	20	22
10	12	19	21	3
11	18	25	2	9

An Actor's Bio *(page 252)*

He won back-to-back Oscars for "Captains Courageous" and "Boys Town." He also starred in "Father of the Bride." Who is he?
Spencer Tracy

Jigsaw *(page 252)*

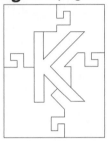

Capital Scramblegram *(page 253)*

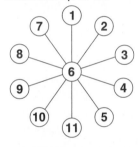

Word Ladder *(page 253)*

Answers may vary.
WORK, pork, perk, peak, peat, plat, PLAY

Counting Up *(page 254)*

The next number is 50. These numbers represent the value of U.S. coins.

Rhyme Time *(page 254)*

1. wind kind; 2. hard yard; 3. warm dorm; 4. tram scam; 5. pork fork; 6. rare chair; 7. regal eagle; 8. sweet treat; 9. troupe group; 10. groovy movie; 11. dental rental; 12. skeeter meter

Sudoku *(page 255)*

3	2	5	7	1	6	4	8	9
1	9	6	5	4	8	7	2	3
4	7	8	9	2	3	1	6	5
8	3	2	4	6	9	5	7	1
6	1	7	8	3	5	9	4	2
5	4	9	1	7	2	6	3	8
2	5	4	6	8	1	3	9	7
9	6	3	2	5	7	8	1	4
7	8	1	3	9	4	2	5	6

Ring of Numbers *(page 255)*

The 6 must go in the center circle, and each set of opposite circles must add up to 12.

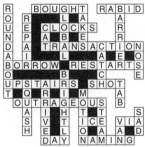

Crisscross Puzzle *(page 256)*

Isometric Rogues *(page 257)*

The rogue in each row is: Group I: The third figure from the left; Group II: The second figure from the right; Group III: All the figures match in this row; Group IV: The figure on the far right; Group V: The third figure from the left

H. H. *(page 258)*

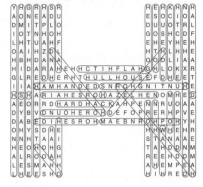

Leftover letters spell: "Hertford, Hereford, and Hampshire" (a line from the song "The Rain in Spain" from the musical "My Fair Lady").

Five-Letter Anagrams *(page 259)*

1. drove/Dover; 2. pains/Spain; 3. stain/satin; 4. trail/trial; 5. Stale/least; 6. stare/tears

All in the Family *(page 259)*

MOM is MIA. DAD is SID. SIS is IDA. Each appears 4 times. Their hometown is MIAMI.

Four Sisters *(page 260)*

Robert is not married to Roberta, Paula, or Alberta so his wife is Carla. Albert is not married to Alberta or Roberta so his wife is Paula. Paul is not married to Roberta so his wife is Alberta. Therefore, Carl's wife must be Roberta, whose last name is not Carlson or Robertson or Paulson; it is Albertson. Robert and Carla's last name is not Robertson or Carlson so it is Paulson. Since Robert Paulson is not the man in the second half of Clue 3, Albert and his wife Paula's last name is Robertson. This leaves Carlson to be the last name of Paul and Alberta. In summary:
Alberta Paul Carlson; Carla Robert Paulson; Paula Albert Robertson; Roberta Carl Albertson

Coin Dilemma *(page 260)*

50¢, 25¢, 10¢, 10¢, 10¢, 10¢, 1¢, 1¢, 1¢, and 1¢.

ANSWERS

Word Paths (page 261)
1. Waste not, want not; 2. Look before you leap; 3. Practice what you preach; 4. A stitch in time saves nine

Fifty-State Highway
(pages 262–263)

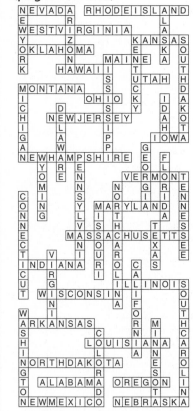

Crypto-quotes (page 264)
1. "Debt, if owed to ourselves, is not debt but an investment."
   —Franklin D. Roosevelt
2. "Let us endeavor so to live that when we come to die even the undertaker will be sorry."
   —Mark Twain

Times Square (page 264)

3	5	5	2	150
9	3	8	2	432
9	5	8	7	2520
9	3	8	7	1512

2187 225 2560 196

ABCD (page 265)

	A	B	C	D			
A	1	2	1	3	0	2	
B	2	2	2	0	2	1	
C	3	0	1	2	2	1	

A	B	C	D				
0	2	2	1	2	2		
3	1	1	1	A	B	A	C	D	A
2	0	2	2	C	A	D	A	C	D
0	3	1	2	B	D	B	D	B	C
3	0	2	1	C	A	D	A	C	A
0	3	1	2	B	D	B	C	B	D
1	2	2	1	C	B	C	A	D	B

Bookend Letters
(page 265)
DANGLED; ECLIPSE; PRIMP; STRAITS

The International Scene
(pages 266–267)

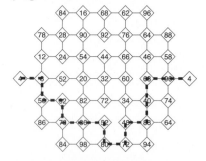

Circles and Numbers
(page 267)
Replace the question mark with a 2—the numbers in each circle total 25.

A Four-midable Maze
(page 268)

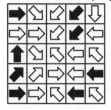

Four-Letter Anagrams
(page 268)
1. salt/last; 2. team/meat; 3. aunt/tuna; 4. pale/leap; 5. sink/skin; 6. note/tone

Shoe Sale (page 269)

Jigstars (page 270)
The pairs are: A and G, B and K, C and F, D and L, E and H, I and J.

1 +, 2 - (page 270)
123 - 45 - 67 + 89 = 100

Sudoku (page 271)

9	1	3	2	5	6	4	7	8
4	5	6	9	8	7	1	2	3
8	2	7	4	1	3	9	6	5
7	3	5	1	9	4	6	8	2
2	8	1	7	6	5	3	4	9
6	4	9	8	3	2	7	5	1
3	6	4	5	2	9	8	1	7
5	9	8	6	7	1	2	3	4
1	7	2	3	4	8	5	9	6

Arrow Web (page 271)

Rhyme Time (page 272)
1. why try; 2. stew crew; 3. rich witch; 4. time crime; 5. ford board; 6. swell bell; 7. clock lock; 8. brunch bunch; 9. clever lever; 10. coerce verse; 11. muzzle puzzle; 12. beneath teeth; 13. never endeavor; 14. after laughter; 15. boring flooring

Mondrianize It! *(page 273)*

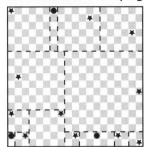

Word Jigsaw *(page 273)*

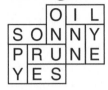

Snow *(page 274)*

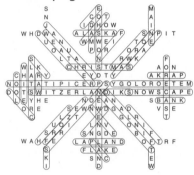

Leftover letters spell: "Snow White and the Seven Dwarfs."

Name That Nickname *(page 275)*

The man nicknamed Tubba is 44. He drives a station wagon, is a beer-bottle capper, and roots for the Raiders.

The Upper Crust by Alpha Sleuth™ *(page 276)*

Mind Stretcher *(page 277)*

"One for the money, two for the show…"

Dissection *(page 277)*

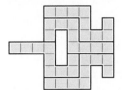

Diagonal Jump *(page 278)*

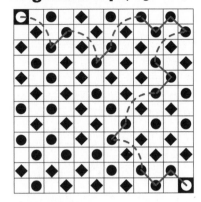

Word Jigsaw *(page 278)*

You Said It! *(page 279)*

1. No one seems to know for sure what people want these days, except that they won't accept a penny less.; 2. Today's travelers have proven that the world is certainly round. It is their wallets that are flat.; 3. Snow is nature's peanut butter. It's crunchy, kids love it, and it clings to the roof of your house.; 4. Few things are so embarrassing as watching your boss do what you just said could not be done.

Times Square *(page 279)*

						120
3	2	4	1	2		48
2	2	2	2	5		80
3	1	5	1	2		30
4	3	1	4	1		48
2	3	1	4	2		48
144	36	40	32	40	240	

Curvaceous Cube Construction *(page 280)*

Cube B is correct.

Fitting Words *(page 280)*

A	M	A	S	S
M	O	V	I	E
P	R	I	Z	E
S	E	D	E	R

Red, White, and Blue *(page 281)*

	A	B	C	D	E	F
1	B	W	R	R	B	W
2	R	W	B	W	R	B
3	W	B	R	B	W	R
4	R	B	W	R	W	B
5	W	R	B	W	B	R
6	B	R	W	B	R	W

Gram's Birthday *(pages 282–283)*

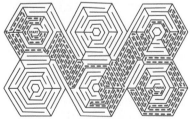

Hexagonal Shift *(page 283)*

Anagram President *(page 284)*

1. hardy; 2. amble; 3. rumba; 4. rinse; 5. yanks; 6. tuber; 7. relay; 8. urban; 9. melon; 10. alter; 11. Nepal
President Harry Truman

ANSWERS

Finding a Digit (page 284)

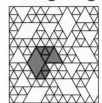

Word Columns (page 285)

No one knew who was attacking the castle until we learned it was the forces of Sir Nymbas of Cumulus, the legendary Dark and Stormy Knight.

Word Ladder (page 285)

PLANE, plant, plait, plain, blain, brain, TRAIN

Crypto-Animal Families (page 286)

1. Chicken, goat, cow, horse, goose, duckling, sheep, swine, rabbit, hound; 2. Hippopotamus, rhino, tiger, giraffe, elephant, gorilla, zebra, kangaroo, snakes, lion; 3. Whale, seal, turtle, stingray, dolphin, lobster, oyster, starfish, jellyfish, shark

Psychics for Hire (page 286)

None. It's impossible to only predict 4 out of 5 because that means they would automatically know that the 1 stock left is in the fifth drawer; they actually would have predicted 5 out of 5.

Sudoku (page 287)

3	5	1	4	2	7	8	6	9
7	2	8	1	9	6	4	5	3
6	4	9	5	3	8	1	7	2
1	3	5	8	4	2	6	9	7
2	7	6	9	5	1	3	4	8
8	9	4	6	7	3	5	2	1
9	1	7	3	6	5	2	8	4
5	8	2	7	1	4	9	3	6
4	6	3	2	8	9	7	1	5

Don's Diner and Part-Time Arcade (page 287)

1. Upside-down exit sign; 2. monster arm reaching out of video game; 3. customer's hat floating; 4. no stool under customer on far left; 5. tail around leg of video game player; 6. second stool from left is too tall; 7. second customer from right has no head; 8. section of the counter is missing; 9. third customer from left's head is backward; 10. far right customer has no eyes; 11. spider hanging from ceiling; 12. no chain for hanging light

Star Power (page 288)

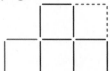

Four Squares to Three (page 288)

Frame Games™ (page 289)

Positive feedback

Weird Word Search (Part I) (page 289)

Weird Word Search (Part II) (page 290)

GHOSTLY, UNCANNY, CHILLING, BIZARRE, STRANGE, FREAKY, ARCANE, MACABRE, CREEPY

Logidoku (page 290)

5	9	2	3	4	1	6	8	7
4	7	8	6	2	5	3	1	9
6	3	1	7	8	9	4	2	5
8	1	3	4	7	2	9	5	6
2	5	7	9	6	8	1	4	3
9	6	4	5	1	3	8	7	2
7	4	9	8	5	6	2	3	1
1	8	6	2	3	7	5	9	4
3	2	5	1	9	4	7	6	8

Bungled Burglary (page 291)

1. Woman coming out of painting; 2. glass of water sitting on edge of window; 3. curtains don't match; 4. fish out of water; 5. thief has Santa hat; 6. thief has one bare foot; 7. dresser has zippers instead of knobs; 8. thief brought gifts; 9. bulldog has cat tail; 10. flowers have no stems into vase; 11. drawers hanging in mid-air; 12. Tiny's bowl is a hat; 13. screwdriver instead of knitting needle; 14. ball of yarn turns into a snake; 15. chair's arms turn into teddy bear feet; 16. slippers and socks attached to no one; 17. weeds growing in room

Jelly Bean Jar Maze (page 292)

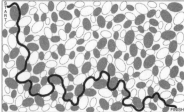

Fitting Words (page 292)

B	A	R	D	S
E	Q	U	I	P
A	U	G	E	R
N	A	S	T	Y

Go Figure *(page 293)*
Answers may vary.

1	5	4	3	1	4	6	5	29
2	3	1	4	3	9	5	8	35
4	2	6	8	2	7	8	6	43
2	3	5	7	6	1	3	4	31
1	6	4	6	5	7	8	5	42
3	5	3	8	7	4	7	2	39
4	2	8	7	5	3	2	3	34
1	8	7	5	9	6	4	1	41

35 (top)
18 34 38 48 38 41 43 34 29

Alphabet Fill-In *(page 293)*
1. solid; 2. khaki; 3. bayou;
4. venom; 5. relax; 6. junta;
7. zilch; 18. query; 19. egret;
10. green; 11. clump; 12. wharf;
13. lingo

Amusement Park by Alpha Sleuth™ *(page 294)*

Inward/Outward Bound *(page 295)*

Rhyme Time *(page 296)*
1. meek eek; 2. drab crab;
3. need speed; 4. buff enough;
5. couth youth 6. hound sound;
7. sharp escarp; 8. devout scout;
9. tourist list; 10. crabby cabbie;
11. flabby tabby; 12. sublime crime;
13. exalted malted; 14. cheaper sweeper; 15. grandstand band;
16. tourney journey

Decorating Dilemma *(page 297)*
The daughter doesn't want wallpaper, paneling, or Day-Glo paint, so she must want the checkerboard carpeted wall and be Lee, and she is the upstairs resident. Dale doesn't want wallpaper or paneling—he wants Day-Glo paint. If that's true, Dale must be the son. His bedroom is either next door or in the converted garage. Pat, writing the letter, by several references is the father, and he wants paneling. This leaves Leslie to be the mom, who wants wallpaper. Pat refers to "an occupant" of the next room, which implies a husband and wife, making the son the resident of the converted garage.
In summary:

Name	Relation	Decor	Room
Dale	Son	Day-Glo Paint	Converted Garage
Lee	Daughter	B&W Carpet	Upstairs Room
Leslie	Mom	Wallpaper	Next Door Room
Pat	Dad	Paneling	Next Door Room

ABCD *(page 298)*

	A	0	1	3	1	2	2
	B	2	2	0	2	1	2
	C	2	2	0	3	0	2
A B C	D	2	1	3	0	3	0
2 1 2 1	C	B	A	C	D	A
1 3 1 1	B	C	D	B	A	B
1 1 3 1	C	B	A	C	D	C
2 2 0 2	D	A	D	B	A	B
1 2 2 1	B	D	A	C	B	C
2 0 1 3	D	C	D	A	D	A

A Capital Puzzle! *(page 298)*
1. Lansing (MI); 2. Topeka (KS);
3. Denver (CO); 4. Salem (OR);
5. Boston (MA)

Big Screen Letterbox *(page 299)*

1	2	3	4	5	6	7	8	9	10	11	12	13
M	X	N	S	J	O	L	I	E	V	A	W	F

14	15	16	17	18	19	20	21	22	23	24	25	26
Y	B	T	P	G	C	R	U	Z	H	D	Q	K

Go Figure *(page 300)*
Answers may vary.

1	5	3	6	7	4	9	7	8	50
4	2	7	4	3	5	6	6	9	46
9	8	3	7	1	5	4	2	7	46
8	3	4	4	2	3	5	5	9	43
1	9	3	2	7	2	6	7	8	45
8	2	5	4	3	9	9	4	5	49
7	6	3	9	3	7	8	1	4	48
2	4	9	8	2	1	3	2	9	40
9	8	3	7	4	6	8	5	3	53

48 (top)
49 47 40 51 32 42 58 39 62 39

Code-doku *(page 300)*
ONE SMALL STEP ON A PALE MOON

O	A	L	T	M	E	N	S	P
E	T	S	N	O	P	M	A	L
P	M	N	A	L	S	E	O	T
T	S	M	E	P	N	A	L	O
N	O	A	S	T	L	P	M	E
L	E	P	O	A	M	S	T	N
M	N	T	P	S	O	L	E	A
A	L	E	M	N	T	O	P	S
S	P	O	L	E	A	T	N	M

Word Columns *(page 301)*
After eating an entire bull, a mountain lion felt so good he started roaring. He kept it up until a hunter came along and shot him. The moral: When you're full of bull, keep your mouth shut.

Crypto-quote *(page 301)*
"There are two things that are more difficult than making an after-dinner speech: Climbing a wall which is leaning toward you and kissing a girl who is leaning away from you."

—Winston Churchill

Acrostic Anagram *(page 302)*
A. incapacitated; B. perished;
C. usefulness; D. survey; E. forehead;
F. fishing; G. witting; H. willow;
I. sorority
"Virtue is its own reward. There's a pleasure in doing good which sufficiently pays itself."

ANSWERS

Sudoku *(page 303)*

9	6	3	2	5	7	8	4	1
1	8	7	3	4	9	5	2	6
5	4	2	1	6	8	3	7	9
7	1	4	5	2	6	9	3	8
6	2	8	9	3	1	7	5	4
3	5	9	7	8	4	1	6	2
8	3	1	6	7	2	4	9	5
2	9	5	4	1	3	6	8	7
4	7	6	8	9	5	2	1	3

A Can-Do Candle Attitude
(page 303)
Dan bought 94 candles for 50 cents each, one candle for $5.50, and 5 candles for $9.50.

TV Documentaries
(page 304)

	First word	Second word	Director
1	Stealing	Money	Spoolbag
2	Cutting	Bread	Alhen
3	Painting	Newspapers	Rodrigo
4	Eating	Cloth	Torrentino
5	Ripping	Wallpaper	Jockson
6	Making	Pizza	Capri

Digital Sudoku *(page 304)*

Word Ladder *(page 305)*
CLUSTER, bluster, blaster, plaster, platter, PLANTER

Oddball of the Group
(page 305)
Figure D, because it's the only figure that doesn't have an unconnected single straight line in its configuration.

More than a Word
(page 306)

Rhyme Time *(page 307)*
1. ray day; 2. blog log; 3. night bite; 4. steel heel; 5. trial smile; 6. grand brand; 7. found pound; 8. chrome home; 9. thrill hill; 10. attack back; 11. bring string; 12. spare prayer; 13. turkey jerky; 14. sweeper keeper; 15. mention intention

Starboard Course Maze
(page 308)

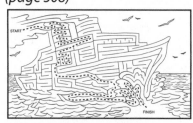

Tiny's Sock Drawer
(page 308)
Tom would have to pull out 3 socks. Because there are only 2 different colors, if he pulls out 3, at least 2 will be the same color.

Word Web *(page 309)*

Wacky Wordy *(page 309)*
Tomatoes (tom 8 Os)

Go Figure *(page 310)*
Answers may vary.

1	5	4	3	1	4	6	5	29
2	3	1	4	3	9	5	8	35
4	2	6	8	2	7	8	6	43
2	3	5	7	6	1	3	4	31
1	6	4	6	5	7	8	5	42
3	5	3	8	7	4	7	2	39
4	2	8	7	5	3	2	3	34
1	8	7	5	9	6	4	1	41

18 34 38 48 38 41 43 34 29

The Perfect Square
(page 310)

Masyu *(page 311)*

Someone Will Get This Right! *(page 311)*
Choice B is correct. The number on the left side of the colon is the sum of the digits on the right side of the colon in each set.

Star Power *(page 312)*

Frame Games™ *(page 312)*
Mixed feelings

Cross-Math *(page 313)*

5	+	9	−	8	=	6
+		−		+		
2	×	4	−	6	=	2
+		+		÷		
3	÷	1	+	7	=	10
=		=		=		
10		6		2		

Prime Suspect *(page 313)*

	Nationality	Hair	Coat	Build
1	Italian	none	green	round
2	English	red	blue	thin
3	Chinese	gray	purple	slim
4	Spanish	white	cream	medium
5	African	dark	yellow	hunched
6	Mexican	brown	mauve	fat

Animal House *(pages 314–315)*

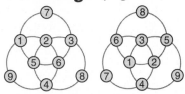

Fitting Words *(page 315)*

V	A	S	E	S
E	R	O	D	E
I	M	A	G	E
L	Y	R	E	S

Pretzel Logic *(page 316)*

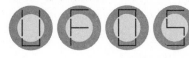

Name Calling *(page 316)*

Man should live if only to satisfy his curiosity.

Stately Letterbox *(page 317)*

1	2	3	4	5	6	7	8	9	10	11	12	13
Q	J	R	A	U	V	C	L	D	X	E	S	Z
14	15	16	17	18	19	20	21	22	23	24	25	26
P	H	B	W	Y	O	M	I	N	G	F	K	T

Acrostic Anagram *(page 318)*

A. counterbalance; B. dossier;
C. goldfish; D. thornier; E. heartaches;
F. thereafter; G. wafts; H. venue;
I. without
"A hurtful act is the transference to others of the degradation which we bear in ourselves."

Sudoku *(page 319)*

8	3	5	4	7	2	6	1	9
1	7	2	3	9	6	5	8	4
4	6	9	8	1	5	3	2	7
7	2	6	1	5	4	8	9	3
5	8	1	2	3	9	4	7	6
3	9	4	6	8	7	1	5	2
2	5	8	9	6	3	7	4	1
9	1	3	7	4	8	2	6	5
6	4	7	5	2	1	9	3	8

Money for a Bunny *(page 319)*

The odds of the 2 balls falling in the same hole are still 1 in 50.

Japanese Culture *(page 320)*

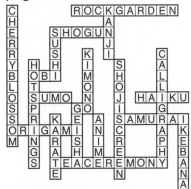

Alien Revolution *(page 320)*

Rotate each inner circle 90 degrees counterclockwise so the lines in the inner and outer circles form the letters U, F, O, and S.

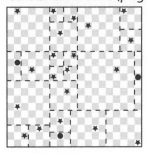

Mondrianize It! *(page 321)*

Fitting Words *(page 321)*

P	A	G	A	N
O	B	E	S	E
T	U	N	I	C
S	T	E	A	K

Cole Porter Songs *(pages 322–323)*

ABCD *(page 323)*

	A	3	0	0	2	2	2
	B	0	3	2	1	2	1
	C	1	3	2	1	1	1
A B C D	D	2	0	2	2	1	2

2	2	1	1	A	B	C	A	B	D
1	1	2	2	D	C	B	D	A	C
3	2	0	1	A	B	D	A	B	A
1	1	1	3	D	C	B	D	A	D
0	3	3	0	C	B	C	B	C	B
2	0	2	2	A	C	D	C	D	A

Get It Straight *(page 324)*

ANSWERS

The Friendly Skies by Alpha Sleuth™ *(page 325)*

```
        J
        U
        M
        B
  C     R          H
  O Z O N E        E A V Y
  C     Q
  K     R U N W A Y
F L A P           X
  W I N G         
  J E T     T A X I S
  D
```

F L I G H T   M A N U A L

Red, White, and Blue
(page 326)

	A	B	C	D	E	F
1	R	B	B	W	R	W
2	B	B	W	R	W	R
3	R	W	W	B	R	B
4	W	R	R	B	B	W
5	W	R	B	R	W	B
6	B	W	R	W	B	R

Odd-Even Logidoku
(page 327)

8	4	7	5	1	9	3	2	6
9	6	3	2	8	4	1	5	7
2	1	5	7	6	3	4	8	9
5	9	4	1	2	8	7	6	3
7	2	1	4	3	6	8	9	5
6	3	8	9	5	7	2	1	4
4	5	2	6	7	1	9	3	8
3	7	6	8	9	2	5	4	1
1	8	9	3	4	5	6	7	2

Word Columns *(page 327)*
"An enemy can partly ruin a man, but it takes a good-natured injudicious friend to complete the thing and make it perfect."

Mirror Images *(page 328)*
1. Different wallpaper; 2. different mirror frame; 3. "Hair" instead of "Style" on page taped to mirror; 4. heart charm instead of circle on necklace hanging on mirror; 5. daisies instead of roses in vase; 6. one less bottle on tray; 7. jar now behind vase; 8. perfume bottle is different; 9. drawer is open; 10. no necklace on table; 11. different table legs; 12. hair in reflection is different; 13. full lock of hair, not just strands, sticking out from back of hairdo; 14. woman wearing necklace;

15. woman wearing a ring; 16. dress has sleeves; 17. dress has belt; 18. chair pad has ruffles; 19. woman's shoe is different; 20. only one slipper under chair; 21. no baseboard; 22. purse flat on floor

Hitori *(page 329)*

4	4	1	8	5	2	7	5
7	5	3	2	6	3	1	4
8	4	3	7	5	5	6	1
4	6	3	5	4	8	4	2
5	3	8	8	7	1	2	4
8	1	5	3	5	7	2	6
3	5	7	4	1	6	8	5
6	8	4	8	2	2	5	1

Frame Games™ *(page 329)*
Pride comes before a fall

Menagerie Nursery
(pages 330–331)

```
P A I R S     I L S A     K N O B
E D D I E     N U N N     I O N A
C A L F M U S C L E       T O M B
O N E L I N E R     M I C K E Y
S O R E   C R E M O N A
        S A T   I N G R A T E
B A C K U P S     S E E S R E D
O R R I N           S O N N Y
A L A D D I N     A P T N E S S
R O M A I N E     S A S
        R A C E C A R   A H A B
N A P O L I     A R E A C O D E
A C L U     S A M U E L C O L T
I R O N   O P E L     S T P A T
L E W D   R O L E     O S S I E
```

Word Ladder *(page 331)*
HILL, hilt, halt, halo, hall, gall, gale, PALE

Star Power *(page 332)*

```
      2 3 7
  2 7 1 ★ 8 3 7
  8 ★ 4 6 5 ★ 2
3 5 6 3 ★ 1 4 6 2
8 ★ 2 8 7 2 8 ★ 1
4 7 1 ★ 5 ★ 3 5 7
  3 6 4 1 6
```

Six-Letter Anagrams
(page 332)
elapse/asleep/please

Painterly Logic *(page 333)*
Trailer 101: violet roof, orange doors, indigo walls; Trailer 102: red roof, blue doors, yellow walls; Trailer 103: green roof, yellow doors, red walls; Trailer 104: indigo roof, green doors, violet walls; Trailer 105: blue roof, red doors, orange walls

Odd-Even Logidoku
(page 333)

9	1	7	2	3	8	4	5	6
6	3	2	5	4	7	9	1	8
8	4	5	1	6	9	3	2	7
2	9	3	6	7	5	1	8	4
1	5	6	4	8	3	2	7	9
4	7	8	9	1	2	6	3	5
3	6	4	8	5	1	7	9	2
5	2	1	7	9	6	8	4	3
7	8	9	3	2	4	5	6	1

Digital Sudoku *(page 334)*

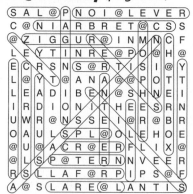

Six-Letter Anagrams
(page 334)
1. course/source; 2. recent/center; 3. warden/wander; 4. talent/latent; 5. aboard/abroad

Th@'s Wacky *(page 335)*

```
S A L @ P   N O I @ L E V E R
C @ N I A R B R E T @ C S   S
@ Z I G G U R @ I N M N   C F
L E Y T I N R E @ P O @ H @ Y
E C R S N S @ R T I S I @ T I
L @ X Y T @ A N A @ @ P O T N
L E A D I B E N @ S H N E R E
I R D I O N I T H E E S R B R
U W R @ N S S E I @ R @ B O E
O A U L S P L @ O L E H O X
@ U @ A C R @ E R F L I X @
R S L L A F @ R P I P S @ F
A @ S L A R E @ L A N T I S
```

Quilt Quest *(page 336)*

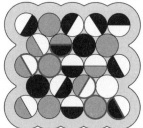

Star Power (page 336)

	2	7	4			
1	★	5	4	3	8	7
3	6	8	★	1	★	5
4	★	2	7	6	2	4
2	5	1	7	4	★	8
7	★	8	★	3	1	5
4	3	6	5	2	★	6
			4	8	7	

Codeword (page 337)

```
M I C R O N   S C R U F F
I   O   M   S O P     R I
S A R D I N E   M   D   I
L   R   T   L E P T O N S
A C I D S   F   L     K
Y   D     I   E N J O Y
  D O   A D M I X     U
L Y R I C   P       D   S
I   Q   O   M I G H T
A V E N U E S   A   M   R
I   M   I   E V I L E Y E
S   I   R   D   Z   N   W
E A R N E R   B E A T E N
```

1	2	3	4	5	6	7	8	9	10	11	12	13
G	N	M	A	H	Y	B	O	C	F	T	U	E

14	15	16	17	18	19	20	21	22	23	24	25	26
J	R	K	P	W	V	L	X	Z	S	I	Q	D

Sudoku (page 338)

8	5	1	3	2	4	7	6	9
2	9	7	1	5	6	8	4	3
3	6	4	7	8	9	2	1	5
4	1	3	5	9	8	6	2	7
7	2	5	6	3	1	4	9	8
6	8	9	2	4	7	3	5	1
1	3	2	4	7	5	9	8	6
9	4	6	8	1	3	5	7	2
5	7	8	9	6	2	1	3	4

A Puzzling Perspective (page 338)

Elephantine

ABCD (page 339)

		A	B	C	D			
	A	2	2	1	1	1	2	
	B	2	0	2	3	1	1	
	C	1	1	2	0	3	2	
A B C D	D	1	3	1	2	1	1	

2	0	1	3	D	A	D	A	D	C
1	1	3	1	C	D	C	B	C	A
1	3	1	1	B	A	B	D	B	C
3	1	1	1	A	D	A	B	C	A
1	2	1	2	B	C	B	D	A	D
1	2	2	1	A	D	C	B	C	B

For Your Eyes Only (page 339)

All 4 arrows are the same length.

Hashi (page 340)

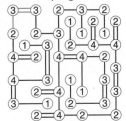

Odd-Even Logidoku (page 340)

7	2	9	4	5	8	3	6	1
1	4	5	3	6	2	7	9	8
3	6	8	9	7	1	5	4	2
8	3	6	2	1	4	9	5	7
5	7	1	6	3	9	8	2	4
2	9	4	7	8	5	1	3	6
9	1	2	8	4	3	6	7	5
4	8	7	5	9	6	2	1	3
6	5	3	1	2	7	4	8	9

Codeword (page 341)

```
S T A R T I N G   E T C H
A   E   K   R   X   U
A B L A Z E   E M P I R E
L   P   B O A   I   V
H E N S   A   T U R K E Y
A       N       E
E U R E K A   M I D W A Y
      J       A     L
S E V E R S   J   L A S T
Q   C   I C E   U   O
Q U O T E D   S E C U R E
A   E   E   T   R   A
F L E D   S O Y B E A N S
```

1	2	3	4	5	6	7	8	9	10	11	12	13
L	P	K	N	I	A	J	T	D	S	C	H	X

14	15	16	17	18	19	20	21	22	23	24	25	26
E	Q	F	U	R	M	B	O	Y	Z	W	V	G

Make Sense of the Symbols (page 341)

Option D is next, because if you rotate each of the symbols 90 degrees counter-clockwise, you'll see the initial letters of the traditional 9 planets in our solar system (before Pluto was demoted to dwarf planet status).

Red, White, Blue, and Green (page 342)

	A	B	C	D	E	F	G	H
1	G	B	W	R	W	R	G	B
2	R	W	B	R	G	G	B	W
3	W	G	R	G	B	W	B	R
4	G	W	R	B	G	R	W	B
5	W	B	G	W	R	B	R	G
6	B	R	G	W	R	B	W	G
7	B	R	W	G	B	W	G	R
8	R	G	B	B	W	G	R	W

Name Calling (page 343)

Don't rejoice at your enemy's fall, but don't rush to pick him up either.

Word Ladders (page 343)

Answers may vary.
1. RIVET, river, Rover, rower, bower, bowel, TOWEL; 2. BADGER, bagger, dagger, danger, manger, manner, BANNER

Mondrianize It! (page 344)

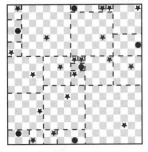

Dissection (page 344)

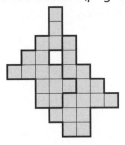

Acrostic Clues (page 345)

"When tillage begins, other arts follow. The farmers, therefore, are the founders of human civilization."
A. Daniel Webster; B. vegetation; C. teetotal; D. loafing; E. House of Usher; F. lazier; G. affirms; H. French horn; I. Mother; J. whirl

ANSWERS

Buy Buy Buy
(pages 346–347)

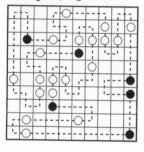

C	P	A	S		A	P	B	S		J	U	T
H	O	B	O		Z	I	O	N		O	N	O
E	L	B	A		A	L	T	A	R	B	O	Y
F	O	R	M	A	L	L	O	G	I	C		
		I	C	E	A	X		P	O	O	H	
I	R	A		E	A	R		T	U	R	B	O
D	E	N	N	I	S		H	O	P	P	E	R
E	A	T	I	T		E	O	N		S	Y	N
A	L	E	X		B	A	S	T	E			
		C	O	M	E	S	T	O	R	E	S	T
O	P	E	N	A	R	E	A		A	X	E	L
W	A	D		T	R	I	G		S	E	A	R
E	Y	E		S	A	N	E		E	S	P	N

Star Power *(page 347)*

		3	4	6		
6	5	7	★	1	6	5
2	★	8	5	2	★	8
7	1	4	3	★	4	7	3	1
5	★	6	7	1	6	5	★	2
3	2	8	★	4	★	8	4	6
		5	2	3	2	7

Masyu *(page 348)*

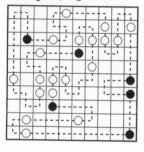

Number Crossword
(page 348)

	4	9	5	
5	5	1	4	4
1	6		3	8
2	7	3	2	4
	8	4	1	

Rhyme Time *(page 349)*

1. top crop; 2. try thigh; 3. pipe
type; 4. cool pool; 5. mall stall;
6. small ball; 7. stale mail; 8. stash
cash; 9. faint taint; 10. clock stock;
11. hokey pokey; 12. green marine;
13. light flight; 14. horse course;
15. better setter

Cross-Math *(page 350)*

5	+	7	×	2	=	24
×		+		+		
3	+	4	-	1	=	6
+		-		×		
9	-	6	×	8	=	24
=		=		=		
24		5		24		

Pattern Placement
(page 350)

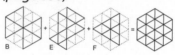

Fitting Words *(page 351)*

M	A	C	A	W
A	L	I	B	I
L	O	T	U	S
T	E	E	T	H

Pythagorize It! *(page 351)*

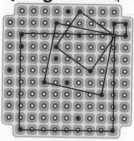

Think ABCD *(page 352)*

	A₂		C₁		A₁	
B₂	D	B		A	C	A₂
	A	C		B	D	D₁
	B	D	C			A
A₁			A	D	B	C
C₁	C		B		A	D
		A	D	C		B	C₂

D₂ D₂ B₁

Frame Games™ *(page 352)*

One giant leap for mankind